By NORMAN FOERSTER

NATURE IN AMERICAN LITERATURE:
Studies in the Modern View of Nature.

AMERICAN POETRY AND PROSE:
A Book of Readings, 1607–1916.

AMERICAN CRITICISM

AMERICAN CRITICISM

A Study in Literary Theory from Poe

to the Present

BY

NORMAN FOERSTER
Author of 'Nature in American Literature'

Norman Foerster

TOVT
BIEN OV
RIEN

BOSTON AND NEW YORK

HOUGHTON MIFFLIN COMPANY

The Riverside Press Cambridge

1928

142140

The Riverside Press
CAMBRIDGE · MASSACHUSETTS
PRINTED IN THE U.S.A.

Before we can have an American literature, we must have an American criticism. — LOWELL.

The criticism which alone can much help us for the future ... is a criticism which regards Europe as being, for intellectual and spiritual purposes, one great confederation, bound to a joint action and working to a common result; and whose members have, for their proper outfit, a knowledge of Greek, Roman, and Eastern antiquity, and of one another. Special, local, and temporary advantages being put out of account, that modern nation will in the intellectual and spiritual sphere make most progress, which most thoroughly carries out this programme. — ARNOLD.

Those precious legacies — accumulations! They come to us from the far-off — from all eras, and all lands — from Egypt, and India, and Greece, and Rome — and along through the middle and later ages, in the grand monarchies of Europe — born under far different institutes and conditions from ours — but out of the old insight and inspiration of the same old humanity — the same old heart and brain — the same old countenance yearningly, pensively, looking forth. What we have to do to-day is to receive them cheerfully, and to give them ensemble, and a modern American and democratic physiognomy. — WHITMAN.

PREFACE

Since about the year 1912, and especially since the Great War, America has experienced a new self-consciousness. We have been increasingly eager, not only to reveal our present inadequacies, but also to understand and revalue our achievement in the past — particularly our literature. We have expressed ourselves in a literary criticism probably less perfunctory, more fresh and alert, more energetic and abundant, than that of any previous epoch in our three centuries of history. We have grown deeply interested in criticism itself, in criteria and methods, and also in the development of criticism in America: in the conditions that have shaped it, in the aims and temper of the critics, in the standards that they employed, and in the issues that they debated.

When the final volumes of the 'Cambridge History of American Literature' were published a few years after the war, the editors candidly admitted that 'the number of pioneer tasks still to be undertaken in the study of American literature was larger than could be entirely foreseen.' In a review of the work I ventured to point out, as one of the most important of the untried tasks, an account of the history of our literary criticism. After considering undertaking this task myself, I came to the conclusion that the time for it was not ripe; that before it could be carried out with anything like finality a number of monographs would have to be written on special periods and problems. I came to feel, also, that some of these limited studies would be of more immediate value than an historical survey. Among these studies I eventually selected a critical analysis of the literary creeds that have been most impressively set forth in this country. It seemed to me that if these creeds were thoroughly exam-

ined we might come to a better understanding of the dominant motives of our creative literature in the past.

Since light on the past is always light on the present and
future, it seemed to me, furthermore, that a serious confron-
tation of the standards adopted in the nineteenth century
might in some measure illuminate the chaos into which our
criticism has fallen. Admittedly, there is a striking contrast
between the standardization of our life in general and the
absence of standards in our literature and our thinking about
literature. In the main our critics appear to have abdicated
their responsibility and privileges in favor of an open-
mindedness that is with difficulty distinguished from vacuity.
By so doing, they have given up their powers to the publishers and the editors, whose standards, being mainly commer-
cial, are mainly low. Publishers and editors are chiefly concerned, not with what the public ought to want and the best
of the public does want, but with what the majority want or
are supposed to want. If the professional critics are to regain
leadership, they will have to learn to be leaders rather than
mere observers. So long as their open minds contain nothing
but the passing winds of doctrine, so long as they dally with
the fashions of the moment instead of putting on the armor
of tried standards, they will be impotent to lead. It is a hopeful sign when a writer like Floyd Dell, in the concluding paragraph of his 'Intellectual Vagabondage, an Apology for the
Intelligentsia,' looks forward to a younger generation that
shall have the courage to formulate *conventions* (italics his).
The paramount need of the times, in literary criticism as in
other activities, is a convention (a 'coming-together') that
shall wisely use and not willfully reject the traditions of the
past. Upon the assertion, 'The dead writers are remote from
us because we *know* so much more than they did,' the only
sensible comment is that of T. S. Eliot: 'Precisely, and they
are that which we know.' Perhaps we are beginning to sus-
pect, as our interest in outlines and stories of philosophy,

science, history, etc., would seem to indicate, that 'that which we know' is never remote and irrelevant, but always present and serviceable.

I am indebted to several persons who have been so kind as to read portions of this book in manuscript or in proof-sheets; particularly Charles Cestre, Professor of American Literature and Civilization in the University of Paris; Friedrich Schoenemann, Lecturer in American Literature and Civilization in the University of Berlin; and Chester Penn Higby, Professor of Modern History in the University of Wisconsin. I am indebted to the editors of 'Studies in Philology' (1923, 1927) and 'Publications of the Modern Language Association' (1926) for permission to reprint three excerpts that first appeared in those journals and are now incorporated in this book; and in the Introduction I have sketched a rationale of American literary history similar to that which I first published in the preface of 'American Poetry and Prose' (Houghton Mifflin Company, 1925) and in an article in the 'Saturday Review of Literature' for April 3, 1926. Portions of the book were originally presented as lectures in the universities of Illinois (1925) and Munich and Berlin (1928).

NORMAN FOERSTER

CONTENTS

INTRODUCTION

LITERARY criticism in America has not had the support of a native cultural tradition. The discovery of America provided a new setting, or theater, for European culture; the New World had everything to receive, nothing to give, in respect to the higher interests of humanity. Although the frontier soon began to transform Europeans into such Americans as Jefferson, Jackson, and Lincoln, the continuous influx of immigrants and of foreign ideas postponed indefinitely the achievement of a distinctive culture. Two hundred years after the settlement at Plymouth, Washington Irving still found America a land of youthful promise and preferred to let his imagination dwell upon 'the accumulated treasures of age' in the Old World. Even Emerson, who authoritatively declared our cultural independence, conceded in 1844 that Europe extended to the Alleghany Mountains. His disciple Whitman, in the same paradoxical manner, heralded with trumpet blasts the beginning of a new order, the fulfillment of which he left to the bards of a remote future. In our own time, three centuries after the Plymouth plantation, countless voices are crying that America has come of age, although all signs still point to the future. In a word, America has had no native tradition guiding her art and her criticism — no national background of ideas offering firm support to those who would rest upon the past, or firm resistance to those who would revolt. If our critics wish to be American, they must deploy in a vacuum.

Inevitably, therefore, our culture and our criticism have been mainly derivative. While the whole of the European tradition has been ours to draw upon at will, we have naturally tended to use most freely, in each of the periods of our history, those streams of tendency which contemporary Europe itself was following. As Cotton Mather observed, the discovery of America nearly coincided with the Renaissance and the Reformation; of the two, however, the Reformation chanced to be much the stronger in determining the foundations of our culture. A transplanted Puritanism, contrasting oddly with the crudities of the frontier and the primitive culture of the aborigines, established in America a remarkable moral discipline and spiritual idealism. Supplemented in later times by other forms of dissent, the Puritan spirit became a leading factor in American life, American literature, American criticism.

As Puritanism was the great contribution of the seventeenth century, so was the Enlightenment the great contribution of the eighteenth. Jehovah became the absentee landlord of the deists; natural depravity was set aside for natural goodness; the moral discipline and spiritual idealism of the Puritans was followed by reliance upon common sense and reason. While Jonathan Edwards represented the surviving Puritan spirit, Franklin represented the worldly spirit of the new age. The interests and the thought of the eighteenth century produced the American Revolution, as in Europe they produced the French Revolution, and the Colonies became a self-conscious nation.

In the nineteenth century the national spirit, surpassing the bounds of the political realm, aspired to the creation of a national culture comparable with that of each of the great countries of Europe. This passion gave impetus to the literature of the century of Cooper, Poe, Emerson, Hawthorne, Thoreau, Longfellow, Whitman, Mark Twain, and Howells. While it is true that this literature had distinctively American elements because it faintly reflected the frontier frame of mind, the fact of primary importance is that it was dominated by the European tradition in its contemporary aspect. In the early decades of the century Europe was experiencing the so-called Romantic Movement; its writers were concerned with revolt, feeling, imagination, ideality, genius, the ego, nature, the national past. To a nation like the United States, eager to exploit its selfhood, the romantic break with tradition offered a favorable opportunity that was soon recognized. Romantically we insisted upon the value of our own experience — and imitated the romanticism of Britain and Germany. The Puritans subsided into distant ancestors, the reasonable school of Pope fell into contempt and oblivion, and throughout the country literary taste was plainly romantic. New England Transcendentalism — 'romanticism on Puritan soil' — imitated Wordsworth, Coleridge, the young Carlyle, and the Germans; while even at the Middle Western frontier scarcely a verse-maker escaped the influence of Scott and Byron. After the movement had passed its *Blütezeit*, and our major authors had done their best work, a host of lesser romantics like Taylor and Stoddard kept the romantic tradition in power.

As this high-strung cult of feeling and intuition relaxed, vitality passed into those elements of experience that romanticism had tended to slight. Ethical restraint and convention once more became popular; an America founded in Puritanism offered a favorable soil for the staid middle-class morality that flourished here a little later than in Victorian England. And the common sense and rationalism of the eighteenth century reasserted themselves in the scientific spirit of the period after the Civil War, when the growth of natural knowledge altered our minds as the Industrial Revolution altered our landscapes. In America as in Europe, romanticism was succeeded by realism. The quest of reality had also actuated the romantics, who had sought it in the 'ideal' as opposed to the 'actual.' It was this rejected actual to which the new writers devoted themselves, observing and representing it under the inspiration of the scientific spirit. Walt Whitman, obedient to both the romantic and the realistic impulse, marks the passage from the old movement to the new; the future belonged, in his time, to Howells, James, Mrs. Wharton, Stephen Crane, and the writers of the present century.

These various streams of tendency have determined the course of American speculation on the nature and function of literature. In our speculation as a whole, the issues most commonly debated are:

1. What is the relation of literature to morality?

2. What is the relation of literature to reality?

3. What is the relation of American literature to the national spirit?

Since American literary history is in the main a history of the rise and development of the Romantic Movement in the New World, we shall naturally find that the most impressive answers to these questions, prior to the twentieth century, have been formulated by leaders in that movement: Poe, Emerson, Lowell, and Whitman.

AMERICAN CRITICISM

AMERICAN CRITICISM

.˙.

CHAPTER I

POE

§ 1

WITH his usual critical acumen, Poe saw that a people's literature may be provincial in either of two opposite ways. At the beginning of his essay on Drake's overrated poem 'The Culprit Fay,' he wrote an analysis of the state of American criticism which to this day may be read with profit. First, there is the older type of provincialism: a servile respect for European opinion. 'That an American book could, by any possibility, be worthy perusal, was an idea by no means extensively prevalent in the land; and if we were induced to read at all the productions of our native writers, it was only after repeated assurances from England that such productions were not altogether contemptible.' This cringing form of provincialism, however, as Poe is careful to point out, is related with an important virtue — a due respect for what is really superior. It would be folly, he says, to place ourselves on a level with the mature nations of Europe, 'the earliest steps of whose children are among the groves of magnificently endowed Academies, and whose innumerable men of leisure, and of consequent learning, drink daily from those august fountains of inspiration which burst around them everywhere from out the tombs of their immortal dead, and from out their hoary and trophied monuments of chivalry and song.' Of this sustaining power of the past, it must be admitted, Poe himself had but a dim understanding.[1] The second and opposite form of provincialism, prominent in Poe's day and still too common, is a blindly patriotic sense of our own importance. We may look down, as well as up; may be 'snobbishly arrogant' as well as 'snobbishly mean,' as Thackeray said in 'Punch.' Declaring that 'We are becoming boisterous and arrogant in the pride of a too speedily assumed literary freedom,' Poe bids his readers not to 'forget, in the puerile inflation of vanity, that *the world* is the true theatre of the biblical histrio. . . . So far from being ashamed of the many disgraceful literary failures to which our own inordinate vanities and misapplied patriotism have lately given birth, and so far from deeply lamenting that these daily puerilities are of home manufacture, we adhere pertinaciously to our original blindly conceived idea, and thus often find ourselves involved in the gross paradox of liking a stupid book the better, because, sure enough, its stupidity is American.'

Making it his task to wage incessant warfare against these two forms of provincialism, especially the superficially patriotic form, Poe wrote more criticism than any other kind of composition, and became known in his own time chiefly as a literary critic. In place of the idols that he cast down, he set up the ideal of adherence to principles, 'the purest rules of Art,' discovered by philosophical analysis. He did not hesitate to assume the existence of absolute, universal principles, fixed in the nature of literature and in the mind of a rightly thinking man, though he recognized the extreme difficulty of stating them. Words cannot hem in the spiritual nature of poetry, he says, for the intangible necessarily eludes defini-

---

[1] 'He read books of contemporary fame, especially such English books as were reprinted in Philadelphia, and magazines and newspapers, for which he always showed avidity; he had little familiarity at any time with literature earlier than Byron, and never showed love or devotion to great masters of the past. He had, in the narrowest sense, a contemporaneous mind, the instincts of the journalist, the magazine writer.' (Woodberry, *Life*, i, 132.)

tion; yet definitions are requisite in human discussion — and Poe never hesitates to define. In 1831, when he had scarce attained manhood, he set forth his poetical creed in the 'Letter to B——' prefacing his own poems, and again and again, in the years that followed, he repeated it with remarkable consistency. Seeking to avoid the conventional rules, whether classic or romantic, and at the same time merely personal preferences and antipathies, he aimed at a criticism that should be both impersonal and deductive and therefore valid. Whether an art or a science (he used both terms) he never doubted that criticism is or ought to be 'based immovably in nature,' on 'the laws of man's mind and heart,' upon which the arts themselves are based. Authority thus resides in principles not in persons, in reason not in precedent, in rationale not in rule. The rational critic will give praise to what has been well done; but he will look less at merit than at demerit, less at 'beauties' than at 'defects,' because it is the business of the critic to hold up as the model of excellence, not the good, nor even the best that has been done, but the best that can be — he must 'see the sun, even although its orb be far below the ordinary horizon.'[1]

To this rational method and this high standard Poe adhered with a faithfulness amazing in the America of the thirties and forties. While the great majority of our criticasters never

[1] Perhaps the best statement of his ideal in criticism is the following passage from his prospectus for *The Penn Magazine*: 'It shall be a leading object to assert in precept, and to maintain in practice, the rights, while in effect it demonstrates the advantages, of an absolutely independent criticism; — a criticism self-sustained; guiding itself only by the purest rules of Art; analyzing and urging these rules as it applies them; holding itself aloof from all personal bias; acknowledging no fear save that of outraging the right; yielding no point either to the vanity of the author, or to the assumptions of antique prejudice, or to the involute and anonymous cant of the Quarterlies, or to the arrogance of those organized *cliques* which, hanging like nightmares upon American literature, manufacture, at the nod of our principal booksellers, a pseudo-public-opinion by wholesale. . . . It will endeavor to support the general interests of the republic of letters, without reference to particular regions — regarding the world at large as the true audience of the author.' (Quoted, Woodberry, *op. cit.*, I, 274.)

saw the sun or mistook flashy meteors for the supreme lumi-
nary, while they judged in accordance with petty provincial
instincts instead of sovereign reason, Poe held clearly before
himself a lofty vision of the critical activity and pursued its
dictates with a devotion that shows his possession of a passion for criticism as well as for poetry. Although he could be
impatient, disdainful, and even as brutal as the Scotch re-
viewers whom he censured, he did not deserve the charge that
he had the polemical rather than the critical temper. He had
ground for his boast that in ten years' time he did not write a
single critique either wholly destructive or wholly laudatory,
or state a single opinion of importance without supporting it
with some show of reason. He developed a theory of literary
principles and applied it without shrinking from the fatigue
of thought. Rejecting the essay form of the British reviews
as an evasion of the critical task, he read his books carefully,
analyzed them patiently, and generalized deliberately, despite the pressure of poverty and such temperamental handi-
caps as few writers in any age have labored against. For
polemics as such he had little enough taste; but he guarded his
literary principles with passion and had the reformer's zeal in
seeking to make them prevail.

Poe derived his principles of criticism from his own conception of art, which may be studied indifferently in his creative
or in his critical work: it is implicit in the one, explicit in the
other. Frequently it is held as a reproach — as a mark of
limitation — that his creation and his criticism are substantially the same. This may be regarded, however, as a
great merit, not merely because it attests to his honesty, his
fidelity to principle, but more especially because, as Poe himself says, it is the only proper relation of theory and practice
— of that theory of literature which regulates the critical
activity and that practice of literature which is the embodi-
ment of theory. As an English critic of our own day puts it,
literature is the consciousness of life and criticism is the con-

sciousness of literature. An artist may, of course, be deficient
in the critical faculty ('Poets are by no means, necessarily,
judges of poetry,' says Poe); but when he possesses the critical faculty, his theory and practice will tend to coincide. It
would assuredly be absurd if they conflicted, if, for example, Poe's poetic principle and poetic creation clashed with
each other, or his conception of the tale were antagonistic
to his own tales.[1] Nevertheless, one must add, as Poe himself failed to add, that in any artist who falls short of the
ideal artist — practically, therefore, in any artist who has
ever lived — theory should include more than practice, the
artist as critic should perceive more than he can himself
carry out. As critic, he must allow for modes of excellence
that are denied himself, and his achievement in criticism will
depend largely on the degree of clearness with which he perceives these excellences. It is precisely in this respect, as we
shall see, that the criticism of Poe was most deficient. Just
as the primary weakness of his art was want of range, so the
primary weakness of his criticism was want of range. He was
right in making his theory and practice harmonious; he was
wrong in allowing them absolutely to coincide.

Holding that poets are not necessarily judges of poetry, Poe
also holds that critics, on the contrary, *are* necessarily poets;
they must have, he means, 'the poetic sentiment, if not the
poetic power — the "vision," if not the "faculty divine."'
It was one of the signal results of the Romantic Movement of
the early nineteenth century that it established firmly this

[1] The unity of Poe's creation and his criticism and of both with his life has
been studied by J. W. Krutch, in *Edgar Allan Poe*, 1926, in the uncertain light
of the 'new psychology.' Endeavoring to discover 'the relationship which
exists between psychology and æsthetics,' Mr. Krutch in the end concedes that
'the present state of knowledge is not such as to enable any one satisfactorily
to determine that relationship.' This being so, I cannot but think that the
literary critic should indefinitely continue to prefer what Mr. Krutch terms
'the level of art' to 'the level of psychology.' Even if the day of a securely
scientific psychology of art should ever arrive, the literary critic will still find
artistic results far more important than psychological causes.

relation of the critical and poetical natures, and Poe played an important part in establishing it in America. He asserts that 'to appreciate thoroughly the work of what we call genius, is to possess all the genius by which the work was produced' — all the genius but not, he adds, the constructive ability. Had he been a disciple of Goethe, he would have accepted the dictum,

Du gleichst dem Geist den du begreifst,

but though in some sort a disciple of Schlegel, he could not accept the assertion that 'Genius . . . is taste in its highest activity,' an assertion that has become central in the 'expressionist' criticism of our day. It apparently never occurred to him that he might have performed the entire critical function when he had entered by sympathy into the mind of genius and occupied the genial point of view: for Poe this was the indispensable preliminary and condition of sound criticism, but criticism itself was the later process of comparison with other examples of literature and with the ideal example, ending in the formulation of deduction and judgment. It is one of the leading distinctions of Poe's theory of criticism that it gave full weight at the same time to the element of sympathy and the element of judgment.

Now, what were in his mind the central principles upon which sound judgments might be based? They may be summed up in few words:

The end of art is pleasure, not truth. In order that pleasure may be intense, the work of art must have unity and brevity. In poetry, the proper means of arousing pleasure is the creation of beauty; not the beauty of concrete things alone, but also a higher beauty — supernal beauty. Music is an indispensable element in poetry, and is especially valuable in the poet's straining toward the supernal, since music comes nearer this goal than any other art. In the prose tale, on the other hand, the artist may seek to produce effects other than those

of poetry, — effects of horror, terror, passion, — limiting him-
self in each case to a single effect.

This was Poe's artistic creed, exemplified in nearly all that
he wrote: in his poetry, his tales, his essays on literary theory,
and his criticism of literature — on nearly every page of his
sixteen volumes. In its simplest form it can be stated, as I
have stated it, in a few lines; but even when stated completely, it would remain brief. Poe was as direct and laconic,
in his exposition of literary principles, as his master Coleridge
was discursive and circumlocutory; so intent was he, indeed,
on the avoidance of metaphysical fogs that he went to the
other extreme and was satisfied with a rather barren formu-
lism, to which he tended by nature. His phrases of greatest
import — his formulæ — recur again and again, without
significant variation, from the 'Letter to B——' onwards,
and too few of them receive their share of Poe's ratiocinative
faculty. Sometimes whole passages are lifted from an earlier
context and planted in a new one, without much regard for
an organic accommodation, such accommodation as Matthew Arnold, for instance, usually effected when he quoted
from his previous writing. Yet it seems clear that such trans-
plantation, even when successful, implies weakness of
thought — apparently it was so in the case of Arnold, whose
formulæ and self-quotations are symptomatic of a relative
sterility of ideas, and apparently it was so in the case of Poe,
who at the beginning of his career in letters adopted a neat
little set of guiding principles and seemingly never suspected
that they might be inadequate. In the main, fortunately,
they were admirable principles, and his fidelity to them gave
his work as a whole singular consistency, definiteness, and
impact, three qualities very dear to him. Temperamentally
wasteful of emotional and intellectual energy, Poe nevertheless contrived to make the whole of his literary achievement
march unmistakably in one direction, just as in the composition of a single tale he managed to make every word and

image move convergingly to a premeditated end or 'effect.'
The result of such devotion to an artistic purpose was impressive. But it must not be allowed to obscure the fact that
Poe's guiding principles of creation and criticism, admirable
so far as they went, did not go far enough; that the failure of
Poe to enlarge his controlling conception of art, while it helps
to explain his striking achievement, also helps to explain
why this achievement was not greater.

§2

Let us begin our study of the artistic creed of Poe (perhaps
the only creed he had) with an examination of his first canon:
The end of art is pleasure, not truth. By truth he means both
intellectual and moral truth, neither of which, he holds, is the
legitimate aim of the artist.

Living, as it seemed to him, in a land of the philistines —
in a puritanical, humanitarian, and materialistic environment
hostile to the æsthetic vision of life — Poe was subject to
charges of superficiality and eccentricity which his temperamental weaknesses rendered plausible, and apparently regarding the offensive as the soundest defensive strategy, he
carried the war into the enemy's country, upholding the
standards of Beauty and Pleasure as supreme in art (supreme, for that matter, in life itself) and attacking, with an
effective use of light artillery, the 'heresy of the Didactic' so
strongly intrenched in England and America. Both moralism
as the end of art and realism as the end of art, however
widely respected, he held to be heresies, somewhat as Milton
regarded those who are heretics in the truth; and he fought
them with fine energy — especially the moral heresy, in that
day the more formidable of the two. The particular objects
of his contempt were 'the moralists who keep themselves
erect by the perpetual swallowing of pokers'; such moralists,
one may imagine, as the principal of a school that Professor
Trent tells us of, who was capable, a century after the birth

of Poe, of proscribing Mr. Trent's history of American literature from the school library on the ground, not that the
author had treated Poe badly, but that he had treated him
at all: 'School children, according to my correspondent,
ought not to know that such a life as Poe's was ever lived.'
This is almost as perverse as the case of the prince whom
Eckermann reports as saying that if he had been the Deity he
would have left the world uncreated rather than create a
world that should contain Schiller's 'Robbers.'

In so far as Poe's attack is directed against the philistine
type of moralist who thrives in America, it is so obviously
sound that it need not detain us here. The assumption that
the artist is to regard himself as a moral physician administer-
ing pills (whether plain or sugar-coated) is none the less
ridiculous because it has occasionally been made by noble-
minded persons; and it is doubly ridiculous when the *materia
medica* is not morality itself but a temporary moral code — is
grounded, not in the nature of man, but in more or less
arbitrary and shifting social relations. It is unquestionably
true that art has a moral result, and that man's struggle to
clarify his moral values is carried on within the domain of
fine art as well as outside of it; yet at the same time within its
domain art has its own purpose, and that purpose is not moral
but æsthetic. No amount of moral excellence alone will
constitute a composition a work of art, and on the other hand
it may have a quite negligible moral content and yet be a
work of art. If it does not give pleasure, it is not art; if it
does give pleasure, it is.

Had Poe stopped here — had he contented himself with
showing that the artist must not aim at morality and that
the critic must not identify artistic and moral values — he
would have performed an inestimable service to American
letters. But in his impetuous attack on the moralists, he
sometimes overstated his doctrine and thus invited an effective counter-attack. The apostles of art for art's sake have

so often made their gospel odious through their own art, and have so often discredited themselves by their criticism of art — by their preference for the inferior — that we have grown suspicious of any one who uses their expressions. The poet, says Poe, can have no more noble purpose than 'this poem which is a poem and nothing more — this poem written solely for the poem's sake.' Blind and mad, he says a moment later, is he who would 'reconcile the obstinate oils and waters of Poetry and Truth.' These would seem to be far-reaching ideas, involving, to use Poe's favorite word, heresies of the first magnitude. Yet they really do not. For, viewed strictly and philosophically, a 'poem for the poem's sake' is surely meaningless; and viewed loosely and practically, as Poe doubtless used it, it is commonplace — it asserts only that a poem is a poem, not something else. As for the oils and waters, Poe is plainly at the mercy of his metaphor, which not only enables him to express his meaning — to drive home his distinction between the moral and the æsthetic — but forces him to suggest more than he means. As the context indicates, he is insisting only that there is a sharp difference in 'modes of inculcation' between Truth and Poetry, the intellect aiming at perspicuity, precision, terseness, dispassionateness, while poetry aims at the 'exact converse' of these qualities (though here again, to secure force, Poe overstates his point). In the spirit and method of their endeavor, Truth, or the didactic in its full sense, and Poetry, the handmaiden of taste, are indeed, as Poe asserts, as nearly opposite as possible, are as unrelated as oil and water. But Poe does not say and does not mean, as he is often understood to say and mean, that Truth and Poetry in all respects manifest this elemental alienation, that they are in all respects mutually incompatible.

For, in the first place, they unite in their subject-matter. The poetic and the moral, while very different in spirit and method, are alike in that they both concern themselves with man's moral nature. 'We would not be misunderstood,' Poe with good reason reminds his reader; for he is entirely willing to admit that Poetry, the handmaiden of taste, 'is not forbidden to moralize — in her own fashion. She is not forbidden to depict but to reason and preach, of virtue. As, of this latter, conscience recognizes the obligation, so intellect teaches the expediency, while taste contents herself with displaying the beauty: waging war with vice merely on the ground of its inconsistency with fitness, harmony, proportion — in a word with τὸ καλόν.' Too often the reader of Poe remembers 'the radical and chasmal difference' between truth and poetry, the 'obstinate oils and waters,' and forgets that at the same time, as Poe dimly perceived, they have an intimate relation, that in a very real sense truth, beauty, and goodness are one. Thus, according to Mr. Brownell, Poe's theory is that 'poetry has absolutely nothing to do with truth (to which he had an intellectual repugnance), that it is concerned solely with beauty (which he does not define, but assumes, in opposition to more conventional opinion from Plato to Keats, to be absolutely divorced from truth).' On the contrary, it is clear that Poe accepted, if he did not really understand, the 'conventional opinion':

Beauty is truth, truth beauty.

In his 'Marginalia' he asserts that 'the *highest* genius is but the loftiest moral nobility.' In his review of 'The Culprit Fay,' he objects that the Sylphid Queen is a fanciful compound of incongruous natural objects 'unaccompanied by any *moral* sentiment,' though his use of the word that he italicizes is not altogether clear. More significantly, in his review of Longfellow's 'Ballads,' while deprecating the poet's inveterate didacticism, he approves those poems in which, as he thinks, the moral element is rightly introduced because it is æsthetically treated: in 'The Wreck of the Hesperus,' for example, 'we have the beauty of childlike confidence and innocence, with that of the father's stern courage and affection,' in 'The Skeleton in Armor,' 'we find the beauty of bold courage and self-confidence, of love and maiden devotion, of reckless adventure, and finally of life-contemning grief,' and in 'The Village Blacksmith,' 'we have the *beauty* of simple-mindedness as a genuine thesis; and this thesis is inimitably handled until the concluding stanza, where the spirit of legitimate poesy is aggrieved in the pointed antithetical deduction of a *moral* from what has gone before.' Here is no absolute divorce, but a highly intimate relation between beauty and moral truth. In such passages Poe shows plainly that he is at least on the way to an adequate conception of the relation of art and morality. But other passages indicate that he has far to go before arriving at a full sense of the vital fusion of the two.

For, in the second place, he seeks to demonstrate the compatibility of poetry and morality by his doctrine of 'collateral relations.' Instead of moving toward a conception of their organic union, he was accustomed to regard them mechanically as lying side by side in a work of art, as 'collateral,' or as placed one above the other — Beauty above, as an upper-current, and the Didactic beneath, as an under-current. This mechanical distinction, however, really grants the whole case to the moralist, permitting him to exercise a moral purpose in a work of art so long as he succeeds in making his moral purpose subordinate, contributing collaterally, or as an under-current to the main theme, or, to use another expression that Poe favored, incidentally. This sophomoric conception of the relation of art and morality is unworthy of a critic who is in so many respects close to the central principles, and it may even suggest that, beneath the rebel against Puritanism, there was a moribund Puritan nature. Fighting 'tooth and nail' against the didactic, he yet concedes, altogether unnecessarily, that poetry is not forbidden to moralize 'in the right way' (surely, poetry ought never to affect a moral *purpose*), and then habitually accepts, as the right way, a direct moral purpose which is made to seem casual or subordinate. The obstinate oils and waters have become the lion and the lamb. And Poe is finally reduced to the feeble argument that, the two elements being altogether capable of accord, the poet who would 'introduce didacticism' into his poem is accepting a superfluous handicap which he can overcome only by 'a feat of literary sleight of hand.' All of our high principles of the inviolable nature of poesy have vanished, and nothing remains but a question of ingenious technique — a *tour de force*.

Thus Poe's theory of art and morality, which ever lay in the foreground of his mind, turns out to be a mass of ill-sorted and discordant ideas surprising in a critic of his ratiocinative powers. How shall we account for so fundamental a confusion? How did it happen that a critic who discoursed so pungently on the inalienable right of poetry to the pursuit of happiness and beauty betrayed his high cause by conceding the moral purpose so long as it was decently subordinated? Why did Poe, though moving in the direction of a sound view of art and morals, perceive this sound view so dimly, through such a veil of conflicting and irrelevant distinctions? Inherent in his recognition of a unity in subject-matter — inherent but never extracted and expressly stated — is the recognition of a necessary fusion of the moral and the æsthetic in art as in life, from which it follows that a great art which is at the same time an immoral or unmoral art is impossible, that a weak or distorted conception of man's moral nature results in a mode of beauty correspondingly weak or distorted.[1] Why does this view of art and morality, expressed with considerable distinctness by his guide Coleridge, remain merely latent in Poe?

The answer would seem to be plain: because Poe was him-

[1] *Troilus and Criseyde*, for example, 'is a great work of art, and as such, I believe, inevitably ethical.' (G. L. Kittredge, *Chaucer and His Poetry*, 144.)

self so astonishingly deficient in ethical development. Perhaps there is no better instance in all literature of important achievement in despite of ethical weakness; which is but another way of saying that Poe just falls short of the heights because of ethical weakness. He was singularly wanting in interest in the actual life of experience which the great artists have represented and interpreted; he was as remote from the world of Shakspere as any writer of his caliber could be. He was so indifferent to the phenomena and the problems of actual life that he barely managed to secure the materials for his own private house of art — his dream-world within the Shaksperian dream-world of actual life.[1] While a writer like Shakspere, as Coleridge rightly insisted, is in the march of the human affections, attuned to the law of human nature, a writer like Poe pursues his solitary way as if ignorant of the meaning of the human spectacle, and, although he orders his experience in shapes that are exquisite, leaves the major part of our human nature unresponsive. As a consequence of his lack of interest in humanity, his art is lyrical — limited to the re-creation of a mood, whether in his poems or in his tales. The subjective mood objectified and depersonalized is his almost unvarying substitute for the impersonal representation of life which is the aim of the realist and the impersonal imitation of the ideal which is the aim of the classicist. All high types of realism and classicism demand a grasp on man's 'pathos' and 'ethos,' on the fluctuant life of emotion and the deeply established life of character, to both of which Poe was a stranger. His knowledge of character was obviously rudimentary (contrast Jane Austen, who was writing in his boy-

[1] In an article on 'Poe in Relation to his Times' (*Studies in Philology*, xx, 293–301), Killis Campbell contends that Poe was 'as genuinely interested in his age and in what was going on about him as was the average American of intelligence in his day.' While this is doubtless sound, it should be observed (1) that as a writer of genius Poe might have been expected to have an exceptional interest in his world; (2) that his interest was superficial, showing no ethical insight; (3) that his most important interest was in contemporary books, not in the human relations of actual life.

hood, or even Scott, another writer of his time, or the author of 'The Scarlet Letter'), and his knowledge of the play of emotions in our reaction to the happenings of life was little more sophisticated — he knew only, or at least used only, a very few kinds of emotion, and used them broadly, elementarily, and not with subtlety, delicacy, or a sense of their multitudinous interrelations, as they are represented by Tolstoy, or Meredith, or Henry James. It may be that he chose his materials deliberately; but this is not to say that he could have chosen otherwise had he so desired — the more one reads Poe, the more one feels that he used with supreme power the scant and inferior materials that he possessed. He was a master of creative imagination, but the chaos to which he gave form was but a small fragment of the whole.

Deficient in ethical development, Poe was almost as limited in intellectual development. And again there are curious inconsistencies betokening a fundamental confusion.

Sharing the Transcendental disparagement of the ordinary reason, regarding truth as 'the quirks and quibbles of chopped logic,' he was at the same time an adept at logic, which he used with great deliberation in his creative work as well as in his criticism, and which he sometimes seems to have abused to obscure the truth so long as it served his immediate purpose. It is when he is most rigorously logical that we are least sure of Poe's sincerity — most suspicious of quirks and quibbles. His immense powers of analysis and ratiocination, his instinct for definition, division, cause and effect, and the irresistible syllogism, needed the ballast of humor, common sense, and ethical control, and so tended to deploy in a universe logical rather than human. This is the universe of Poe's tales, both those of ratiocination and those of 'terror, or passion, or horror, or a multitude of such other points.' Separating poetry and prose with unromantic rigor, Poe contends that the creation of beauty is the province of the poem and that 'Truth is often, and in very great degree, the aim of

the tale.' Brought into relation with his primary canon that
the end of art is pleasure and not truth, this contention would
seem to involve the view that the tale is scientific and not
æsthetic — a paradox from which Poe escapes, not too plausibly, by making pleasure the ultimate end of both the prose
tale and of science, as in the following passage of chopped
logic:

It is a truism that the end of our existence is happiness; if so, the
end of every separate part of our existence — everything connected
with our existence should be still happiness. Therefore the end of
instruction should be happiness; and happiness is another name for
pleasure; — therefore the end of instruction should be pleasure. . . .
He who pleases, is of more importance to his fellow men than he
who instructs, since utility is happiness, and pleasure is the end
already obtained which instruction is merely the means of obtain-
ing.[1]

Extracting the drift from these scholastic twists and turns,
one may infer that Poe means that, while science and philosophy aim directly at truth, which results in pleasure, poetry
aims at pleasure by way of beauty, and the prose tale aims at
pleasure by way of truth. Truth is thus, after all, not the aim
of the tale; it is the means, the material used, for that pleasurable effect which is the end of all art. Poe is contemptuous of
the realism that is often called photographic — the grapes of
Zeuxis, the Jan Steen, type; he is equally contemptuous of
the realism or naturalism that seems to regard the truthful
and the disagreeable as synonymous — 'If an artist must
paint decayed cheeses, his merit will lie in their looking as
little like decayed cheeses as possible.' Both types, Poe
would maintain, err in aiming at truth, instead of aiming at
pleasure by way of truth, as he did in his own tales; though it
must be admitted that in his evocation of pleasure Poe made
a very free use of the psychological kinship of pleasure and
pain, so often is the effect dominantly painful.

[1] Cf. Wordsworth's Preface of 1800, Grosart, II, 90–92.

In a word, contemning mere logic and logical truth, Poe excels in them, using them in his tales with a view to a pleasurable effect. So far, he is on strong ground; but not content with the Transcendental degradation of mere logic and logical truth, he rejects also the kind of reason and truth which was the avowed basis of Transcendentalism — the higher reason of immediate insight, and an order of truth that might be called, in Poe's own language, supernal. Once, at least, he seems to have caught a full glimpse of the romantic vision of the unity of the highest beauty and the highest truth, when he attributes to the faculty of ideality our admiration of earthly and heavenly beauty, and, 'mingled up inextricably' with our thirst for beauty 'the unconquerable desire — *to know.*' 'Poetry,' he adds, 'is the sentiment of Intellectual Happiness here, and the Hope of a higher Intellectual Happiness hereafter.' This is Transcendental enough; and yet he never misses an opportunity to ridicule the profundity of the Germans, the pantheism of Wordsworth and the moonshine of Coleridge, the metaphysical nonsense of Carlyle, whom he dubbed an ass, and of his 'respectful imitation,' Emerson. He may have been entirely right in refusing to enlist in the Transcendental quest of truth, but he only revealed his own severe limitation in refusing for a false reason. He might have maintained that the Transcendentalists were experiencing a dubious kind of immediate insight into the supernal, but instead he threw up the whole quest of truth as unworthy of a creator of beauty, except as a collateral interest. Examining critically Bryant's long poem 'The Ages,' he writes a single sentence on its 'philosophy,' and then expatiates at length on technical matters because 'it is only as a poem that we wish to examine "The Ages."' That is, the poet's opinions may be what they may be: for us they are irrelevant — our concern is with the poem. Again, in his important 'Exordium,' Poe sets forth as a leading critical principle that he will 'limit literary criticism to comment upon *Art*. A book is written —

and it is only *as the book* that we subject it to review. With
the opinions of the work, considered otherwise than in their
relation to the work itself, the critic has really nothing to do.
It is his part simply to decide upon *the mode* in which these
opinions are brought to bear.' The critic has no right to consider the truth or value of the author's conception — of his
intuition, as the expressionist critic of our day would say; he
is simply to consider the mode in which the conception has
been carried out, its expression and externalization. The
mode is the art, the art is the mode, and art and criticism
alike have no serious interest in truth.

Here Poe departs, of course, from his own critical masters,
Wordsworth and Coleridge; from Wordsworth, who associates pleasure and truth so intimately that we are at a loss to
know which of the two he regards as really central in poetry,
and from Coleridge, who affirmed that 'No man was ever yet
a great poet, without being at the same time a profound
philosopher' and who found in Shakspere 'the morning star,
the guide and pioneer, of true philosophy.' In holding to this
conviction these romantic critics were, as they realized, leaning upon the classical doctrine of Aristotle. Thus, Wordsworth wrote in his famous preface to the 'Lyrical Ballads':
'Aristotle, I have been told [how charmingly naïve!], has said
that poetry is the most philosophical of all writing: it is so: its
object is truth, not individual and local, but general . . .' But
Poe accepts neither Aristotle's dictum nor Wordsworth's en-
dorsement of it; in *his* preface, that to the poems of 1831, he
writes: 'Aristotle, with singular assurance, has declared
poetry the most philosophical of all writings — but it required a Wordsworth to pronounce it the most metaphysical.
He seems to think that the end of poetry is, or should be, instruction.' Apparently Poe misconceived both Aristotle and
Wordsworth. His reference to Aristotle is obviously based,
not on Aristotle himself, but on Wordsworth's free rendering,
the ambiguity of which ensnared Poe. The 'Poetics' affirms

that pleasure, not truth, is the end or object of poetry, and yet a pleasure limited by the demands of truth; whereas Wordsworth bluntly says, 'Its object is truth,' and then goes on to argue that man has no knowledge save what has been acquired by pleasure and exists in him by pleasure, and so leads up to the memorable assertion that 'Poetry is the breath and finer spirit of all knowledge; it is the impassioned expression which is in the countenance of all science' — an assertion that Poe gives no sign of having understood.

The dependence of art upon truth for the quality of the pleasure that it evokes is thus conceded alike in the classicism of Aristotle and in the romanticism of Wordsworth and Coleridge. Classicist and romanticist may have viewed 'truth' and 'philosophy' variously (there is a wide difference between the Stagyrite law-giver and the Devonshire critic whose 'towering intellect' abashed Poe), but Aristotle and Coleridge, Aristotle and Wordsworth, are in fundamental accord as to the need in art of a vital fusion of truth and beauty, knowledge and pleasure. It is not they, but Poe, who displayed 'singular assurance.'

This is equivalent to saying that Poe showed the same weakness in his criticism that he showed in his creative work. Unmoral and unphilosophical in his poems and tales because he was himself unmoral and unphilosophical, he was unable to attain in his criticism a larger vision of the principles of art than he could himself exemplify. It has already been remarked that his creation and his criticism should harmonize but not coincide. If his criticism was to be more than an exposition of his own artistic practice and a measuring of others by himself, he must possess the power of enlarging his guiding principles — of seeing the sun — of seeing, at all events, more than himself and his kind. His own art he saw, indeed, with extraordinary vividness: he could even caricature himself, as in 'The Philosophy of Composition.' And his kind — Coleridge, Shelley, Keats, and Tennyson (or a part

of Tennyson) — these are the *sole* poets, he writes in a letter
to Lowell — he valued only as they fulfilled his own predilections as a poet. It was not the fine, if tame, humanity of
Tennyson that he had in mind when he hazarded the opinion,
in his most important essay on the nature of poetry, that
Tennyson was the noblest poet that ever lived. It is possible
that he had a more conventional respect for Shakspere, Milton, the Bible, and other classics of his own literature than he
was willing to display; apparently he had no respect at all for
the art of the Athenian dramatists. Ancient classicism —
'the glory that was Greece' — was in the main closed to him;
the same is true of modern realism, that of the eighteenth
century and of his own day in Europe; he had within his
view little more than romanticism, and romanticism of a
highly limited type. *That* he saw in full light, and analyzed
searchingly. If his own type of art had been central rather
than eccentric, what a critic he would have been! But it was
palpably absurd to apply to all authors, both contemporary
and past, the yardstick of the Poesque brief lyric and brief
tale. His principles were inflexible because, save in the process of formulating them, his mind was essentially unphilosophic. In this sense, he was as unintellectual as he was unmoral.

Whatever glimpses he may have had, then, of the intimate
relation of truth and beauty, of truth and pleasure, however
he may have at times assumed their organic fusion in the
work of art, Poe habitually disregarded the romantic doctrine of the union of opposites that lay ready to his hand, and
in effect proclaimed the radical alienation of truth and pleasure in art. He banished truth from art, and, turning to the
other member of the ancient marriage, sought to give a totally satisfying content to pleasure. His first canon becomes
simply 'The end of art is pleasure,' and all the rest of his
creed is an amplification of this canon.

§ 3

It was perhaps to be expected that, having banished truth, Poe would conceive of pleasure in a purely quantitative sense. Since truth has commonly been assumed to be the determinant of the quality of pleasure — the highest pleasure, that is, being possible only when the work of art conforms to the laws of man's mind and heart — it would be natural to suppose that Poe, having divorced truth from art, would elaborate a philosophy of pleasure in terms of quantity alone. But not so; though he was emphatic in his insistence on quantity, he was if anything more emphatic, as we shall see, in his insistence on quality.

Turning first to his discussion of quantitative pleasure, we come upon two of his most characteristic doctrines, applicable to poem and tale alike: the doctrines of unity and brevity. Unity is primary, in Poe's view, and brevity secondary; unity the proposition, brevity the corollary. •

In the entire history of criticism since Aristotle, no one has insisted more constantly on the importance of unity than Poe the romanticist. Though he did not, like Aristotle and the great romantic critics Schlegel and Coleridge, establish its basis in another and larger doctrine, that of organic form, probably because his own art had a distinctly mechanical tendency, he perceived with exemplary clearness the service of unity in the production of æsthetic pleasure. He conceived of unity in both the classical and the romantic senses. With Aristotle, he demands the unity of plot or action, at least in all cases where plot forms a part of the contemplated interest. '*Plot* is very imperfectly understood,' he writes, 'and has never been rightly defined. Many persons regard it as mere complexity of incident. In its most rigorous acceptation, it is *that from which no component atom can be removed, and in which none of the component atoms can be displaced, without ruin to the whole.*' Elsewhere, in his mechanical way, he likens it to a building, 'so dependently constructed, that to change the position of a single brick is to overthrow the entire fabric.' This is indeed a rigorous definition, as he goes on to acknowledge in both passages; a good tale, a good drama, will sometimes be found to depart widely from this gospel of perfection. Yet the true artist will keep his eyes directed to 'that unattainable goal,' even though it is for God alone to construct the perfect plot. He, only, sees the whole as a perfect web of causes and results entirely adapted to each other; He, only, has vision free of confusion and irrelevancy. 'The plots of God are perfect. The Universe is a plot of God.' He is the master plot-maker, and the model of all true artists. We must not say of them, as we may say of mediocre tale-writers, that 'they seem to begin their stories without knowing how they are to end; and their ends, generally — like so many governments of Trinculo — appear to have forgotten their beginnings.' Sound artists will take a hint from the Chinese, who '*begin their books at the end*,' so that their plots may possess an 'indispensable air of consequence, or causation,' may have, as Poe says in the hoary phrasing of Aristotle, a beginning, middle, and end. Poe does not undervalue a good beginning — 'At all risks, let there be a few vivid sentences *imprimis*' — nor good 'points' in the development — but he holds that 'of all literary foibles the most fatal, perhaps, is that of defective climax.' Here, at the end, where all converges, is the height of interest; here is lost or achieved that pleasurable result which was the aim of the writer; here is the sum or degree of pleasure determined. It is true that Poe was aware of the architectonic or, as he terms it, sculptural aspect of unity of plot, the pleasure residing in 'totality of beauty'; but this, he points out, is a pleasure for the few and not for the many, and consequently his emphasis falls, not on this intrinsic æsthetic value of unity of plot but on the value of the intense conclusion which it renders possible. He offers no idealistic explanations of our deep satisfaction in architectonic form, though they might be found inhering in his sen-

tence 'The plots of God are perfect'; he associates unity of
plot, not with the poem, in which the supernal aim demands
a high quality of pleasure, but with the short tale, where the
dominant consideration is intensity or quantity of pleasure.

This same end, quantity of pleasure, is subserved by the
romantic unity of effect or impression, which Poe exemplified in his many tales of horror, terror, and the like, as he
exemplified unity of plot in his tales of ratiocination. Just as
in the tale of ratiocination the writer must foresee the
dénouement, so in the tale of effect he must select in advance
the particular effect to be produced; 'and no word should be
then written which does not tend, or form a part of a sentence
which tends to the development of the dénouement, or to the
strengthening of the effect.' As means for the attainment of
the effect, the writer may rely upon incidents or tone, or both.
If the incidents are to predominate, they must have a logical
relationship — unity of plot will then serve unity of effect.
If the tone is to predominate, it must be a single tone — unity
of tone will then serve unity of effect. Although Poe uses all
these terms loosely at times, what seems to be his meaning
may be indicated by saying that he would have regarded
his 'Purloined Letter' as an example of unity of plot, his
'Murders in the Rue Morgue' as an example of unity of effect
served by unity of plot, and his 'Masque of the Red Death'
as an example of the unity of effect served by unity of tone.
Himself a master of unity in every sense, he seems to have
given most attention to the unity of tone — 'tone, by means
of which alone, an old subject, even when developed through
hackneyed incidents, or thoughts, may be made to produce a
fully original effect,' as he writes when discussing a form, the
drama, in which tone is relatively neglected. What most impressed Coleridge in some early work of Wordsworth's was
'the original gift of spreading the tone, the atmosphere, and
with it the depth and height of the ideal world around forms,
incidents, and situations . . .'; this was what Poe sought to

do, in his own way, in his poems, while in his prose, in which the ideal world seemed to him inappropriate, he constantly aimed at the creation of other tones, other atmospheres. Tone he apparently regarded — as the word itself suggests — as the equivalent in prose for the music in verse, an element in which the theme floats and is carried to the culminating effect. Sometimes, even, his 'tale' is composed of little more than the tone. As Mr. Brownell says — and Mr. Brownell is caution itself in his praise of Poe — 'He understood to perfection the value of tone in a composition, and tone is an element that is almost invaluable. In this respect he has no American and few foreign rivals.'

If the reader's pleasure is to be intense, then, unity of some sort — some principle of concentration — is essential. The false note, the irrelevant incident, the pointless detail, the confusion of effects, are therefore to be guarded against with unremitting care. And for the same reason the artist must avoid excess of length.

For unity and magnitude are, Poe declared with emphasis, incompatible because of the nature of the human mind. Beginning with his early preface, in which he asserted that we do not really, whatever we may say, enjoy epics, Poe consistently maintained that brevity is the soul of art. A long poem does not exist; it is a contradiction in terms, for if it is long it is not a poem but a collection of poems linked with prose — at least half of 'Paradise Lost' is prose. The artist professes to produce a certain unique pleasure; an unique pleasure demands unity, totality; and unity is impossible if, as in the epic or the novel, the artist disregards the formidable fact that 'through a psychal necessity' all excitements are transient. The feeling flags, a revulsion occurs, and every sort of unity is annihilated. Moreover, if the work is too long to be read at one sitting, the activities of our workaday life intervening between readings render impossible a unified impression. A single sitting is therefore an absolute limit, and within this, there is the further limit imposed by the aforesaid psychal necessity — in 'The Poetic Principle' Poe allows a half-hour at the utmost, in his review of Hawthorne's 'Twice-Told Tales' one hour. He reduces the matter to a definite law when he affirms that 'the brevity must be in direct ratio of the intensity of the intended effect,' adding, as a proviso, that, as there is a limit to magnitude, so there is a limit to brevity — a work may be so short as to prevent the formation of an intense and lasting impression. Poe's general position is thus precisely the same as Aristotle's when, in the 'Poetics,' he requires 'a certain magnitude,' neither too great nor too small; but, curiously, while the classical theorist is generous, the romantic law-giver is rigid. It was well for Poe, whose powers could not compass the sustained flight, to accept his limits and perfect himself within them — if all artists did so, we should have vastly more supremely fine art. He deserves the fullest credit for seeing so clearly what he could do, and doing it with all his energy. At the same time, he gravely erred in carrying over into his theory of art the limits of his creative art, transforming his deficiencies into essential principles of art and rules for the guidance of other artists. In this matter of brevity, his wisdom as an artist was his fatuity as a critic.

So far as his own work was concerned, Poe was eminently right in believing that intensity demanded brevity. In the tale of ratiocination, the reader is unable to retain all the complicated data from one reading to another. If his enjoyment is to be full — if all the evidence and points of relation are to be perceived as a perfect web woven by a master spider, the tale will lose with every extension beyond a certain length. If the reading must be broken off, some of the evidence, some of the points of relation, will inevitably be effaced or obscured, unless the design is exceptionally simple. Again, in all the tales of effect in which the tone or mood is central, a cessation of reading will almost invariably injure or destroy the illusion. A psychological state of the 'mood' type is by nature fragile and transitory, liable to annihilation at any moment if the artist errs ever so little or the reader suffers a slight interruption — the delicate illusion is snapped and can hardly be restored — the contagion is spent — the garish light of day floods the shadowy mood and either obliterates it (as the sun obliterates a bright fire) or subjects it to the alien criticism of practical life. In narrative that is more representative of human experience, in certain kinds of tales and novels that involve more of human nature than is involved in the mathematical tale of ratiocination and the lyrical tale of mood, the reader may return to the text, after an interruption, without serious loss — in a moment the old feeling revives, and he is again at the artist's command. But in the Poesque tale, this is not so: the author must say, 'Let me have your undivided attention,' and the reader must give it — that is, if the intensity at which the author aimed is to be realized. The narrator is telling his story, not in the market place at noon, but by the fire side on a dark and gusty night in November when an intruding visitor is expected: narrator and audience alike, knowing that the prosy everyday world will presently reassert itself, abandon themselves to the mood of the story in order to have it over before the intrusion occurs.

Intensity, then, is to be achieved by means of unity and brevity, as Poe uniformly states. It may be partly achieved, also, by the choice of a special kind of subject-matter — horror, terror, and the like. Although Poe does not discuss this means as if it were coördinate in importance with the other two, does not in this regard legislate for all artists on the basis of his own experience, he plainly associates certain 'effects' with his doctrine of intensity or quantity of pleasure. When he discusses effects, he is obviously not thinking of the intensity which Jane Austen, for instance, attained in her magical delineation of the commonplace; he is thinking of intensity won by the skillful use of the extraordinary — the terrible, the repulsive, the ghastly, the weird (a word to which he gave new life), the unaccountable, the unprecedented. He addresses, not the understanding of his readers, their common sense, their habitual moral sense, their instinct for the normal and representative in life, but the very opposite of these — their occasional feelings of mystery, of dark powers at work in the universe, of inexplicable things that are neglected precisely because they seem inexplicable, of ugly and harrowing things from which men customarily avert their eyes, of the strange functioning of the senses, the nerves, the subconscious self. These things he sought to express, not with the relish of the sentimentalist, but with the artful deliberation of the melodramatist. He possessed the faculty, as Mrs. Browning said, 'of making horrible improbabilities seem near and familiar' — near, at all events, if not quite familiar. Intensity to him implied thrills, and thrills implied the merely extraordinary, the merely strange. To the merely strange — the strange, that is, viewed in its strangeness rather than related to the meaning of life — he gave admirably complete and shapely expression, which is beauty. Nothing could be too strange, too rare, too ugly to bring into the realm of art. Assuredly, he believed in 'the addition of strangeness to beauty.'

§4

While Poe, developing his theory of the short story, a relatively new form of art, was so engrossed in the means to a maximum intensity that he failed to provide for a qualitative beauty, he gave to quality the fullest recognition in his theory of the lyric poem. For the good poem, in his view, must produce not only a pronounced pleasure, but also a high pleasure, an elevated kind of pleasure; and of the two considerations, degree and kind, he elects to emphasize kind.

Truth and Passion, to which the writer gives pleasurable

form in the tale, Poe expressly excludes from the domain of
the poet. The concern of the poet is with Beauty alone,
which satisfies the soul, and not with Truth, which satisfies
the intellect, or with Passion, which satisfies the heart. Since
the satisfaction of the soul is the supreme satisfaction, pre-
eminence in literary art belongs to the poet, the creator of
beauty. What Poe meant by beauty, as thus divorced from
the mind and heart of man, is not very clear to us and seems
not to have been very clear to him, though he repeatedly
confronted the term with his dialectic.

He distinguishes three kinds of beauty. First and hum-
blest is the beauty of the concrete, perceived through the
senses, and the beauty of human sentiments — 'the manifold
forms, and sounds, and odors, and sentiments' in the midst of
which man has his being. At the close of 'The Poetic Principle' Poe instances, in a kind of enthusiastic catalogue, some
aspects of concrete beauty: the stars, the waving grain, far
mountains, cloud groupings, gleaming rivers, quiet lakes, the
songs of birds, the sighing night-wind, the scent of the violet,
and the like. But the list is somewhat confused; among these
physical beauties is included 'the suggestive odor that comes
to him, at eventide, from far-distant, undiscovered islands,
over dim oceans, illimitable and unexplored,' an odor whose
existence, apart from its romantic percipient, may well be
doubted. Continuing his catalogue, Poe avails himself of
specifically ethical 'beauties,' such as 'all noble thought,' 'all
unworldly motives,' 'all holy impulses,' 'all chivalrous, generous, and self-sacrificing deeds.' And finally, for the climax,
he gives us a rhapsody, not without a tincture of sentimentalism, on the beauty of woman, partly physical, partly moral:
'the grace of her step,' 'the lustre of her eye,' 'the melody of
her voice,' 'her sigh,' 'the harmony of her rustling robes,'
'her winning endearments,' 'her burning enthusiasms,' 'her
gentle charities,' 'her meek and devotional endurances'; 'but
above all — ah, far above all — he kneels to it [beauty] —

he worships it in the faith, in the purity, in the strength, in the altogether divine majesty — of her *love.*' Perhaps three quarters of all the items are physical, because, it would seem, they are indubitable examples of the existence of beauty outside the poetic consciousness. Merely to repeat these forms, sounds, colors, odors, and sentiments, and thus to yield a duplicate delight, is only the work of an accomplished realist. 'This mere repetition is not poetry.'

The function of this beauty of things and sentiments in the divine economy is to incite in us a desire to contemplate and to seize for our own the supernal Loveliness. The poet who is indeed a poet cannot content himself with the superficial beauties of the world in which he lives; he aspires, he struggles, he thirsts, for the Beauty above. 'It is the desire of the moth for the star.' The expression of this longing by those who have felt it keenly has given us all the true poetry that we possess. Man's soul is immortal; and the poet, through his perception of ideal beauty, renders us conscious of our eternal nature, satisfies the human soul, and so affords the highest pleasure that is possible in this present life.

In seeking to envisage the supernal, the poet creates a kind of beauty that is intermediate between the inferior beauty of things and sentiments and the superior beauty of the eternal. 'Inspired by an ecstatic prescience of the glories beyond the grave, we struggle, by multiform combinations among the things and thoughts of Time, to attain a portion of that Loveliness whose very elements, perhaps, appertain to eternity alone.' Since a vision of this arch loveliness is denied by 'any existing collocation of earth's forms,' the task which the true poet assays is to recombine these forms in such a manner as to adumbrate heavenly beauty — a task impossible of complete performance, but one which he makes a 'wild effort' to achieve. All of his predecessors having failed, his hope lies in the novelty of his combinations, whether he is combining the existing earthly forms or is combining those combinations which his predecessors, 'toiling in chase of the same phantom, have already set in order.' It will be observed that Poe here provides, not only for the revolutionary artist who would discard tradition and build afresh, but also for the classical artist endeavoring by emulation to transcend the accomplishment of the art of the past.

The poetic principle, then, Poe defines as 'The Human Aspiration for Supernal Beauty,' and the kind of pleasure proper to the art of poetry as 'an elevating excitement of the Soul,' a pleasure in comparison with which all other human emotions are 'vapid and insignificant.' Passion, as he repeatedly insists, is not the proper effect of poetry, nor the vehicle of poetry. It is prosaic, homely; it is a cause of the poetic sentiment, but as the poetic sentiment grows, the cause surceases. Passionate grief, for instance, may lead to poetic feeling, but is not itself poetic feeling — it becomes poetic feeling only when it is subdued, chastened, transformed. When the poet's grief is no longer grief, when he has become not most passionate but most dispassionate, then first is his mood poetic. 'A passionate poem is a contradiction in terms.'[1] Tennyson's 'Locksley Hall' Poe adduces as an example of a passionate composition that falls short of being a poem, while 'Œnone,' on the other hand, instead of stirring us to passion, elevates the soul by means of its image of ideal beauty. In his insistence on this distinction, Poe uses language that has a ring more ethical than æsthetic: 'In regard to Passion,' he writes, 'alas! its tendency is to degrade, rather than to elevate the Soul,' a conception reminiscent of the moralist Plato's condemnation of poetry because it exercises and waters the emotions.

Poe's entire conception of poetry, indeed, may seem, if superficially regarded, Platonic. Like Plato he averts his

[1] Cf. Schiller: 'An art concerned with passion there is; but passionate art is a contradiction, for the inevitable result of artistic beauty is freedom from passions.' (*Ueber ästhetische Erziehung, Brief 22.*)

gaze from this life, this dream within a dream; like Plato he disparages those who would imitate the things and sentiments of the dream-world; like Plato he is ardent in the quest of ideal beauty. Is he a Platonist, or, like Shelley, a pseudo-Platonist?

From Plato and Aristotle he derived nothing of importance, perhaps nothing at all. Unlike nearly any great writer with whom one might compare him, he was void of enthusiasm for any artist or spiritual leader of the past. For the ideality of his creed, he was indebted, not to the Aristotelian doctrine of the universal, nor to the Platonic conception of ideas, nor to Emerson's curious combination of Platonism, Puritanism, and German Transcendentalism, but to the diffused romantic idealism of his time, especially in its English expressions in Byron, Moore, Coleridge, Wordsworth, and Shelley. In one of his early reviews, in the course of his discussion of the faculty of ideality Poe quotes in a footnote two entire stanzas from Shelley's 'Hymn to Intellectual Beauty.' They tell of an experience of illumination:

> Sudden thy shadow fell on me —
> I shrieked and clasped my hands in ecstasy!

and of a consequent dedication, joined with an humanitarian purpose:

> ... never joy illum'd my brow,
> Unlink'd with hope that thou wouldst free
> This world from its dark slavery,
> That thou, O awful *Loveliness*,
> Wouldst give whate'er these words cannot express.

Ignoring the humanitarian purpose — he was not fond of what he liked to term the mob, the herd, the rabble — Poe italicized the word Loveliness, and used it repeatedly later, along with Supernal Beauty. Its content in Poe's criticism is plainly not Platonic but Shelleyan; that is, its associations are not with the Platonic love of reason and character, but with the Shelleyan emotional abandon. It implies, not a

laborious dialectic transcended by insight into the highest
Good, but an uncritical indulgence in expansive desire leading to an illusive (shall we say delusive?) vision of perfect
happiness. A second footnote on the same page indicates
another source of Poe's conception of ideality. Echoing
Coleridge, he writes: 'Imagination is, possibly in man, a
lesser degree of the creative power in God.' This is the romantic equivalent for the classical doctrine of the imitation
of the universal; emphasis falls no longer on what is broadly
human, the ethos, an unchanging reality which the artist
is humbly to imitate, but on an intoxicating sense of the
artist's freedom to give expression to his individuality and
in so doing to create a valid image of the ideal. The exaltation of the ego, in a sense reminiscent of the German romantic mingling of flesh and spirit, is an essential element, if
not the dominant element, in the romantic idealism of Shelley, and Coleridge, and Poe.

Poe's entire discussion of the ideal is obviously remote from
Platonic and Aristotelian modes of thought. As instances of
the ideal he mentions, in an undiscriminating list, the 'Pro-
metheus Vinctus' of Æschylus, the 'Inferno' of Dante, the
'Destruction of Numantia' by Cervantes, the 'Comus' of
Milton, the 'Ancient Mariner,' the 'Christabel,' and the
'Kubla Khan' of Coleridge, the 'Nightingale' of Keats, the
'Sensitive Plant' of Shelley, and the 'Undine' of De La
Motte Fouqué.[1] This is scarcely the list that Plato or Aristotle would have drawn up if they had had both the ancients
and the moderns to choose from; they might have chosen one
or two of these, at most. The selection of 'Comus' instead of
'Paradise Lost' is instructive; so is the emphasis on romantic
examples, particularly the selection of three poems by Coleridge — all three as romantic, as un-classical, as possible. In
a later essay, 'The Poetic Principle,' Poe can remember in
the whole of English literature no poem 'more profoundly —

---

[1] Poe uses this list, with slight modification, a second time.

more weirdly *imaginative*, in the best sense, than the lines commencing — "I would I were by that dim lake," — which are the composition of Thomas Moore.' And a moment later he offers us, as 'one of the truest poems ever written' Tom Hood's 'Haunted House.' 'It is, moreover, powerfully ideal — imaginative.'

§ 5

The two last terms, 'ideal' and 'imaginative,' are used almost interchangeably by Poe; and they are used almost interchangeably with other terms such as 'the mystical' and 'harmony.' Imagination he seeks to define by contrasting it with fancy, availing himself of hints from Coleridge and Wordsworth, and involving himself, as they did, in inconsistencies and vaguenesses. The true distinction, he writes in his review of Moore's 'Alciphron,' though it is 'still but a distinction *of degree*' has to do with the idea of the mystic. 'The term *mystic* is here employed in the sense of Augustus William Schlegel, and of most other German critics. It is applied by them to that class of composition in which there lies beneath the transparent upper-current of meaning, an under or *suggestive* one.' This secondary meaning '*spiritualizes* the *fanciful* conception, and lifts it into the *ideal*.' In the merely fanciful poem there is no under-current. But in the imaginative poem, at every stroke of the lyre we hear a ghostly echo; in every glimpse of beauty 'we catch, through long and wild vistas, dim bewildering visions of a far more ethereal beauty *beyond*.' Through the magic casements of the Palace of Art we behold as in a dream the realms of faëry land forlorn. No view of art could be less classical than that.

Elsewhere, in an article on N. P. Willis, Poe approaches the definition of imagination from a different angle. Imagination, Fancy, Fantasy, and Humor, all alike involve combination and novelty. But they differ. Imagination selects elements that are harmonious, from either beauty or deformity, and by combining them creates something new. This will be beautiful according to the thoroughness of the harmony and the richness or force of the materials used. Fancy, on the other hand, relatively neglects the process of combination, and gives us, in addition to novelty, unexpectedness. Fantasy involves not only novelty and unexpectedness of combination, but also a positive avoidance of proportion, and, while the novelty gives pleasure, the incoherence gives pain. Humor goes a step beyond, seeking incongruous or antagonistic elements, and, doing so palpably, gives pleasure — humor being 'a merry effort of Truth to shake from her that which is no property of hers.'

Imagination, so distinguished, is the instrument by which the poet creates visions of harmony. His visions satisfy the soul because of their harmony, and satisfy in proportion as they give order to rich materials. When the imagination is most vigorous and is employed in its highest tasks, earthly passion quite melts away and is replaced with a divine serenity — the lofty ardor, perhaps, of the angel Israfel. Then come to his song 'the golden, easeful, crowning moments' (in the phrase of another critic), when the poet seems indeed to dwell where Israfel hath dwelt, in a skiey region where are none of the conflicts of our world of sweets and sours, where all is harmony, order — a harmony, an order, so rich in content, so intense with force, that it is one with ecstasy.

The two conceptions of the imagination, though as Poe leaves them they seem to clash, are not incompatible. Had he brought them together, he might have said that the principle of harmony or order is a divine principle, and that consequently every step toward a complete harmony is in so far a step toward supernal harmony. By means of imagination, the poet creates a harmony; but his harmony does not satisfy him — beyond it he glimpses, again by means of the imagination, a more ethereal harmony which he cannot express but which he can indicate through suggestion, an under-current of meaning, an ideal 'tone' or echo. Thus he brings us to the gates of the supernal not only by his creation of a high harmony, but also — in the language of Coleridge — by 'spreading the tone, the atmosphere, and with it the depth and height of the ideal world around the forms, incidents, and situations' that constitute this harmony.

In this conception of the workings of imagination there is much that may be accepted without hesitation, at least by those of the ideal persuasion. But if it is regarded in the light of Poe's own practice — as the unity of Poe's criticism and his creation gives us a right to regard it — it will be found to contain implications that reveal its inadequacy. Poe understood well enough the advantages of intensity, both as relating to 'the force of the matters combined' and to the unifying energy that shaped them into harmony; but he did not understand the differences of quality in the matters combined — he wanted what he himself terms 'the facility of discovering combinable novelties worth combining.' Wonderful as was his power of expressing forcibly the order that he created in each of his best tales, wonderful as was his power of achieving harmony in each of his best poems, so that, in tale and poem alike, every word counted toward the production of an intense effect, we cannot avoid feeling that in his tales the order is aimless and that in his poems the harmony is premature. Only too well did he describe, in one of his tales, his own use of the imagination in prose fiction: 'Imagination,' he wrote, 'feeling herself for once unshackled, roamed at will among the ever-changing wonders of a shadowy and unstable land.' If his intensity holds us as we read, it does not hold us afterward: we have scarcely turned the last page of the tale when the order begins to appear arbitrary and fanciful, the illusion of unreality rather than the illusion of a higher reality. And in his poems — yield ourselves as we may to the spell of harmoniously combined im-

ages and of haunting music — we cannot escape, in retrospect, the feeling that their exquisite harmony is fragile,
bodiless, premature.

Our dissatisfaction with the quality of Poe's ideality is in
large measure owing to his adoption of the romantic doctrine
of the indefinite, which appears in his first preface and per-
sists thereafter as a major law of his criticism. He apparently derived it — like so much else — from Coleridge, who
in his lectures on the drama distinguished, as Schlegel had
done before him, between the ancients and the moderns by
asserting that the Greeks idolized the finite, which may be
expressed by definite forms or thoughts, and the moderns
revere the infinite, which demands an indefinite vehicle. It is
a pretty contrast, and an unsound one, as pretty contrasts are
liable to be; but Poe accepted it in his literal way and applied
it with his customary deliberate directness.

Inseparably associated with this doctrine of the indefinite,
in Poe as in the romantics generally, is its corollary doctrine
of the supremacy of music over all the other arts. 'It is in
Music, perhaps, that the soul most nearly attains the great
end for which, when inspired by the Poetic Sentiment, it
struggles — the creation of supernal Beauty. It *may* be,
indeed, that here this sublime end is, now and then, attained
in fact. We are often made to feel, with a shivering delight,
that from an earthly harp are stricken notes which *cannot*
have been unfamiliar to the angels.' This perfect harmony,
this vision — this very experience — of supernal loveliness,
music may attain because of its freedom from earthly things,
its indefiniteness, its vagueness. Poe seems never to have
suspected that music, instead of offering the purest spiritual
experience, may often be merely a refuge for the dreamer
from the realities of life, an evasion of life rather than a
transcendence. Severing the art from the artist, he assumed
that the art was divine, infinite, while the artist might be a
plain mortal much like the rest of us. It did not occur to him

that what he took to be the language of the angels might be the fevers of the flesh.[1] He affirmed that a passionate poem was a contradiction, but not that a passionate musical composition was a contradiction — the composer's excitement he assumed to be of the soul. His test, so far as he applied any, was apparently quantitative: if the music invaded his whole being, stormed the citadel of sovereign reason, and made him yield in any ecstasy of passiveness, it was supernal. He exerted no effort to distinguish, as the Greeks had done, between music that is relaxing and music that is tonic. He did not urge a re-examination of musical experience in retrospect, a criticism of its effect, a determination of its quality. If it offered a ravishing harmony in place of the discords of actual life, he was satisfied without questioning the contents of that harmony, the elements of experience that were successfully shaped into unity. If it profoundly satisfied his desires, he did not ask *what* desires.

One infers that he agreed with the German romanticists, as did Pater, that all the arts constantly aspire to the condition of music: at least, he held this to be true of poetry. 'The *vagueness* of exaltation,' he wrote to Lowell, 'aroused by a sweet air (which should be strictly indefinite and never too strongly suggestive) is precisely what we should aim at in poetry' — an assertion of which his own poems are an illustration, together with those poems of the ideal that he listed, most notably, perhaps, 'Christabel' and 'Kubla Khan.' Music, he believed, has powers of expression beyond words, of which poetry seeks to avail itself in being a rhythmical

[1] 'An art that came out of the old world two centuries ago with a few chants, love songs, and dances, that a century ago was still tied to the words of a mass or opera, or threading little dance movements together in a "suite," became, in the last century, this extraordinary debauch, in which the man who has never seen a battle, loved a woman, or worshipped a god may not only ideally, but through the response of his nerves and pulses to immediate rhythmical attack, enjoy the ghosts of struggle, rapture, and exaltation with a volume and intricacy, an anguish, a triumph, an irresponsibility unheard of.' (D. S. MacColl, *Nineteenth Century Art.*)

creation of beauty. In rhythm, the divine mathematics of music is organically united with the mental images that are the stuff of poetry — rhythm, the basis of which is time, 'the inviolable principle of all music.' Verse he thought of as 'an inferior and less capable Music.' But at the same time — as in his conception of the poetic and the didactic — he provided for a mechanical, collateral relation of the two elements. He believed in the combination of the poem and the song, looking back regretfully to the age of bards and minnesingers, and approving Thomas Moore, who, 'singing his own songs, was, in the most legitimate manner, perfecting them as poems.' [1] He failed to observe that a true marriage of the two, rather than a mere combination, is impossible, for although sound may be wedded to image, it is not in the full sense musical sound, music being properly free of limiting images. When music ceases to be abstract, it is no longer fully music, as Poe well understood in his objections to 'programme music.'

In making music supreme among the arts, Poe, along with many other romanticists, may have been entirely right — the hierarchy of the arts, if there be such a thing, is anything but self-evident. Certainly it is plausible to assert that the expressiveness of music begins where the expressiveness of words leaves off, that the indefiniteness of pure sound offers the best sensuous medium for the externalization of spiritual experience. If this is so, music provides not only a maximum intensity of beauty, but also the highest kind of beauty, and through a synthesis of maximum quantity and highest quality attains a position foremost among the arts. Such, one may admit, is its power, potentially; but it does not follow that it actually exerts this power in such music as the world now possesses. In the ancient world, the art was in its infancy; in the Middle Ages, it was in its childhood, so that

[1] Cf. Wordsworth in his list of the molds into which the materials of poetry may be cast: '3rdly, The Lyrical, — containing the Hymn, the Ode, the Elegy, the Song, and the Ballad; in all which, for the production of their *full* effect, an accompaniment of music is indispensable.' (Preface to the poems of 1815.)

another art, architecture, became the vehicle for the concrete
expression of the infinite; only toward the close of the modern
'classical' age did it develop rapidly, and cnly under romantic
auspices did it attain the exuberance of youth. It must be
remembered, when we compare music with other arts, that
it is to this day still in its youth, and that the vast majority
of so-called classics of music are a product of the romantic
spirit. To appraise it is to appraise romanticism itself: a task
beyond our scope here. We can only sketch the argument,
with constant reference to Poe.

§6

The main point at issue is perhaps the content of that
indeterminateness, or indefiniteness, which is characteristic
of music and of other arts in so far as they are musical. By
the infinite, which is perforce indefinite in finite experience,
Poe means the spiritual principle active in human life. Does
it follow that, since the infinite is indefinite, the indefinite is
also the infinite, the spiritual? To argue so is to commit one
of the grossest of logical blunders, as Poe, with his analytical
mind, might have been expected to demonstrate. But he did
not; it was, at bottom, his own argument. In the verbal song
as in music itself, we must have, he declares, 'a certain wild
license and *indefiniteness* — an indefiniteness recognized by
every musician who is not a mere fiddler, as an important
point in the philosophy of his science — as the *soul*, indeed,
of the sensations derivable from its practice — sensations
which bewilder while they enthral — and which would *not* so
enthral if they did not so bewilder.' There is every suggestion, here, of an irresponsible indefiniteness. After suggesting, in the next sentence, that the feelings produced by sweet
sound may have no loftier origin than the 'merely mathematical recognition' of equality as the root of all beauty, he
sets down as a certainty that 'the *sentimental* pleasure derivable from music, is nearly in the ratio of its indefiniteness.'

Give it a determinate tone and you deprive it of its essential character, its ethereal, its ideal character. Then, in an illuminating sentence, he indicates only too clearly his conception of the ideal: 'You dispel its dream-like luxury: — you dissolve the atmosphere of the mystic in which its whole nature is bound up: — you exhaust it of its breath of faëry.' What in other passages professed to be a spiritual exaltation now turns out to be a dreamlike luxury. The voices of the angels have become the breath of faëry.

To this land of faëry we are transported bodily in 'The Island of the Fay.' Beginning with a comment on '*la musique*,' to the effect that those who love it for its own sake and for its 'spiritual' uses may appreciate it to the full only when they listen in solitude, he remarks that solitude is even more essential to the contemplation of nature. Then he tells how, in his wanderings in a remote region of mountains, sad rivers, and melancholy tarns 'writhing or sleeping within all,' he came by chance upon a certain rivulet and island, and reclined beneath an odorous shrub 'that I might doze as I contemplated the scene.' One end of the island was 'all one radiant harem of garden beauties'; the other, somber, gloomy, mournful, sad, solemn, spectral, unsightly. 'I lost myself forthwith in reverie'; and while in this state, with half-shut eyes, he beholds a Fay proceeding slowly from the light end to the dark end of the island, standing erect, 'in a singularly fragile canoe.' This she does repeatedly, circling the island, till he beholds her magical figure no more, and returns, presumably, to real life.

Nor is this all. The aspiration for the infinite, or highest reality, turns out to be not merely the fascination of an unreal fairyland, a land of idle dreams; it reduces itself, at length, to an insatiable thirst for rather material luxury. Mr. Ellison, of 'The Landscape Garden,' one of Poe's several studies of private paradises, is obviously an 'idealized' version of Poe himself. To him the laws of Bliss are four: exercise in the open air, the love of woman (*by* woman, he means, and of course by the loveliest of the sex), the contempt of ambition, and an object of unceasing pursuit. The last two being difficult of attainment in this world of necessities and distractions, Poe provides Mr. Ellison with a fortune, inherited at the age of twenty-one, amounting to *four hundred and fifty millions of dollars* (the italics are the author's), a very tidy sum in the first half of the last century.[1] Having the poetic sentiment, this person so admirably equipped in external goods was enabled to express himself in the 'creation of novel forms of Beauty.' Since his mind chanced to be tinged, as Poe says, with materialism, he became neither poet nor musician — 'although no man lived more profoundly enamored both of Music and the Muse' — but aimed at a 'purely physical loveliness.' This he attained, along with an incidental and somewhat obscure spirituality, in the construction of a landscape garden surpassing even the dreams of twentieth century millionaires. In a longer form of this study, 'The Domain of Arnheim,' Poe composed a detailed description of this landscape garden, lavishing upon it his rare dexterity in selection, emphasis, tone, and the like.

Here, then — in the island of the fay and the domain of Arnheim — is the indefinite at last made definite, its content disclosed. Here is the tendency of the mystic, the ideal, the supernal, revealed. 'Here, indeed, was the fairest field for the display of imagination in the endless combining of forms of novel beauty.' The novelty of beauty no one will be disposed to deny, but there are, of course, novelties and novelties; there is, for example, not only the novelty of 'The Domain of Arnheim,' 'The Haunted Palace,' and 'Kubla Khan,' but the novelty of 'Paradise Lost' and 'King Lear.'

[1] With his usual artistic 'intensity' and his American love of statistics, Poe computes that at three per cent the annual income amounted to $13,500,000 — $1,125,000 per month, or $36,986 per day, or $1541 per hour, or $26 per minute. According to press reports (February 4, 1927) Mr. Henry Ford has latterly bettered this, having an income of $190.25 per minute.

From 'King Lear' a writer in the London 'Times' some time ago quoted the lines beginning

We two alone will sing like birds i' the cage

as an instance of those moments when the play ceases for us and we are transported by the magical music of the lines to the universal, the absolute. These moments occur, we must agree, in all the greatest literature; but when the writer of the article goes on to quote the first stanza of 'To Helen,' and to remark, 'They are like music rising at the wave of a great conductor's wand . . . ; it is an expression of the passion for the absolute,' one cannot but feel that he has unconsciously changed the subject — that the absolute of Poe's poem is not the same as the absolute of Shakspere's. The harmony Poe has attained is as complete as Shakspere's, but, as in so much of romantic poetry and romantic music, it is a premature harmony, it does not contain enough, it does not rise above the normal experience of life but sinks beneath it. It is the harmony of the *tour d'ivoire*, of the Palace of Art, as Stedman says, 'a lordly pleasure-house, where taste and love should have their fill, regardless of the outer world.' The ideality implied by Poe's cult of beauty was more or less delusive because of his ethical and spiritual shortcomings. Life to him was not a dream, but a nightmare, in which he was rarely the actor, but was acted upon by impulse, sensitiveness, pride, and morbid melancholy.[1]

One more qualitative aspect of Poe's æsthetic remains to be considered: his dictum, which appears early and late in his criticism, that 'a species of melancholy is inseparably connected with the higher manifestations of the beautiful.' The species of melancholy that he has in mind is clearly enough not that of Greek tragedy, with its awful sense of

[1] 'My life has been *whim* — impulse — passion — a longing for solitude — a scorn of all things present in an earnest desire for the future.' (From Poe's 'spiritual autobiography,' Woodberry, *Life*, II, 93.)

moral powers related with but transcending the moral consciousness of man, nor that of Shaksperian tragedy, in which
nobility and falsity meet in a fatal combat whose significance
must remain perpetually indeterminate. It is, rather, that
which was fashionable in Poe's time — the romantic nos-
talgia, the quest of the Blue Flower, the satisfaction of the
heart yearning infinitely for an unethical perfection. In the
lectures of Schlegel, which may have been Poe's 'source,' this
melancholy of the North is contrasted with the joy of the
Greeks, and is explained as a relic of the Middle Ages, when
the sentiment of the infinite drew the spirit of man away from
this fleeting world to an eternal in which alone lay happiness.
'When the soul,' says Schlegel, 'resting as it were under the
willows of exile, breathes out its longing for its distant home,
what else but melancholy can be the keynote of its songs?'
With the abysmal differences between this ethical, ascetic,
impersonal type of melancholy and the æsthetic, indulgent,
egotistic type of melancholy characteristic, with whatever
modifications, of the romantics, Poe, no more than Schlegel,
concerns himself. 'And thus when by Poetry — or when by
Music, the most entrancing of the Poetic moods — we find
ourselves melted into tears — we weep then — not as the
Abbate Gravina supposes — through excess of pleasure, but
through a certain, petulant, impatient sorrow at our inability
to grasp *now*, wholly, here on earth, at once and forever,
those divine and rapturous joys, of which *through* the poem,
or *through* the music, we attain to but brief and indeterminate
glimpses.' On the meaning of this sentence, it will suffice to
ask two questions: Is the true mystic 'petulant'? What kinds
of poems and music has Poe in mind as suggesting divine and
rapturous joys? The answers are not doubtful. Does not
Poe himself say, in 'The Philosophy of Composition,' that
beauty *of whatever kind*, in its highest development, brings
the sensitive soul to tears?

Of this association of beauty and melancholy Poe avails

himself with an erring literalness. Explicitly does he add the latter to the former, almost as an embellishment, as in his portrait of the Marchesa Aphrodite, in which he bluntly tells us that in the expression of her face, 'which was beaming all over with smiles, there still lurked (incomprehensible anomaly!) that fitful stain of melancholy which will ever be found inseparable from the perfection of the beautiful.' Since perfection demands melancholy, Poe gives it to us, not perceiving that (incomprehensible anomaly!) the melancholy is essentially in the beholder of beauty and not in the object itself — that it is inseparably related with beauty as the ultimate sentiment evoked by perfect beauty, and that the quality of the melancholy varies with the quality of the beauty. With the same literalness, the same dependence on 'mere logic,' Poe reaches the conclusion that of all topics death is the most melancholy, and that death is most melancholy when it is the death of a beautiful woman. That death is the most melancholy fact in life is sufficiently indicated by the history of the human spirit, but that death is most melancholy when it is the death of a beautiful woman by no means follows. If 'beautiful woman' means, as in Poe it seems to mean, a woman of extreme physical charm, Poe's conclusion is palpably unsound. Incomparably more melancholy is the death of a Hamlet or Lear, because it is in man's nature to give the highest place in life to moral grandeur.

From the melancholy fact of death Poe passes, by a transition easy in that day of graveyard literature, to the triumphs of the Conqueror Worm. In 'The Poetic Principle,' for example, he quotes Bryant's not very remarkable poem 'June,' and subjoins these observations: 'The poem has always affected me in a remarkable manner. The intense melancholy which seems to well up, perforce, to the surface of all the poet's cheerful sayings about the grave, we find thrilling us to the soul — while there is the truest poetic elevation in the thrill. The impression left is one of a pleasurable sadness.'

The term 'pleasurable sadness,' in this connection, is certainly a synonym of sentimentalism, with which Poe's ideality is often visibly tinged. He indulged not only the luxury of dreams, but also the luxury of melancholy. Yet in the main, with his fine sense of the strength of restraint, which makes his later work seem objective in comparison with the tendency to insincere vaporing in his first poems, he avoided the unashamed confidences of many of the romantic brotherhood, giving us, in place of sentimentalism and an excess of self-expression, an artful creation of the strange. The tone of melancholy remains, but emphasis falls, not on the expression of melancholy feeling but on the strange, conceived as a kind of externalization or objectification of melancholy.

Long before Pater defined romanticism as the addition of strangeness to beauty, Poe availed himself of this collocation of ideas in his discussion of romantic art. Thus he writes of Shelley, 'the author of "The Sensitive Plant"': 'His quaintness arose from intuitive perception of that truth to which Bacon alone has given distinct utterance: "There is no exquisite Beauty which has not some strangeness in its proportions" [sic].' Ignoring the ethical aspect of this sentence in its context in Bacon's essay 'Of Beauty,' Poe used it again and again, in both his critical and his creative work, in support of *bizarrerie*, quaintness, grotesqueness, fantasticality, as an effective addition to the kind of harmony that he contemplated. The quaint in phrasing and the grotesque in rhythm, for instance, if deliberate and not accidental, he holds to be 'very admissible adjuncts to Ideality.' Thus he commends Mrs. Browning for her use of unexpected repetitions in her verse, which produce 'a fantastic effect,' a phrase that would here seem to be synonymous with ideality. Illustrations occur everywhere, of course, in his own prose and poetry. The features of Ligeia, for example, were wanting in that regularity which is falsely insisted upon 'in the classical labors of the heathen'; whereupon he quotes Lord Veru-

lam and speculates at full length upon the elusive strangeness
in the face, concluding that the cause resided in the black
eyes, which in moments of excitement gave her 'the beauty
of beings either above or apart from the earth, the beauty of
the fabulous Houri of the Turk.' Of such is the kingdom of
Ideality — a kingdom surely 'apart from the earth' rather
than above it. Strangeness is added, again, to the beauty of
the domain of Arnheim, that very explicit vision of loveliness to which we must return for a moment. In the funereal
gloom of the chasm, as the reader may recall, 'the windings
became more frequent and intricate, and seemed often as if
returning in upon themselves, so that the voyager had long
lost all idea of direction. He was, moreover, enwrapt in an
exquisite sense of the strange.' Nature's works take on 'a
weird symmetry, a thrilling uniformity, a wizard propriety.'
The gloom deepens apace, until suddenly the voyager gazes
upon a vision of pure beauty — rich, warm, soft, dainty,
voluptuous, with 'a miraculous extremeness of culture that
suggested dreams of a new race of fairies.' Now the visitor
quits his vessel and enters a canoe of ivory 'stained with
arabesque devices in vivid scarlet.' Of itself, this 'fairy bark'
swings round and advances, producing mysteriously a
'soothing yet melancholy music.' New beauties and new
wonders disclose themselves, till at length 'the whole paradise
of Arnheim bursts upon the view':

There is a gush of entrancing melody; there is an oppressive sense
of strange, sweet odor; there is a dream-like intermingling to the
eye of tall, slender Eastern trees, bosky shrubberies, flocks of
golden and crimson birds, lily-fringed lakes, meadows of violets,
tulips, poppies, hyacinths, and tuberoses, long, intertangled lines of
silver streamlets, and, upspringing confusedly from amid all, a
mass of semi-Gothic, semi-Saracenic architecture, sustaining itself
by miracle in mid-air; glittering in the red sunlight with a hundred
oriels, minarets, and pinnacles; and seeming the phantom handi-
work, conjointly, of the sylphs, of the fairies, of the genii, and of the
gnomes.

Although it must be said that such a vision of paradise is exceptional in Poe's prose, as 'Israfel' is exceptional in his verse, it must also be said that in lieu of the strangely supernal he creates the strangely infernal. According to his own theory, this is proper enough so far as his prose is concerned — 'The Fall of the House of Usher' is a masterpiece in the construction of an infernal harmony — but it is a violation of his own conception of poetry. His constant theme, as Mr. Woodberry says, is ruin: death, melancholy, strangeness. Seeking to add strangeness to beauty, Poe really adds beauty to strangeness. And it is an inferior kind of strangeness that he aims at: never awe, but wonder, and wonder of the superstitious sort, arising from a disorganization of the nervous system. His characteristic theme is never spiritual intuition, but instinctive premonition; and though we may yield to him — at his best, with his amazingly dexterous art, he makes us willing instruments — we retain only briefly the 'effect' upon which he expended all his pains. It melts away like an evil dream, or, if it is idyllic, like a castle in the air. His charnel house offers no real terrors, his paradise no real satisfaction. If the æsthetic experience that he gives us is intense, it is also relatively devoid of meaning. Poe was one of those, perhaps the greatest of those, who

> . . . make
> Strange combinations out of common things,
> Like human babes in their brief innocence.

The school of the melancholy poets became, as Chateaubriand observed, a school of poets of despair. Poe was one of them, and with far more reason than can be alleged by most singers of

> Infinite passion and the pain of finite hearts that yearn.

His very entry into the world was ominous: with a temperament and nervous organization portending disaster, he found himself almost from the start without parental sympathy and guidance, in a land averse from if not positively hostile to the æsthetic vision of life; and not far ahead lay poverty, confusion, frustrated ambition, repeated nervous collapse, and a few hours of happiness to heighten the contrast — the whole welter to be brought to a conclusion so tragic that one may not call it premature. 'So have I wondered,' wrote Stedman, 'at seeing a delicate forest-bird, leagues from the shore, keep itself on the wing above relentless waters into which it was sure to fall at last.' If life as he knew it — he could know it no other way, he was so introspective — was life as it is, it could yield only despair. Bitterly he concluded: 'To be thoroughly conversant with Man's heart, is to take our final lesson in the iron-clasped volume of Despair.' Brooding over a little book that might be entitled 'My Heart Laid Bare' — a book more honest, perhaps, than Rousseau's 'Confessions' — he shrank from the terrible thought. 'No man ever will dare write it. No man *could* write it, even if he dared. The paper would shrivel and blaze at every touch of the fiery pen.' Instead of laying open to the public gaze his inner experience, he expressed life, expressed despair, objectively, by a deliberate creation of the hideous, the perverted, the ruined, to which he gave an impressive beauty — that is, shape and order and definiteness (with ever a magical residue of the indefinite) — by means of his masterly technique.

This technique was the conscious application of reason to art, not the organic expression affected by romanticism. Shelley's is of the latter type, according to Poe, the poet's soul being Law itself, but in his own theory and practice reason is always regnant. To be natural meant to him, as it meant to the Augustan age of English literature, to be reasonable. Rousseau's natural man he rejects, or rather Hellenizes: 'Man's chief idiosyncrasy being reason, it follows that his savage condition — his condition of action *without* reason — is his *un*natural state.' Conceding that *Poëta nascitur* is indisputably true as regards the poetic sentiment, he avers that it is absurd as regards the practical result, the concrete poem. If the poetic sentiment or intuition is to be conveyed to others, the poet should possess in high degree the powers of causality, i.e., a perception of the causes needful to produce a desired effect. Similarly, Poe maintains that 'the *truly* imaginative mind is never otherwise than analytic,' a comment that brings into relation the two aspects of his own art; and again, that originality is not 'a mere matter of impulse or inspiration,' as the romantic spirit conceives it, but rather a matter of purposeful construction: 'To originate, is carefully, patiently, and understandingly to combine.' Thus while the majority of our romanticists, including the greatest, have delighted in casting aspersions on man's logical faculty — of which some of them have had, indeed, a quite aspersible quantity — Poe, having a large endowment of it and finding it very useful, was quite as friendly to it as to the 'mystic' and the 'ideal,' ulterior qualities that he could produce at will through his formulæ. It would not be fanciful to say that his whole view of art was mathematical. A certain result — x — unknown to the reader but predetermined by the artist — was to be attained. For this result, a long series of causes was then devised. These were given an order and coherence depending on their nature. By division of the subject, by subtraction of the irrelevant elements, by enumeration of details patiently added to yield a sum or climax, by a multiplication of subordinate sums leading to the ultimate effect, the artist's logical powers could so arrange the data of the senses as to provoke in the reader that x, or sentiment or intuition, which was in the artist's consciousness at the beginning. Poe's interest in mathematics is, of course, well known; in many tales he employed it or discussed its nature, as in his literary criticism he used its terminology ('repetend' being a good example); and his absorption in problems and puzzles of all kinds, from cryptography to plagiarism, is notorious. The new *genre* that he brought into vogue, the de-

tective story, was precisely the contribution to be expected of
him. So far did he carry this exploitation of his logical faculty 'for its own sake,' as he might have said, so innocent
was he of all serious endeavor to understand what he liked to
term, with Goethe and Carlyle, the open secret of life, that
the activity of his reason became aimless, irresponsible, and
unmeaning.

For the rational principle in Poe, unaided by moral imagination, became the accomplice of the senses, or appetitive
principle, and so enabled him to produce only an inferior
range of harmonies — shuddering harmonies of the murky
subconscious, and roseate harmonies of sensuous longing pos-
ing as spirituality. His vision oscillated not between the
earthly and the supernal, but between the infernal and the
Arcadian. Denying Bryant a rank with 'the spiritual Shelleys, or Coleridges, or Wordsworths, or with Keats, or even
Tennyson, or Wilson,' on the ground that 'the objects in the
moral or physical universe coming within the periphery of
his vision' are too limited, Poe sets down as a critical canon
this assertion: 'The relative extent of these peripheries of
poetical vision must ever be a primary consideration in our
classification of poets.' This is surely a sound canon, if properly understood; it explains why Chaucer, for example,
great as he is, is not among the greatest — his periphery is
short. But Poe forgets that precisely what makes Chaucer
great despite his restricted periphery, is his extraordinary
truth and completeness of vision within his limits, and that
the spiritual Shelleys (along with the Wilsons) are inferior to
him because, with all their reach of vision, they are wanting
in this truth and completeness. Reality, it would seem,
whether the reality of concrete things or of the human spirit,
is irrelevant in Poe's conception of art. If a man has but an
ample reach of vision, an extensive periphery, if he can look
over — or even overlook — a vast number of objects in the
physical or moral universe, and can express his vision, it

matters not that his picture is a fair mirage, fascinating in its fluid harmony, rather than an illusion of a higher reality that speaks to all of man's nature. In Shakspere, in Milton, 'even in Tennyson,' we feel that we are moving toward a superior truth and beauty, a unity perceived by them, not arbitrarily created. In them, as in Poe, reason is supreme; but it is reason aided by the senses and the will, as in Plato's figure of the charioteer and the two horses endeavoring to mount toward the heavens. Reason in Poe, wanting moral support, must rely upon but one of the horses, the rebellious one who is black, 'a large misshapen animal . . . , gray-eyed and bloodshot.' Seeking the celestial harmonies, he can make no progress thither — the true 'awful Loveliness' is never in sight. The senses, goaded onward, bring him to a spurious loveliness, a beautiful limbo where the 'sweets' of life lie spread in an ordered profusion, or, more often, they plunge to a nether region where the 'sours' of life are made horribly perfect. 'The fact is,' as Poe himself tells us, 'that in efforts to soar above our nature, we invariably fall below it' — unless we rise, as the great have ever risen, in life itself and its reflection, literature, with the aid of the other winged horse, he whom Plato describes as white and as 'a lover of honor and modesty and temperance, and the follower of true glory.'

CHAPTER II

EMERSON

§ 1

In Poe, the concentration of brilliant powers to a definite end — to art for the sake of art — gave to all his literary activity a compactness, a unity, a luminous exterior, that were wanting in the work of his chief critical contemporaries, Emerson and Lowell. The disparate interests of Lowell were never brought to a focus, a unity of purpose; none of them have the full weight of the man behind them. In Emerson, to be sure, there was an impressive inner harmony, of which everything that he did was a faithful expression — like rays from a shining light. Yet this light shone impartially on all things. Nature, science, history, art, ethics, metaphysics, religion, all were dear to him, all so absorbing that he could surrender none of them. He studied, in his transcendental way, the whole of life, and expressed himself as preacher, moralist, metaphysician, orator, poet, literary critic, summarizing the series with the term 'scholar,' understood in his own sense. If he was anything he was the scholar in his own sense; that is, he was nothing in particular, he was a man — a man thinking. He hated the division of labor, necessary as it seemed, renouncing his first choice of occupation, the ministry, and never assuming another. He would be free, free to live, free to express himself as the spirit chose; and his spirit was avid. In the end he achieved, according to Arnold's plausible verdict, the most important work in English prose of the nineteenth century. Yet it is hardly excessive to say that he was master of no subject, since he never thought anything out, and of no literary form, since nearly all his essays and poems are series of sentences rather than wholes.

Despite this lack of concentration, however, Emerson contrived to express himself abundantly on a great variety of subjects, one of which is the theory of literature. In respect to amount, his literary criticism ranks with that of our chief professed critics, Poe and Lowell. Widely scattered through twelve volumes of 'Works' and ten volumes more of 'Journals,' it would present an imposing bulk if brought together.[1] Equally impressive is its comprehensiveness. Much of it is abstract, concerned with essential principles; for Emerson was even more interested than Poe in the poetic principle and the philosophy of composition. But much, also, is concrete, concerned with individual artists. It contains two treatments of Beauty, two of Art, one of Criticism, one of Books, one of The Poet, one of English Literature, one of Imagination, one of The Comic and one of The Tragic, two of Modern Literature, and more than a dozen of individual authors ranging from Plato to Carlyle. None of the essays is concerned, as was so much of Poe's work, with ephemeral writers. All deal with central principles, or with the classics of literature, or with prominent contemporaries. Rarely, if ever, are the same passages used repeatedly, in Poe's fashion; Emerson restates, attacks again and again, from various angles, the chief problems of art, so that in the end, despite contradictions, we feel that we really understand him. This sense of security is strengthened by the fact that he also wrote essays,

[1] Following is an incomplete list of Emerson's criticism of art and literature: 1. Passages in *Nature* (especially the section on Beauty); 2. Art, in *Essays, First Series*; 3. The Poet, in *Essays, Second Series*; 4. Plato, in *Representative Men*; 5. Montaigne, *ibid.*; 6. Shakspere, *ibid.*; 7. Goethe, *ibid.*; 8. Literature, in *English Traits*; 9. Beauty, in *The Conduct of Life*; 10. Art, in *Society and Solitude*; 11. Books, *ibid.*; 12. The Comic, in *Letters and Social Aims*; 13. Poetry and Imagination, *ibid.*; 14. Persian Poetry, *ibid.*; 15. *Poems* (*passim*); 16. Plutarch, in *Lectures and Biographical Sketches*; 17. Thoreau, *ibid.*; 18. Carlyle, *ibid.*; 19. Robert Burns, *ibid.*; 20. Shakspere, in *Miscellanies*; 21. Walter Scott, *ibid.*; 22. Michael Angelo, in *The Natural History of Intellect*; 23. Milton, *ibid.*; 24. Art and Criticism, *ibid.*; 25. Thoughts on Modern Literature, *ibid.*; 26. Walter Savage Landor, *ibid.*; 27. Europe and European Books, *ibid.*; 28. Carlyle's 'Past and Present,' *ibid.*; 29. The Tragic, *ibid.*; 30. Reviews, etc., in *Uncollected Writings*; 31. Passages in the *Journals*.

on Inspiration, Intellect, History, etc., that have a collateral relation with his æsthetical essays; for his creed, unlike Poe's, embraces far more than beauty.

Emerson's and Poe's conception of criticism compared

alike in believing poet + critic of same genus and in calling for absolute criticism

Unlike:

1) Emerson had fatalistic conception of artistic creation

2) Poe believed in conscious adaptation of means to ends

3) Criticism becomes art when it goes beyond poets words to his thought accor. to Emerson

The general conception of the nature and office of criticism in Emerson's essays is superficially akin to that of Poe. Poet and critic are of the same genus: 'The poet is the lover loving; the critic is the lover advised'; consequently, the specific difference between them lies in the poet's spontaneity and the critic's consciousness — the one loving, the other advised. Unlike Poe, however, Emerson sets the two sharply apart. The poets cannot be served by the critics, assuredly not if their criticism is querulous and destructive. For the poets do as they can, and cannot do otherwise: 'to implore writers to be a little more of this or that were like advising gunpowder to explode gently.' This fatalistic conception of artistic creation is in striking contrast with Poe's belief in the conscious adaptation of means to ends. Emerson is unlike Poe, again, when he asserts that criticism is an art when it goes beyond the poet's words, his vehicle, to his thought, the thing conveyed. But the two are once more in agreement in calling for an absolute criticism, a comparison of the particular work of art, not with inferior art, nor even with superior art, but with supreme art — art that excels the best that has ever been produced. Using a term that Poe abhorred, Emerson demands a 'transcendental' criticism. We must judge books, he says, by absolute standards. 'We must consider literature' — all literature — 'ephemeral, and easily entertain the supposition of its entire disappearance.' Confronted with a new poem, for instance, we are not to ask whether it has as good a right to exist as other mediocre poems, or whether it compares passably with certain good poems that it reminds us of, or even whether it can stand unblushingly beside the works of Homer and Shakspere and Milton, but whether it justifies itself in relation to the hypothetically supreme poem, the very Sun of poems which outshines even our masterpieces. Nay, we must be prepared to go still further; for the very Sun of poems is yet but a poem and not essential truth itself — beyond the ideal poem is the Ideal itself, the criterion of all human striving.

It is necessary to remember that most of the critical judgments of Emerson were actually delivered from this high ground. If at times he seems 'all knife and root-puller,' fastidiously discontent with many favorites of his day and ours, we must bear in mind that his standard was absolute, not in Poe's sense, but completely so. When Emerson applied this standard to Poe himself, Poe became 'the jingle man,' a most inadequate judgment if one is thinking of such other poets as Coleridge and Shelley, but not so inadequate if one refers to Homer and Shakspere or to the ideal poet or to the Ideal itself! He speaks of 'the abortive Homers that we praise, or try to,' such as Browning, Miss Barrett, Bryant, Tennyson. It is a rude way, perhaps, of disposing of half-gods and quarter-gods, but when you have in mind the gods themselves what less can you say? He asks, again, 'How shall I find my heavenly bread in Tennyson? or in Milnes? in Lowell? or in Longfellow?' We can only respond, Do not go to them for heavenly bread, but for an humbler staff of life; whereupon Emerson will put a question that has never been finally answered, But why be content with the lesser when the greater is yours for the asking? Although he himself by no means confined his reading to the best, he returned ever and again, throughout his life, to the indubitable masters. While Poe had no attachment to, or even respect for, any of the great authors, Emerson devoted himself to Plato, to Plotinus, to Plutarch, to Montaigne, to Shakspere, to Bacon, to Milton. While in college, according to a classmate, he came to know Shakspere almost by heart. Looking back to his first reading of Montaigne, Emerson remarked that no book before or since had meant so much to him. His modern masters, like Arnold's, were Wordsworth and Goethe. Of

Goethe he remarks that but for him the literature of our
times would be weak. Always he sought out, earnestly if not
ardently, the great writers.

Granting him his high standard, we are bound to accept
most of his unfavorable verdicts. The most damaging judgments that Emerson pronounced are, rather, favorable ones.
'The poem of all the poetry of the present age for which we
predict the longest term,' he tells the readers of 'The Dial,'
'is Abou ben Adhem, of Leigh Hunt,' a curious opinion also
recorded in his 'Journals.' In his poems 'The Test' and
'Solution,'

the unfading petals five

include, along with the conventional Homer and Dante and
Shakspere and Goethe, his favorite Swedenborg, who is also
one of the heroes of 'Representative Men.' Of the unfavorable verdicts, the most curious is that on Dante, whom he
styled 'another Zerah Colburn,' because of his prodigious
imaginative power — as definite as the senses themselves —
undirected by wisdom or illumination. Too much has been
made of Zerah, however; Emerson's choice of the comparison
is a good instance of his frequent violence of expression, his
fondness for the 'superlative' that he condemned. Elsewhere
he compares Dante with Byron, Burke, and Carlyle, and he
includes him, as has been noticed, among the five unfading
petals. Furthermore, like most readers of Dante, Emerson
had in mind primarily the 'Inferno,' which he read in J. A.
Carlyle's translation and later in that of Parsons, and which
repelled his rainbow optimism. Had he read the whole of the
'Divine Comedy' — it is a reasonable inference that he did
not — he would probably not have denied Dante's wisdom
and illumination: 'I never read him,' he said, 'nor regret that
I do not.'

More serious, all things considered, was the fact that he
rarely read a novel, and of all the novelists cared only for

Scott. In his 'Journals' he refers to 'the poor Pickwick
stuff,' adding the parenthesis, 'into which I have only looked
and with no wish for more.' A little later, however, he is persuaded by friends to try 'Oliver Twist,' and upon complet-
ing it writes an incisive paragraph in which Dickens receives
credit for his acute eye for surfaces and is disparaged for his
deficiency in poetry and in insight into character. Of Jane
Austen's novels he managed to read two, 'Persuasion' and
'Pride and Prejudice,' quite missing their merits but clear-
eyed as to their defects: they are 'vulgar in tone, sterile in
artistic invention, imprisoned in the wretched conventions of
English society, without genius, wit, or knowledge of the
world' — a judgment wholesale yet by no means groundless.
Thackeray he finds wanting in much the same way; in 'Vanity Fair' the author gives us this world of conventional society, apparently accepting the illusions that Bunyan had rejected. Emerson is doubtless blind to some of the finest
qualities of the English novel; yet is he not essentially right
in his condemnation of it as concerned mainly with surface?
'The novel,' he predicts, 'will find the way to our inte-
riors, one day, and will not always be novel of costume
merely.'

To Carlyle, again, he did less than justice, much though he
loved the man himself. Applying his inaccessibly high standard, Emerson writes: 'I always feel his limitation, and praise
him as one who plays his part well according to his light, as I
praise the Clays and Websters. For Carlyle is worldly, and
speaks not out of the celestial region of Milton and Angels.'
And he adds, nine years later, 'I still feel, as of old, that the
best service Carlyle has rendered is to Rhetoric or the art of
writing.' Of Tennyson, Poe's arch poet, he said, as he might
have said of Poe himself, that he 'is a beautiful half of a
poet.' That was before the volumes of 1842 appeared; after
seeing them, he could still only say that, while Tennyson's
work had many merits, 'the question might remain whether

it has *the* merit.' It is 'prettiness carried out to the infinite, but with no great heroic stroke. . . . It is a lady's bower — garden spot.' A little later he wrote the passage on Tennyson (incorporated without the poet's name in 'Essays, Second Series') in which he is conceived as 'a perfect music-box. . . . But is he a poet?' When 'In Memoriam' appeared, Emerson was not impressed, describing it as 'the common-places of condolence among good Unitarians in the first weeks of mourning.' But at last the 'Idylls of the King' caused him to change his tone. 'England is solvent,' he now writes in his journal, 'for here comes Tennyson's poem. . . . The long promise to write the national poem of Arthur, Tennyson at last keeps. . . . The national poem needed a national man.' Perhaps, however, Emerson's best comment on any of the contemporary English writers is one that occupies a single ruthless sentence: 'What a notable green-grocer was spoiled to make Macaulay!'

In his judgment of American writers Emerson avoided, as easily as did Poe, the 'patriotic' type of provincialism. His disparagement of Poe himself has already been indicated. Irving, Bryant, Greenough, Everett, Channing, even Webster ('even' is Emerson's own word, for Webster was long a hero to him), 'all lack nerve and dagger.' Lowell, he writes elsewhere, 'wants the uncontrollable interior impulse.' It is a terrible approval that he writes of his Concord neighbor Hawthorne: 'His reputation as a writer is a very pleasing fact, because his writing is not good for anything, and this is a tribute to the man.' Thoreau, as everybody knows, he admired almost unreservedly; his address on the man is almost as reverent as Lowell's essay is carping. Everybody knows, too, of his extraordinary admiration of Alcott, a noble idealist, 'the highest genius of the time.' But not everybody knows that he saw the weaknesses of his visionary friend: 'Alcott can never finish a sentence, but revolves in spirals until he is lost in air.' 'Alcott is unlimited, and unballasted.'

Bound, bound, let there be bound. . . . Alcott is a pail of which the bottom is taken out.' Poor Bronson!

I have dwelt on the literary judgments of Emerson, not only because they are unfamiliar to most of his readers, but also because they were by no means so capricious and extravagant as they have sometimes been represented; on the whole, they were quite as consistent and central as Poe's. And this is so because, as in the case of Poe, behind them lies a definite and coherent conception of literature, and because, as is not the case of Poe, there lies behind *that* conception a controlling *Weltanschauung* — not a technical philosophy, to be sure, but a large and unified vision of nature and man. If his criticism of the work of art in the foreground is often deficient in warmth, it often attains, by virtue of this background beyond background, a measure of insight only too rare in American, or indeed in any criticism.

It is with the nearer background — Emerson's conception of art and literature — that we are here primarily concerned. First let us view it as a whole:

Art is the creation of beauty by man. Using things as symbols, the artist combines them in new forms to express his intuition of eternal beauty. All great art is organic (the outer depending on the inner), in two senses. 1. From the organism, the intuition, itself, proceeds the appropriate form that expresses it. 2. And the intuition, or thing expressed, likewise proceeds from a reality beyond the artist's understanding. We say that the artist aims to express ideal beauty, but we mean that he lets it express itself through him. This ideal beauty is also ideal truth and goodness, which three are one. Latent in all men is this supreme unity, but completely realized in none. The arts, most of all literature, inspire men, help men to realize their complete humanity. If a man ever attained this end, he would have no further use for the means, for works of art. In proportion as men really live — approximate that vital union of truth, goodness, and beauty — their need for art diminishes.

§ 2

One could not desire a better instance of the need of defining critical terms than is afforded by a comparison of Poe's and of Emerson's definition of art. Since Poe defined poetry as 'the rhythmical creation of beauty,' he would necessarily have defined art in general as 'the creation of beauty.' Now, although Emerson's view of art is in striking contrast with Poe's, he begins with these very words. In his first book, 'Nature,' he says, 'The creation of beauty is Art.' What does he mean?

In the Introduction to 'Nature' Emerson inaugurates his career as a writer with the Aristotelian distinction between art and nature and between useful and fine art. Expanding these distinctions, he discusses Nature in section I, useful art in section II (Commodity), and fine art in section III (Beauty). The love of beauty, or Taste, exists in various degrees in all men; the creation of beauty, or Art, is the capacity of the few. These few, not content with admiring beauty, 'seek to embody it in new forms' — to combine the innumerable forms of nature in such wise as to show that they are fundamentally the same. For 'nature is a sea of forms radically alike,' and 'gliding through the sea of form' is that which makes the forms alike, Beauty.[1] Beauty is an ultimate end, 'eternal beauty,' — 'God is the all-fair.' It cannot, therefore, as Emerson says elsewhere, be defined, lying, like Truth, beyond the limits of the 'understanding.'

But if we cannot define eternal beauty, we can indicate with some definiteness what we mean by 'the creation of beauty.' Much as the artist loves the manifold things of nature, he intuitively perceives that their differences are of small account, that, penetrated with his thought, they are all alike. 'A leaf, a sunbeam, a landscape, the ocean, make an analogous impression on the mind.' It is this intuition, this spiritual ac-

---

[1] The imagery is from the Neo-Platonist Proclus, 'Beauty swims on the light of forms,' quoted in *Journals*, 1843, page 436.

tivity within the artist's mind, that is fundamental. Thought is supreme, and nature is only its vehicle, as Emerson asserts at length in the fourth section of 'Nature' (Language). The objects of nature are symbols of our thought; 'the whole of nature is a metaphor of the human mind.' It is the office of the artist, not to know unity in unity, but to show unity in variety. He must relate the two worlds, connect his thought with an appropriate symbol or mass of symbols. If he dwells at the heart of reality, indeed, he finds all symbols expressive of all meanings — 'In the transmission of the heavenly waters,' Emerson writes in 'Representative Men,' 'every hose fits every hydrant'; or, to return to 'Nature,' we may see in Shakspere a sovereign mastery of the world of symbols: 'His imperial muse tosses the creation like a bauble from hand to hand, and uses it to embody any caprice of thought that is uppermost in his mind. The remotest spaces of nature are visited, and the farthest sundered things are brought together, by a subtile spiritual connection.' His symbols, literally 'far-fetched,' fit the thought perfectly, like print and seal. It is the lesser poets, whose symbols and thought are ill related, that give us figures far-fetched in the usual sense. The great poet shows the equivalence of symbolical value; he can reveal spiritual meaning, or beauty, in all of nature. To him there is no ugly, for what we call the ugly is merely that which is viewed alone — the 'Each' seen out of relation with the 'All.' He takes the objects of nature, any objects of nature, unfixes them, 'makes them revolve around the axis of his primary thought, and disposes them anew.' That is 'the creation of beauty.'

Again and again, in the series of volumes that follows 'Nature,' Emerson returns to these ideas, fully elaborating if not quite defining them. His favorite approach may be indicated by saying that he regarded all great art as organic expression.

This fruitful biological analogy, which had its origin in Plato and Aristotle but was submerged or ignored in the cen-

turies that followed, was revived early in the romantic movement, and has been prominent ever since, markedly in the
æsthetic of Benedetto Croce. Emerson doubtless encountered
it in various places — in Coleridge at the least. In Coleridge,
too, Poe probably encountered it, without being impressed;
for although Poe asserted that Shelley contained his own law,
in the main he thought of artistic laws as being consciously
evolved by the critic and consciously applied — almost mechanically applied — by the artist. To Emerson, on the
other hand, it was a fundamental conception capable of answering all our questions about the nature and practice of
art. It is true that in his own writing, his own practice of art,
Emerson was notoriously deficient in the organic law in its
formal aspect; his essays and poems are badly organized, the
parts having no definite relation to each other and the wholes
wanting that unity which we find in the organisms of nature.
Rarely does he give us even a beginning, middle, and end,
which is the very least that we expect of an organism, which,
indeed, we expect of a mechanism. Yet if he could not observe the law of organic form, he could interpret it; in this
matter his practice and his theory are not equivalent — happily, he could see more than he could do. Moreover, he could
both see and exemplify the workings of the organic law in its
qualitative aspect. He is the friend and aider of those who
would live in the spirit, because of his insight — rare in these
times of inner disharmony — into the life of the spirit, and
because of his power to speak as one having authority. Whatever the lapses into caprice and willfulness of which he was
guilty, in the main he makes us feel that his utterance proceeds from a transcendent reality.

Like Schlegel and Coleridge, Emerson distinguishes between the organic and the mechanic. The conception of
beauty to which the preceding century tended, that it is 'outside embellishment,' he decisively rejects. Seeking analogies
in nature, he reminds us that grace of outline and movement,

as in the cat and the deer, are produced by a happily proportioned skeleton, and that 'the tint of the flower proceeds from its root, and the lustres of the sea-shell begin with its existence.' The difference between mechanical construction and organic form, he writes in the 'Journals,'

. . . is the difference between the carpenter who makes a box, and the mother who bears a child. The box was all in the carpenter; but the child was not all in the parents. They knew no more of the child's formation than they did of their own. They were merely channels through which the child's nature flowed from quite another and eternal power, and the child is as much a wonder to them as to any; and, like the child Jesus, shall, as he matures, convert and guide them as if he were the parent.

The doctrine of the organic, though it does not appear in the earliest writing of Emerson, was readily assimilated into the idealism with which he began. Thus in 'Nature' the way is already prepared in such a Neo-Platonic passage as this:

There seems to be a necessity in spirit to manifest itself in material forms; and day and night, river and storm, beast and bird, acid and alkali, preëxist in necessary Ideas in the mind of God, and are what they are by virtue of preceding affections in the world of spirit. A Fact is the end or last issue of spirit.

The emanation which here explains the concrete facts of nature is paralleled by the inspiration which, in Emerson's philosophy of art, explains the concrete work of art. Fact and poem alike spring from the creative spirit, and the poet, as the romantic critics liked to say, repeats in the finite the creative process of the Infinite Creator, and is the agent of that Creator. So long as he is a faithful agent and reports truly his high message, his verse is necessary and universal. Intuition and expression alike are dictated by that supreme Life or Spirit, and so are organic in the profoundest sense. Spirit expresses itself in the poet's intuition, and the poet's intuition expresses itself in the words and music of the poem. Spirit gives the divine hint to the poet, and the poet passes it on to all men, using a form that is excellent in proportion as it is determined by the hint itself, not arbitrarily devised by the poet. 'For it is not metres, but a metre-making argument that makes a poem — a thought so passionate and alive that like the spirit of a plant or an animal it has an architecture of its own, and adorns nature with a new thing.' Thus the poem, we may say — though Emerson does not use the terms — has organic beauty in a twofold sense, qualitatively and quantitatively. That is, it derives a qualitative beauty from the relative depth of the intuition or hint which the poet possessed, and a quantitative beauty from the degree of success with which he externalized, or expressed concretely, this intuition. If Emerson nowhere states his meaning quite so definitely, it is nevertheless plain that this distinction exists implicitly in his text. We are clarifying his sense, not distorting it.

Which of the two, quality or quantity, interested him the more needs no shrewd guess — he was engrossed in organic quality, as Poe was in mechanical quantity. Yet if he does not say much about the explication of the intuition, what he does say is well worth dwelling upon.

The law of the organic or necessary regarded quantitatively requires above all that there be a fitness of means to end. It holds not only of physical nature — the cell of the bee, the bone of the bird, having this perfect adaptation — but equally of spiritual nature — of the architect's building, of the poem. Emerson quotes Michael Angelo's definition of art as 'the purgation of superfluities' and holds that in artistic structures as in natural structures not a particle may be spared. The simplest expression, the severest economy, is the test of beauty of means. 'We ascribe beauty to that . . . which exactly answers its end.' There must be no fumbling with words, no acceptance of the nearly fit, no satisfaction in the rhythm that may be sung but does not sing itself, no embellishment, no laying on of colors, but the work of art must perfectly represent its thought. 'Fitness is so inseparable an accompaniment of beauty that it has been taken for it' — beauty is more than fitness, but must include fitness. Wanting that, the poem, the picture, the sculpture, however high it may aim, will be frustrate, of negligible effect on the reader or beholder. Having fitness, it will stir men forever. All the great works of art, whatever the intuition they embody, have this perfect adaptation of means to end.

So intimate, indeed, is this adaptation in the work of the supreme artists that we shall try in vain to separate intuition and expression: here Emerson in large measure anticipates the expressionist criticism of Signor Croce. What form should the poet give to his intuition? Let him 'ask the fact for the form. For a verse is not a vehicle to carry a sentence as a jewel is carried in a case: the verse must be alive, and inseparable from its contents, as the soul of man inspires and directs the body.' The superior poem is unanalyzable; word and thought cannot be severed. But in the inferior poem they fall apart, and we can distinguish between the vaguely held thought and the awkward or conventional expression. In any poem, we can measure the degree of inspiration by the degree of necessity in the expression. In the ideal poem, this necessity is absolute, down to the single word. 'There is always a right word, and every other than that is wrong,' Emerson inscribed in his journal when he was but twenty-eight years old, long before Flaubert announced this austere doctrine. Not by calculation, by conscious selection, does the master find the right word: 'There is no choice of words for him who clearly sees the truth. That provides him with the best word.' 'The master rushes to deliver his thought, and the words and images fly to him to express it; whilst colder moods are forced to respect the ways of saying it, and insinuate, or, as it were, muffle the fact to suit the poverty or caprice of their expression, so that they only hint the matter, or allude to it, being unable to fuse and mould their words and images to fluid obedience.' The poet seeks to marry music to thought, 'believing, as we believe of all marriage, that matches are made in heaven, and that for every thought its proper melody exists, though the odds are immense against our finding it, and only genius can rightly say the banns.' 'The poet works to an end above his will, and by means, too, which are out of his will. . . . The muse may be defined, Supervoluntary ends effected by supervoluntary means.' In such passages as these Emerson anticipates the profoundest reaches of recent æsthetics.

Yet on one point he is curiously inconsistent. While holding this conception of the inseparableness of content and vehicle, Emerson was well pleased with translations, which are virtually a denial of this conception. One need not speak very strictly to say that the precious life-blood of a master-spirit cannot be successfully transfused. The intuition that has been expressed we can experience only through its expression; for the translation is the equivalent, not of the original intuition, but of the translator's intuition, and between the two there is commonly a wide difference. Accordingly, Thoreau, for example, says that he does not read the classics in translations, for there are none; and he knows his Homer in Greek, long after college days. His friend Emerson, on the contrary, virtually loses his Greek, and although eager to do justice to Goethe, learns German reluctantly — as when Margaret Fuller administers five or six private lessons in that robust language, 'rather against my will.' Some years later he writes in his journal that to him the command is loud to read foreign books in translation, since not to do so would be as foolish as to forego the use of railroad and telegraph, or, as he says in 'Society and Solitude,' to swim across the Charles River to Boston instead of using the bridge. To tell the truth, Emerson was never the scholar, in our sense of the term rather than his; he shrank from the labor of mastering a language, a mere instrument, and his view of translation is perhaps not so much the statement of conviction as the expression of temperament.

With this abatement, which subtracts little, Emerson set forth clearly the inalienable unity of thought and word, thought and music, thought and color, and the consequent law that the degree of inspiration may be measured by the work's approximation to this unity. Given a certain intuition, how completely has it been realized? — This must be our first question in the criticism of art, though not, as romantic critics have often assumed, the only question. The answer to this question will determine the quantitative beauty of the work of art; but there remains the question of qualitative beauty.

Summary of doctrine of. The organic in its quantitative aspect

§3

When Emerson says that the beauty of a work of art is 'ever in proportion to the depth of thought'; when he says that 'the Poet should not only be able to use nature as his hieroglyphic, but he should have a still higher power, namely, an adequate message to communicate; a vision fit for such a faculty,' he avails himself of a standard of criticism that has to do with the kind, rather than the degree, of inspiration and expression. It is not enough that the poet should receive impressions and express them; he should question the authority of his impressions, whether inferior or superior, as his reader will likewise do. For, as Emerson declares when speaking of the impressionable, myriad-minded Goethe, 'It is not more the office of man to receive all impressions, than it is to distinguish sharply between them.' In the criticism of art we are to consider, then, not only exterior excellence, the virtue of explication, but also, and even more, interior excellence, the virtue of reality. The beauty of a work of art resides in both, and is supreme when there is a synthesis of perfect quality and quantity. This synthesis we find, perhaps, in Michael Angelo, of whom Emerson writes that 'Beauty in the largest sense, beauty inward and outward, comprehending

grandeur as a part, and reaching to goodness as its soul —
this to receive and this to impart, was his genius.'

The vital source of this fusion is ideal Nature. It is by taking a central position in the universe, by submitting to the
guidance of Nature, and helping her, so to speak, to make herself known, that the poet attains his triumphs. Art imitates
Nature — ἡ τέχνη μιμεῖται τὴν φύσιν — this doctrine, substantially in Aristotle's sense, Emerson teaches, most fully in the
essay on Art in 'Society and Solitude,' at the beginning of
which his topic is art in its wide meaning, as embracing both
fine art and useful art. 'The universal soul,' he writes, 'is the
alone creator of the useful and the beautiful; therefore to
make anything useful or beautiful, the individual must be
submitted to the universal mind. . . . Art must be a comple-
ment to Nature.' That this is true of the useful arts may be
seen at a glance; the aeroplane, to take an example that
would have delighted Emerson, is useful, practicable, if it em-
bodies a sort of continuation of nature's law, and fatally useless if it contradicts that law. Likewise 'in art that aims at
beauty must the parts be subordinated to Ideal Nature, and
everything individual subtracted, so that it shall be the production of the universal soul.' Hence the doctrine of necessity, which affirms that in the great poem what was written
must be written; when you first hear it you feel that it was
'copied out of some invisible tablet in the Eternal mind.' To
Shakspere writing his plays, Emerson remarks finely, his
thought must have come to him with the authority of familiar truth, 'as if it were already a proverb and not hereafter
to become one.'

Art is therefore not idle play, nor a pleasurable expressive
activity, but an arrestment and fixation of reality. For Poe,
Wordsworth was far too solemn in his view of poetry as aiming at truth; for Emerson, he was not serious enough. In his
enthusiasm for poetry's lovely revelation of truth, he tells
himself in his journal that poetry is 'the only verity,' add-

Emerson's debt to Aristotle

ing, 'Wordsworth said of his Ode it was poetry, but he did not know it was the only truth.' The term 'realism' or 'realism in literature' recurs in the 'Journals'; Emerson desires, as ardently as any modern realistic novelist, that literature shall give us that of which we can say with the fullest conviction that it *is*. But he will by no means deny reality to the ideal. Even while in college, writing a Bowdoin dissertation, he approvingly quoted Burke's assertion that 'Nature is never more truly herself than in her grandest forms; the Apollo of Belvedere is as much in nature as any figure from the pencil of Rembrandt, or any clown in the rustic revels of Teniers.' He might have substituted, '*more* in nature'; for he adopted, then or later, the classical conception of the ideal in art. For example, though never a lover of Aristotle, he reproduces in his 'Journals' the dictum that poetry is more philosophical and higher than history (more *true* is Emerson's word), attributing it, however, to Plato.[1] He is apparently repeating Aristotle again when he adjudges tragedy higher than the epic; and once more when he praises such statesmen as Pitt, Burke, and Webster, because [italics Emerson's] 'They do not act as unto *men as they are*, but *to men as they ought to be*, and as some are.' His view of art was remote from the equalitarian tendencies of modern realism, which inclines to find its reality in that which is most obviously widespread; it was selective, aristocratic, holding the best to be the realest of realities — men as they ought to be, and as some are.

His debt was far greater, however, to Plato and the Platonists. Of the many doctrines that he owed mainly to them, perhaps the most important is the doctrine of inspiration, which winds its golden course in and out of nearly every poem and essay that Emerson wrote. Aristotle, even when interpreted generously, must have seemed to him too external in his conception of poetry; for ideal imitation is yet imita-

[marginalia: Cf Sidney's Defence of Poesie.]

[marginalia: Emerson's debt to Plato and the Platonists.]

---

[1] This is corrected in another journal passage a quarter of a century later. Cf. *Journals*, 1834, 255, and 1861, 296.

tion, and therefore inferior in inwardness to the Platonic conception of inspiration. He suffered no delusion as to the light in which Plato himself viewed the poet's inspiration, but like many another Platonist chose to disregard the philosopher's disparagement of the poet's unconscious activity. He was content that the poet should be philosophic without being a philosopher:

The universal nature, too strong for the petty nature of the bard, sits on his neck and writes through his hand; so that when he seems to vent a mere caprice and wild romance, the issue is an exact allegory. Hence Plato said that 'poets utter great and wise things which they do not themselves understand.'

Nor does he hesitate to quote Oliver Cromwell as saying that 'A man never rises so high as when he knows not whither he is going.' Mystical in his idea of truth, Emerson set small store by 'knowing' and 'understanding,' as these are usually regarded. 'I am gently mad myself,' he confides to Carlyle after referring to the Transcendental reformers, no doubt secretly persuaded that his was a divine madness. It is true that five years later he felt that mysticism had been rather overdone, and that it ought to go out of style for a long time 'after this generation' — a reservation that fortunately left him free to be inspired and to follow his genius as of old. And perhaps he was right; perhaps we ought occasionally to indulge a whole generation of mystics, in order to see, as Whitman might put it, what can be done 'in that line.'

From universal nature sitting on his neck, the poet derives his power. 'Beyond the energy of his possessed and conscious intellect he is capable of a new energy (as of an intellect doubled on itself), by abandonment to the nature of things.' He must speak somewhat wildly — 'wildly well' says Poe — and with his mind used not as an organ or instrument but 'released from all service and suffered to take its direction from its celestial life.' Using a symbol significantly different from Plato's charioteer and horses, Emerson pictures the poet as a lost traveler who throws up the reins and trusts to the horse's instinct to guide him aright. The Platonic charioteer has abdicated, and there is but one horse, half black and half white, half celestial and half earthy, and there is no saying which half is leading the way, or whither it is carrying him! This apparent preference of abandon to control may be found in conceptual language at the end of the essay on Inspiration, where Emerson says that a chief necessity in life is 'the right government' (the phrase is Greek), 'or, shall I not say? the right obedience to the powers of the human soul' (which is rather Christian and Transcendental). Consequently Emerson is prepared to praise Michael Angelo, for instance, on the ground that he has more abandon than the classical Milton.

Yet while it is true that Emerson leads the casual reader to think of him as urging enthusiasm, obedience to one's genius, without providing against the caprices of romantic emotionalism, nevertheless he does indicate the necessary safeguards. The poet's problem, he writes in his treatise on Poetry and Imagination, is 'to unite freedom with precision'; thus, for example, 'Dante was free imagination, — all wings, — yet he wrote like Euclid.' The inexorable poetic rule is *either inspiration or silence*. 'It teaches the enormous force of a few words, and in proportion to the inspiration checks loquacity.' Here we have abandon with a difference; here we have a test of inspiration that regards it as valid according to its measure of restraint, a criterion that would make short work of the poets who offer us vaporous expansiveness instead of a truly inspired utterance. Again, there is the passage in the essay on Swedenborg, which most readers fail to connect with the ardors of the popular essay on Self-Reliance:

The Spirit which is holy, is reserved, taciturn, and deals in laws. . . . The teachings of the high Spirit are abstemious, and, in regard to particulars, negative. Socrates' Genius did not advise him to act or to find, but if he purposed to do somewhat not advantageous, it dissuaded him. 'What God is,' he said, 'I know not: what he is not,

I know.' The Hindoos have denominated the Supreme Being the 'Internal Check.' The illuminated Quakers explained their Light, not as somewhat which leads to any action, but it appears as an obstruction to anything unfit. But the right examples are private experiences, which are absolutely at one on this point.

This is Emerson's criticism of the bizarre revelations reported by the Swedish mystic; along with other passages [1] it indicates conclusively that he recognized the need of a principle of restraint in inspiration as the credential of its quality. When he did not expressly insist upon that need, it is plain enough that he assumed it.

Nor does he fail to point out certain spurious intoxications that must be differentiated from the raptures of inspiration — the intoxications of alcohol and opium, and of wild passions, such as those of gaming and war, which 'ape' the flames of the gods and are attractive to men who are unwilling to seek genuine inspiration through discipline. He reminds us that the experience of meditative men indicates agreement respecting 'the conditions of perception,' citing Plato again, to the effect that the perception demands 'long familiarity with the objects of intellect, and a life according to the things themselves.' Wine, coffee, narcotics, conversation, music, travel, mobs, politics, love, and the like are, he affirms, more or less mechanical substitutes for 'the true nectar, which is the ravishment of the intellect by coming nearer to the fact.' They do, indeed, release the centrifugal powers of a man, help him out into 'free space'; but it is not the heavens that he attains, but 'the freedom of baser places,' for nature refuses to be tricked. 'The sublime vision comes to the pure and simple soul in a clean and chaste body,' he writes with the Puritan accent, and draws support from the noblest of all the Puritans, who would allow the lyric poet to drink wine but requires of the epic poet that he live sparely and drink water from a wooden cup. To this page on false intoxications in

[1] The most explicit is in *The Natural History of Intellect*, pp. 36–37.

The Poet, writes Emerson in his journal, is to be appended
the confession that 'European history is the Age of Wine,' an
age that is at last waning as the new Age of Water begins.
'We shall not have a sincere literature, we shall not have
anything sound and grand as Nature itself, until the bread-
eaters and water-drinkers come.' What Emerson has in mind,
of course, is simply the ancient virtues of simplicity and self-
control, though he conceives them, it must be acknowledged,
rather ascetically.

§ 4

Closely related with the doctrine of inspiration is the distinction between genius and talent that plays such a large
part in the history of romanticism. Although Emerson's distinction between the two terms differs widely from the orthodox romantic distinction, it nevertheless has its romantic
aspect, or accent. To his teaching of self-reliance, of obedience to the genius or immanent universal, Emerson frequently gives a twist that all but reverses his actual meaning, inviting a willfulness and irresponsibility quite alien to his
intention. 'I would write on the lintels of the door-post,
Whim,' he tells us; and many of his disciples not only would
but did and do write it there. 'No law can be sacred to me
but that of my nature'; this may mean almost anything, and
has consequently been interpreted in the sophistical sense
dominant throughout the past century and a half. 'Insist on
yourself; never imitate.' Here the diction is such that one
naturally infers Emerson's approval of the eccentric man of
genius, living from within with no concern for outer consequences. 'Is it not the chief disgrace in the world ... not to
yield that peculiar fruit which each man was created to bear
... ?' Surely we are to be pardoned if we are here reminded
of Rousseau's declaration that he was made unlike anybody
he had ever seen, and of the monotonous cult of idiosyncrasy
that followed that temperamental declaration of independ-

ence. 'Our moral nature is vitiated by any interference of
our will' and people mistakenly 'represent virtue as a struggle,' writes the genuine 'beautiful soul' of Concord; and again
we cannot but remember the unbroken succession of dubious
beautiful souls from Rousseau down to our own times. In
such utterances as these more is involved than mere 'accent';
for, after all, accent involves meaning, connotation, and
Emerson's man of genius is not without relation to the typical
man of genius in the rampant days of the *Geniezeit*.

Having given this modification all the force that it deserves, we are free to say that the stock antithesis between
genius and talent is transformed by Emerson into one that is
much nearer the truth. 'Genius is but a large infusion of
Deity.' It is inspiration working through the intellect, rather
than through will or affection. When, on the other hand, the
intellect 'would be something of itself' instead of being the
agent of the divine, that is talent. Genius looks toward the
cause, proceeding from within outward, while talent proceeds
from without inward. Genius is organic (here we have the
qualitative organic) — it is 'the organic motion of the soul'
and assumes a union of the man and the high fact; whereas
talent is at best in the position of spectator, and at worst is
merely 'acquainted with the fact on the evidence of third
persons.' Genius is growth; talent is carpentry. Genius instructs; talent amuses. Genius beholds ideas and utters the
necessary and causal; talent derives only power — not light
— from above, and finds its models, methods, and ends in
society, exhibiting itself instead of revealing what is above
itself. Genius is not anomalous, but more like and not less
like other men; content with truth, it may seem cold to
readers 'who have been spiced with the frantic passion and
violent coloring of inferior but popular writers' — these
latter are the men of talent. Genius is broadly representative, 'a larger imbibing of the common heart'; the talent of
most writers is, on the other hand, 'some exaggerated faculty,

some overgrown member, so that their strength is a disease.'
'Genius is always ascetic. . . . Appetite shows to the finer
souls as a disease, and they find beauty in rites and bounds
that resist it.' Talent, on the other hand, is self-indulgent.

Here are distinctions *ad nauseam;* and indeed it must be
confessed that Emerson devoted an excess of attention to
these quarreling twins within his mind, recording in his
journal that he and Alcott 'talked of the men of talent and
men of genius and spared nobody'! and expressing himself in
Transcendental jargon, as when he concludes that 'Miss
Edgeworth has not *genius,* nor Miss Fuller; but the one has
genius-in-narrative, and the other has genius-in-conversa-
tion.' Nevertheless, however much of 'talent' Emerson may
display in making these antitheses, the fact remains that he
displays 'genius' also in his intimate sense of a spiritual
activity expressing itself through the happily endowed man
when he has prepared for its reception by rising above the
low plane of egotism and passion. Moreover, allowance must
be made for the time and place in which Emerson sang the
praises of genius — a time of unblushing materialism on the
one hand, and of self-indulgent emotionalism on the other,
and a country characterized by 'a juvenile love of smartness.'
As Emerson points out in the essay on Goethe, we Americans
set great store by mere talent, as the English do, and the
French even more. While Poe finds himself sympathetic with
the brilliant and logical French mind, Emerson extols the very
Germans that Poe ridiculed, on the ground that they have 'a
habitual reference to interior truth.'

The German intellect wants the French sprightliness, the fine
practical understanding of the English, and the American adventure; but it has a certain probity, which never rests in a superficial
performance, but asks steadily, *To what end?* A German public
asks for a controlling sincerity. Here is activity of thought; but
what is it for? What does the man mean? Whence, whence all
these thoughts?

In another essay he speaks of the Germans as 'those semi-Greeks, who love analogy, and, by means of their height of view, preserve their enthusiasm, and think for Europe.' He has in mind their philosophers; but when he considers their poets, he is obliged to say that the chief of them, Goethe, though deserving of ungrudging praise in such an age, is defective because of his worldly gospel of self-culture. 'The idea of absolute, eternal truth, without reference to my own enlargement by it, is higher.' And for his type of the inspired poetic genius he turns, after all, to the English Shakspere.

There is an early journal passage in which Shakspere is compared with a high mountain seen in the morning by the traveler, who deems he may quickly reach it, pass it, and leave it behind, but who, after journeying till nightfall, finds it apparently as far from attainment as in the morning light. The comparison recalls that of Poe, at the opening of his 'Letter to B——,' where a succession of critics, from the fool onwards, are conceived as occupying ever higher steps on the Andes of the mind, 'and so, ascendingly, to a few gifted individuals who kneel around the summit, beholding, face to face, the master spirit who stands upon the pinnacle.' But although the comparisons are similar, Poe and Emerson themselves differ widely in their attitude toward the poet. Poe begins his career as a critic with a passage of pseudo-romantic veneration, and then an end — never again does he kneel before the master spirit on the pinnacle. Emerson, beholding the mountain in the morning of his life, studying its lineaments with a rapture akin to that of Keats on first reading Homer, strives toward it all his years. To Shakspere, Emerson regularly yields supremacy over all other poets and intellects, and it is noteworthy that among his 'authorities,' in O. W. Holmes's table, Shakspere easily stands first.

He is superior to all other poets in quantitative beauty; 'for executive faculty, for creation, Shakspere is unique.'

Before all other poets, he had an intellect responsive to Spirit, so that his expression was organically necessary. Whatever came into his mind he could express in the fit terms. His writings everywhere bear the stamp of a divine inevitability. And he is equally superior in qualitative beauty; while able to express anything that he could think, he was also able to think more justly than any other man. His mind ever touched reality, and an almost limitless range of reality. He was always wise, equal to the heights and depths of his argument and all that lay between. He was not Shakspere but universal man; 'an omnipresent humanity coördinates all his faculties.' He shows no trace of egotism, commits no ostentation, does not harp on one string, like the man of talent. Talent is the severalty of man, genius the universality, and if ever poet had universality it was this modern Proteus. He spoke truth from the inner depths — unconsciously, like Plato's inspired bard. 'I value Shakspere, yes, as a Metaphysician,' writes Emerson in a Coleridgean passage, 'and admire the unspoken logic which upholds the structure of Iago, Macbeth, Antony, and the rest.' And yet, supreme as he is, we can imagine a still loftier poet. Although he gave us a larger subject than had ever existed and invaded Chaos with human order; although he was no less than an agent of nature, endowed with an unique power of insight, he was nevertheless wanting in such a high seriousness as befits his capacities, content to serve as the master of revels to mankind instead of employing his powers for the spiritual realization of himself and of humanity, so that he remains, after all, like the grim priests and prophets, a half-man, and we must still await the whole man, the reconciler, the poet-priest, who alone can satisfy the human spirit.

§5

Virtually all his artistic principles Emerson avowedly derived from what he regarded as the Greek tradition. His own

words show that he was anything but a romantic mediæval-
ist: for the Middle Age, he observes in his journal, 'delighted
in excessive ornament, in foreign and fabulous particulars.
It was farthest from the nature of things. It did not volun-
tarily clothe truth with fable, but any high-colored, picturesque fiction pleased the savages.' Indeed, the poetic mind,
he asserts elsewhere, is naturally pagan, preferring the gods
of Olympus, the Muses, and the Fates 'to all the barbarous
indigestion of Calvin and the Middle Ages.' In the battle of
the ancients and the moderns, the only modern literature
that he unreservedly supported was that of the Classical Revival in England, a main delight with him from his college
days onward. As a young man of twenty-five, he regards the
work of Shakspere, Jonson, Marvell, Herbert, Herrick, and
Milton as no less than 'the head of human poetry.' 'I have
for them,' he acknowledges, 'an affectionate admiration I
have for nothing else' — their splendor renders pallid such
lights as Byron and Wordsworth, Tasso and Dante, even
Virgil and Homer. Ten years later it is still clear with him
that the best of English literature is that of the age from the
accession of Elizabeth to the death of Charles II. That was
the aspiring age when the English, despite their racial love of
fact, were Platonic; but, as he notes after another ten years,
'the Platonism died in the Elizabethan.' The glory is departed, and now the 'Classicality' of the French mind rules, a
mere 'apery,' cleaving to the form and losing the substance;
'with the French school came into English ground a frivolous
style.' Indeed, to him as to Cotton Mather, 'Frenchy' is
something of an oath. The tendency of the eighteenth century to play 'with trappings and not with the awful facts of
nature' (though he conceded exceptions, notably in Dr. Johnson and Burke) antagonized his inveterate Platonism. With
the waning of that pseudo-classic dispensation came a return
to reality, especially in the German philosophers, in Goethe,
and in Coleridge and Wordsworth; yet in the main, as will

presentiy be observed, Emerson's attitude toward the Romantic Revival was hostile.

Turning away from the romanticism of the nineteenth century, and from the pseudo-classicism that preceded it, Emerson found his examples of great art in the English Renaissance, and still more in the ancient world itself — or, rather, in the Greek world, for Rome, as he avers, did not conquer Greece, but was conquered by her, and never equaled the artistic achievements of her conqueror. At the age of sixteen, he enters in his first Wide World journal 'a resolution to make myself acquainted with the Greek language and antiquities and history with long and serious attention and study; (always with the assistance of circumstances).' Circumstances were niggardly in the Harvard of those days, and serious study was always a little beyond Emerson; yet his devotion to Greek civilization was 'long' if nothing else, and he contrived in the end to visualize the glory that was Greece and to grow familiar with its mode of thought. He perceived that the Greek genius, in all its various manifestations — in history, literature, architecture, sculpture — ever leaves the same impression. Without the aid of a British Museum or an Ashmolean, he knew the Greeks primarily in their literature, and even then largely through the foggy medium of translations. Yet from the beginning he asserted,[1] sincerely and not conventionally, that their literary masterpieces remain unparalleled down to our own times.

To the philosophical literature, especially Plato and the Neo-Platonists, his debt can hardly be exaggerated, though Professor Harrison, in his valuable book on 'The Teachers of Emerson,' perhaps succeeds in doing so. Yet if German thought is highly important in Emerson, as his first book, 'Nature,' shows from title to end, Platonism is truly even more important. With Emerson we may say, 'Of Plato I hesitate to speak, lest there should be no end.' Has he not

[1] See, for instance, the *Journals*, I (1822), p. 158, and VI (1842), p. 268.

converted Homer into philosophy, and summarized European thought in advance? Why should not young men receive their education from this book? It is a prime merit of Plato that he does not set his supernal region inaccessibly afar, without relation to mundane existence, but builds 'a bridge from the streets of cities to the Atlantis,' never writing in pure ecstasy or poetic raptures, but 'carrying up every thought to successive platforms, and so disclosing, in every fact, a germ of expansion.' 'The expansions,' he adds, 'are organic. The mind does not create what it perceives, any more than the eye creates the rose.' With all his subjectiveness, Emerson habitually remains remote from the spirit of romantic Transcendentalism, and near his master Plato. And he was perhaps equally devoted to the Neo-Platonists, whom he did not very clearly differentiate from Plato himself, regarding them, it would seem, as a direct organic expansion of that arch philosopher. Plotinus, for instance, is Plato over again, 'exalted a little under the African sun.' To Plotinus, Emerson was sufficiently devoted to undergo the ordeal, on at least one occasion, of translating into English a long passage from Goethe's German rendering from the Greek!

Among the other ancients Homer, of course (favorite that he is with all types of minds), became one of his standards. Twice in his journal he ventures the assertion that 'Homer's is the only epic,' all others being manifestly derivative. Among the five indispensable Greeks named in the essay on 'Books,' Plato and Homer are included; the others are Herodotus, whose anecdotal method attracted him, Æschylus, 'the grandest of the three tragedians,' and Plutarch, who is at once eminently readable and invigorating. Emerson then urges a study of Greek history, with Aristophanes reduced to an ancillary position. I find no evidence in Emerson's writings that he ever read Thucydides; in the essay on Plutarch we are told that the latter has a hundred readers where the former has one; and apparently Emerson was not that one. Euripides the modern also failed to win him; but he responded to Sophocles, reading the 'Electra' in the original with his brother Charles, who reports him as 'quite enamored of the severe beauty of the Greek tragic muse,' and other plays in English — 'for want of thee, dear Charles!' Pursuing his way with a languid pleasure through the 'Iphigenia' of Goethe, he cannot see how a great genius can be content to make paste-jewels; and indeed, 'when in the evening we read Sophocles, the shadow of a like criticism fell broad over almost all that is called modern literature.' [1] He will admit an ancient subject only if the treatment is simple and original, as in Shakspere's plays. 'The words of Electra and Orestes are like actions. So live the thoughts of Shakspere. They have a necessary being. They live like men. . . . Shakspere is like Homer or Phidias himself.'

§6

We have now to inquire precisely what was the ground of this lifelong enthusiasm for the Greeks, since there are, of course, many kinds of *Gräkomanie*. The kinds may be ranged under two heads: first, genuine Hellenism, or enthusiasm for the Greeks as they were; and secondly, pseudo-Hellenism, or enthusiasm for the Greeks as they were not. Pseudo-Hellenism may be divided again into, first, a formalistic type, the pseudo-classicism of the eighteenth century, and secondly, a sentimental type, the false Hellenism of the romantic movement. Of the formalistic deviation Emerson was totally free; but, while perhaps in the main a genuine votarist, he clearly tended to follow the romantic deviation.

When Emerson himself asks the question, what is the ground of interest that all men have in Greek civilization? he

---

[1] Elsewhere in the journal he writes: 'Do not make modern antiques like Landor's *Pericles*, or Goethe's *Iphigenia*, or Wieland's *Abderites*, or Coleridge's *Ancient Mariner*, or Scott's *Lay of the Last Minstrel*. They are paste jewels.'

finds the answer in the idea that every man passes through a
Greek period of life. The individual repeats the experience
of the race, being Classical as a child, Romantic as a youth,
and Reflective as an adult. If this analogy appeals to us — as
I think it does — the reason is surely, not that it expresses a
truth but that, like most analogies, it expressed what Emerson liked to call a half-truth. Every child, says Emerson, is a
Greek, because every child is natural. What a terrible word,
as Falstaff might have said, is this 'natural'! There are so
many ways of being natural, including several sets of opposite ways! Emerson's use of the word is anything but clear.
'The Greeks,' he writes, 'are not reflective, but perfect in
their senses and in their health, with the finest physical organization in the world. Adults acted with the simplicity and
grace of children.' Taken alone, this statement is definite
enough: the Greeks have the naturalness, the spontaneity, of
the animals and of the young human animal. This is not all,
however. A little earlier in the same passage, Emerson had
defined our Greek period as that 'of the bodily nature, the
perfection of the senses — of the spiritual nature unfolded in
strict unity with the body.' From this it appears that 'natural' has a twofold significance, one of them not natural at all
in the usual sense but 'spiritual'; and this modification virtually destroys the original affirmation that every child is a
Greek, for Emerson saw plainly enough that the young, like
the majority of adults, are 'wicked,' in the sense that they are
'animals' and 'have not yet come to themselves.' Again, he
asserts that the Greek soldiers of the 'Anabasis' were 'a gang
of great boys, with such a code of honor and such lax discipline as great boys have,' immediately after setting down as
the typical Greek virtues courage, address, self-command,
justice, strength, swiftness, a loud voice, a broad chest, freedom from the love of luxury and elegance. If some of these
are boyish traits, some of the most important are not; boys
do not excel in self-command and justice, nor are they averse

from luxury. Once more, Emerson makes much of the 'inborn energy' of the Greeks, which the formalistic classicists had well-nigh forgotten, and, adding to it 'the engaging unconsciousness of childhood,' supposes that the result is the Greek genius. But the recipe is not so simple. Inborn energy — yes; childish unconsciousness — yes; and along with these humanistic control, which Emerson quite fails to throw into relief. The mature Greek was not close to nature, like the child, but in harmony with himself. He was neither immersed in nature nor uplifted to the supernatural, living rather on a plane between the two — the human. We must conclude that Emerson, though himself a humanist in various ways, was dominated to such an extent by the Oriental and Christian sense of a supernatural spirit that, failing to find this sense developed among the Greeks, he could not adequately see them for what they were but ascribed to them the type of spontaneity cultivated by the romantic movement of his own times.[1]

Another answer to the question why Greek life and art are perennially attractive, Emerson gives in his distinction between the classic and the romantic. This distinction grows out of the doctrine of organic art. Classic art is organic art, in the widest sense, 'drawing directly from the soul' both the material and the appropriate form. It unfolds itself from within, and bears the stamp of necessity. It is creative — the creative forces of the Eternal are at work, using the inspired writer as their instrument. Romantic art, on the other hand, is additive, aggregative, external, concealing the high fact with haphazard additions. It is the result of inclination, of caprice, instead of an impersonal necessity. For example, had the Greeks lived in Christian Germany they would have

[1] Is it fanciful to regard Emerson's applause of Whitman as a result of his fulfillment of the Greek union of childlike spontaneity and great energy? Here were no paste-jewels, but naïve truth and 'buffalo strength,' even if he did want 'good morals.' The last phrase, though in the Puritan accent, suggests our third element, humanistic insight.

manifested their classicism by building a cathedral, and we moderns are romantic, not classical, when we build a Parthenon custom house. Or, to illustrate with a political analogy, we may say that democracy, in which 'the power proceeds organically from the people,' is classic, while monarchy, in which 'all hangs on the accidents of life and temper of a single person,' is romantic. If Emerson's example and analogy are dubious, the reason may be inferred from a following paragraph, where he remarks that he does not find the antique in society, nor often in modern books, but always in nature: 'Once in the fields with the lowing cattle, the birds, trees and waters and satisfying curves of the landscape, and I cannot tell whether this is Thessaly and Enna, or whether Concord and Acton.' Always in Emerson we return to Nature, as if she were the ultimate criterion; and although by virtue of his Puritan heritage and classical predilections he brought to her an attitude that rendered her subordinate, he yet responded to her emotionally with something of the romantic infatuation and ever and again relented of the austerities of dualism. Consequently, when he echoes Goethe by asserting that the classic is healthy and the romantic sick, we have some ground for the suspicion that he is condemning the romantic for a reason that is itself romantic, viz., the reason that art must shun the artificial, which is characteristic of society, and cleave to the natural. Certainly, Goethe's meaning is capable of receiving a romantic twist. Yet, after all abatements have been made, all romantic waverings allowed for, I think we must conclude that the main current of Emerson's mind was not the romantic but the classic. If we have some doubt as to the above citation from Goethe, we may reassure ourselves with another echo of Goethe that occurs more than once in Emerson's writings: the unmistakably classical idea that the Greeks 'found the genius of tragedy in the conflict between Destiny and the strong *should*, and not like the moderns, in the weak *would*.' This appears in the

'Journals' as early as 1836, the year of 'Nature,' and it became a main ground of Emerson's somewhat surprising indictment of the literature of romanticism.

The poet who wrote the lines as tonic as any in all modern literature,

> When Duty whispers low, *Thou must*,
> The youth replies, *I can*,

perceived with the antique clarity the weakness of *would* and the romantic tendency to confuse *would* and *should*:

Wishing is castle-building; the dreaming about things agreeable to the senses, but to which we have no right. Will is the advance to that which rightly belongs to us, to which the inward magnet ever points, and which we dare to make ours.

European, especially Continental, romanticism gave an indulgent interpretation to 'that which rightly belongs to us,' making it, often, coextensive with 'wishing,' setting up air-castles as legitimate objects of infinite aspiration and daring to realize them, or trying to, in defiance of the laws of life, holding up as an ideal, not man as he might be, but man as he may not be. In the art of music, most indefinite of the arts, often blending *would* and *should* — the dream-world of the senses and a true supernal world — so intimately that we cannot tell whither we are transported but only that we are in ecstasy, romanticism naturally attained its fullest expression. If music reveals, as Schopenhauer said, 'the innermost essential being of the world,' one might expect Emerson to praise it, in the traditional romantic fashion, as supreme among the arts. While indeed recognizing music as 'the modern art,' Emerson holds that 'Writing is the greatest of arts.' If it be asserted that he undervalues music merely because of his æsthetic insensibility to it, our answer would seem to be that he undervalues it mainly because of the dominant cast of his mind, which in his maturity was keenly alert rather than dreamy. We must not confuse his quest of inspiration with romantic reverie.

Only for a brief period of his life did he really belong with the romantic brotherhood. Looking back from the vantage height of late middle age, Emerson remembers the romanticism of his youth, the 'delicious sensibility' of those early days at college, not fronting the realities of life but fain at any moment to extemporize a holiday. Delightful, eager, shallow responses of youth!

How sufficing was mere melody! The thought, the meaning, was insignificant; the whole joy was in the melody. For that I read poetry, and wrote it; and in the light of that memory I ought to understand the doctrine of musicians, that the words are nothing, the air is all. What a joy I found, and still can find, in the Æolian harp! What a youth find I still in Collins's 'Ode to Evening,' and in Gray's 'Eton College'! What delight I owed to Moore's insignificant but melodious poetry.[1]

Thus, like Poe, he began with an enthusiasm for such poetry as that of Moore; but unlike Poe he did not end there. In the year of his first book he already refers to 'the frivolous brains of the Moores and Hugos and Berangers of the day,' and thenceforth he has little to say in favor of Moore or the greater romantic poets. Had he read the Continental poets of *Weltschmerz* and of the *tour d'ivoire*, it is certain that he would have condemned them roundly, since he rejects the less romantic English poets of the same age. While always fond of 'The Bride of Lammermoor,' he brushes aside the poetry of Scott, along with Moore's, as dealing with society rather than with man. Coleridge, again, while conceded to be a supreme critic, is dismissed as a poet. In his hostility to Shelley, Emerson was cautious but wholesale. Stating in his journal in 1841 that Shelley was 'wholly unaffecting' to him, he admits that, since Shelley attracts many of the best readers, it would be hazardous to overlook him. 'I was born,' he remarks, 'a little too soon' — an explanation to which he re-

[1] *Journals*, IX (1861), 310–11. The same memories are poetized in 'The Harp.'

turns half a dozen years later when he will grant Shelley the
'merit of timeliness' in order to account for his 'imposing on
such good heads.' In a 'Dial' paper in 1840 he must have
shocked some of these good heads with his assertion that,
while full of aspiration and noble traits, Shelley was 'never a
poet . . . imagination, the original authentic fire of the bard,
he has not.' His meaning is apparently indicated elsewhere,
when he records Elizabeth Hoar's criticism that Shelley, like
shining sand, looks attractive and valuable, but that, however carefully you sift him, he yields no riches, but merely
flashes forth his mica-glitter. In the case of Byron, his condemnation is more explicit. Though worried, as many readers
of Byron have been, by Goethe's warm praise of him, he rejects the poet partly by applying the Goethean standards of
health and substance. Byron is a poet of vice and disease,
and has no thoughts. He is not to be cast into outer darkness,
let us note, because of his moral irregularities alone; for, hearing a preacher rail at Byron with 'sulphurous Calvinism,'
Emerson remarks that he prefers the vice of Byron to the
virtue of the Reverend Mr. M. — a very illuminating reaction. The point is, rather, that with all his fine energy
Byron was 'ignorant of the world and its law and Lawgiver,'
indulging his pride and selfishness and petty subjectiveness
at the expense of his power of observing reality outside of
himself.

The only exception that Emerson made in his indictment
of the English Romantics was Wordsworth, although in his
early manhood his attitude was that of ridicule. In a letter
written at the age of twenty-three, he expressed the feeling
that Wordsworth had embarked, like the undisciplined minds
of the Middle Ages, upon an ill-advised enterprise, immod-
estly inquisitive in his search for the essence of things. 'The
worthy gentleman,' Emerson writes quaintly, 'gloats over a
bulrush, moralizes on the irregularity of one of its fibres, and
suspects a connection between an excrescence of the plant and

its own immortality.' By the time he was publishing his papers in the 'Dial,' however, Emerson had found that above the poet's serene egotism was a reverence and insight, fitfully displayed and often obscured by defect of the shaping power and of the accomplishment of verse, yet genuine in an age of spurious aspiration. Dedicating himself to the spirit that hovered over Helvellyn and Windermere, faithful to the conscience and will within him, mindful of the high office of the poet, Wordsworth in the end achieved 'more for the sanity of this generation than any other writer.' 'We saw stars shine, we felt the awe of mountains, we heard the rustle of the wind in the grass, and knew again the ineffable secret of solitude. It was a great joy.' Wordsworth expressed for Emerson that profound love of nature for which he was ready, gave utterance and passion to feelings half-nascent in his heart, and confirmed him in that quest — perhaps after all ill-advised — of essential reality conceived as present in external nature. 'We say now, with Wordsworth, to the scholar, Leave your old books; come forth into the light of things; let Nature be your teacher.' Wordsworth he held to be the greatest poet since Milton.[1]

That the vision of life and of art dominating the writings of Emerson was fundamentally classical is surely suggested by his outspoken dissatisfaction with the Romantic Movement as a whole. Aside from his love of Wordsworth, his admiration of Coleridge as a critic, and his guarded approval of Goethe, the writers of the great age just before his own hold a small place in his esteem. His attitude is the more significant because, as we have repeatedly noted in the foregoing pages, he himself was in various respects constitutionally romantic. He had to the full the modern affection for Nature and the tendency to question her for light; he sympathized

[1] An extended study of the influence of Wordsworth upon Emerson has been made by Frank T. Thompson in a dissertation (University of North Carolina, 1925) on 'Emerson's Debt to Coleridge, Carlyle, and Wordsworth,' excerpts from which have been published in *Studies in Philology*.

with the romantic rejection of tradition; he disparaged logical
thought and expression; he opposed to a conventional decorum the new emphasis on the self or genius; he welcomed
the revival of wonder; and in many other ways he apparently
aligned himself with the romanticists and became one of
their eloquent spokesmen. Again and again he tempts us to
place him, not only with Wordsworth, but with Rousseau
and Shelley and Byron. And yet, however responsive he may
have been to the romantic mood that still prevailed in his
times, we are bound to feel, the more we study him, that he
was even more responsive to the spirit and doctrine of
Christianity and of Greek humanism. His own reasons for
this preference have already been indicated in part, with a
certain vagueness for which he himself is more or less responsible. We have now to throw into relief, as the chief of these
reasons, his recoil from the romantic ego and attachment to
what he terms 'the general mind of man.'

Although, as a child of his age, Emerson had his idiosyncratic side, cherishing at times the romantic sense of the
uniqueness of men, it is evident enough that the romantic
age in which he lived distorted his doctrine of the self, as he
himself complains:

A curious example of the rudeness and inaccuracy of thought is
the inability to distinguish between the private and the universal
consciousness. I never make that blunder when I write, but the
critics who read impute their confusion to me.

Possibly he went a little far in saying that he never made that
blunder himself; but it is clear that he made it rarely, and with
reference to externals mainly, and that he was early aware
of the ambiguity of the idea of self. Thus, in 1834, he observes in his journal that a man has not only 'his own genius,'
but also 'his own conscience,' and that self-indulgence and
self-respect are two things. 'All these doctrines contained in
the proposition, Thou art sufficient unto thyself (*Ne te quœ-*

siveris extra) are perfectly harmless, on the supposition that
they are heard as well as spoken in faith.' The supposition is
a large one, as Emerson presently found when his critics
imputed their own confusion to him; and with his romantic
disrelish for mere logic he was ill equipped to defend himself
and render his meaning clear. One of his clearest statements
is in his 'Thoughts on Modern Literature' in the 'Dial,'
where he discusses with some approach to system the 'per-
nicious ambiguity in the use of the term *subjective*.' He distinguishes a healthy subjectivism, in which 'I' does not mean
the individual, a subjectivism arising from the perception
'that there is One Mind, and that all the powers and privileges which lie in any, lie in all,' and on the other hand a
vicious subjectivism, in which personality is central, a luxuri-
ous cultivation of individual thought and feeling. 'The great
always introduce us to facts; small men introduce us always
to themselves.' Goethe, gathering up into himself all that
was typical of his times, was at once great and small, sharing
the subjectiveness of his age in both senses.

This antinomy of the idiosyncratic and the universal self
is rendered clearer by other opposed terms habitually used by
Emerson. The former is related with 'the evanescence of
things,' the latter with the 'centrality'; the former with the
plane of surface, the latter with the plane of substance; the
former with the law for thing, the latter with the law for man;
the former with Devil, the latter with God; the former with
'fate, or the order of nature,' the latter with 'the ideal, or
laws of the mind.' 'The dualism,' as he says himself, 'is ever
present, though variously denominated.' For the lower member of the dualism, Emerson's favorite term is fate. Fate is
the brute force of nature, indifferent to man, apparently even
maleficent, holding on its mysterious course to an end beyond
our understanding:

What front can we make against these unavoidable, victorious,
maleficent forces? What can I do against the influence of Race, in

my history? What can I do against hereditary and constitutional habits, against scrofula, lymph, impotence? against climate, against barbarism, in my country? I can reason down or deny everything, except this perpetual Belly; feed he must and will, and I cannot make him respectable.

The animals live wholly in this order of nature; the child, and most adults, mainly; they are content with 'the drag of temperament and race,' submissive to the egoistic forces at work within them, to the law of nature. But although Fate confronts mankind with a necessity that none may wholly neglect, the wise perceive that there is 'a Necessity contra-distinguished from the vulgar Fate' by means of which they may attain a certain liberation from nature. 'So long as I am weak, I shall talk of Fate; whenever the God fills me with his fulness, I shall see the disappearance of Fate.' We have a double consciousness, one natural and the other human, so that we cannot live exclusively in either: they are discrete, not reconcilable. Vain the attempt to resolve them into harmony; base the life immersed in the lower law, and happy the experience of him who hearkens to the voice of humanity that speaks within. While the animal reaches its highest perfection by yielding to nature, the man reaches his by virtue of his sense of relation with a superior order. 'In the measure in which he has this sense he is a man, rises to the universal life.'

Between men as they are and men as they might be, men as we know them in history and the idea of the 'Standard Man' — what a 'yawning difference'! Those who think of Emerson as a visionary should bear in mind that his was never the idealism that regards this as the best possible of worlds. It was usual with him to speak of actual men as 'lop-sided, one-eyed half men,' or as pupas, tadpoles, bugs, spawn. He could scarcely find words expressive enough to match their meanness; Poe's mob, rabble, herd are tame in comparison. With sulphurous Calvinism still fresh in his

nostrils, even the saintly Emerson recoiled from the natural
man with something like horror. Yet he believed — and
herein was he the visionary — that the yawning chasm between the actual and the imagined could be bridged, not by
strenuous ethical work, but by the simple expedient of self-
reliance, i.e., reliance upon the influx of spirit. By virtue of
inspiration, a man's *posse* becomes his *esse*.

Now, the vision of this attainable superior self or Standard
Man is glimpsed through the imagination — this, with Emerson, as with the Greeks, is the true function of the imagination. He perceives that 'we live by our imaginations,' that
'even the shopboy smoking his cigar assumes the attitude
and air of a rich gentleman, and is raised in his own eyes,'
that the romantic imagination, like the shopboy's, tends to
be egocentric, however alluring in its subtle coloring, and
that the highest type of the imagination is humanistic or
ethical. This type we find, for example, in Milton:

> He is identified in the mind with all select and holy images, with
> the supreme interests of the human race. If hereby we attain any
> more precision, we proceed to say that we think no man in these
> later ages, and few men ever, possessed so great a conception of the
> manly character. Better than any other he has discharged the
> office of every great man, namely, to raise the idea of Man in the
> minds of his contemporaries and of posterity — to draw after Na-
> ture [that is, the universal] a life of man, exhibiting such a composi-
> tion of grace, of strength and of virtue, as poet has not described
> nor hero lived. Human nature in these ages is indebted to him for
> its best portrait.

We find the ethical type of imagination, again, in Jesus, in
whom it was so highly developed that he has been regarded
as the perfect man, the ideal incarnate. Yet Emerson held
the imitation of Christ to be inadequate, feeling in him the
absence of qualities eminently developed in ancient Greece —
such qualities as cheerfulness, love of natural science, love of
art. 'I see in him nothing of Socrates, of Laplace, of Shak-

spere. The perfect man should remind us of all great men.'
Quite in the spirit of Greek humanism, Emerson sought a
pattern that would lift humanity 'to new heights of spiritual
grace and dignity, without any abatement of its strength.'
The senses and emotions are not to be destroyed, as they
ever tend to be by the religious imagination, but to be transcended, as in the wise anthropomorphism of Greece. 'The
excellence of men consists in the completeness with which
the lower system is taken up into the higher — a process of
much time and delicacy, but in which no point of the lower
should be left untranslated.' Emerson remarks the union of
aspiration and restraint in the sculpture of the Greeks, who
held themselves in control and at the same time fixed their
vision upon ideal beauty, attaining thus a lofty serenity,
'permitting no violence of mirth, or wrath, or suffering.'
'This,' he adds, 'was true to human nature.' When a man
is thus 'centred,' in harmony with himself, he shows us that
'all melancholy, as all passion, belongs to the exterior life.'
And such in the main was the serenity of Emerson himself,
in contrast with the melancholy of Poe and most of the
romantics.

§7

Operating thus from the ethical center of human nature,
the imagination advances securely to its vision of the complete life — the 'triple face' of Truth, Beauty, Goodness.
Although Emerson like Plato habitually conceives of the
One as the Good, he holds all three members of the trinity
to be ultimate, equal, and interchangeable, requires as a
condition of true vision a balance of the three elements in
the observer, and regards now one now another as worthy of
preference. This wavering may perhaps be explained by
saying that, while the goal is always the same, the several
approaches offer characteristic obstacles and advantages,
like the several trails to a mountain summit.

When for instance it is beauty that allures, he perceives that

> Beauty is its own excuse for being.

Then is beauty 'the form under which the intellect prefers to study the world,' and he is at one with the Transcendentalists, who make it 'the sign and head' of the trinity, and who disparage the other approaches to the ideal. 'We call the Beautiful the highest, because it appears to us the golden mean, escaping the dowdiness of the good and the heartlessness of the true.' Goodness is grim and unwinning, intellect is devoid of affection, but beauty is warm and lovely and draws us on — *zieht uns hinan* — toward a rapturous vision of the Celestial. In this mood Emerson writes his essays on Beauty and Love, closely following his master Plato, and his poems on Initial, Dæmonic, and Celestial Love. In the last of the three poems he brings us to a vision of the heavenly harmony, of that pure realm

> ... where all form
> In one only form dissolves;
> . . . . . .
> And every fair and every good,
> Known in part, or known impure,
> To men below,
> In their archetypes endure.

Here is that Supernal for which Poe yearned so confusedly, here the source of that music

> Which only angels hear

echoed by wise Merlin and wise Saadi, who are Emerson himself in his best moments.[1] There are passages in Emerson's writings that bear a striking surface resemblance to Poe's passages on the indefinite; for example, the paragraph

---

[1] It is instructive to compare 'Israfel' with such poems as 'Merlin I,' 'Merlin II,' 'Merlin's Song,' and 'Saadi'; and also Keats's 'Ode to a Nightingale' with Emerson's 'Bacchus.'

in the essay on Love in which Beauty is described as un-
approachable:

What else did Jean Paul Richter signify, when he said to music,
'Away! away! thou speakest to me of things which in all my endless
life I have not found and shall not find.' The same fluency may be
observed in every work of the plastic arts. The statue is then beautiful when it begins to be incomprehensible. . . . The same remark
holds of painting. And of poetry the success is not attained when it
lulls and satisfies, but when it astonishes and fires us with new endeavors after the unattainable.

Is not this once more Poe's and Shelley's desire of the moth
for the star? The answer is obvious: Emerson's indefinite is
not Poe's, because he does not sever beauty from the other
aspects of the ideal — this very paragraph, indeed, begins
with the sentence, 'The ancients called beauty the flowering
of virtue,' a reference to 'The Republic' which would have
suffered the contempt of Poe. Not beauty alone, according
to Emerson, but also truth and goodness, each vitally inter-
fused with the others, are requisite for the eye that would
penetrate to the ultimate. Else, the universe is 'opaque.'

Thus, when Emerson places beauty at the head and front,
and celebrates art as the creation of beauty, he never divorces
it from virtue. While he thinks of them as equal, he always
assumes or asserts their mutual dependence. For morals
alone, independently of the other ultimates, he expresses an
aversion. 'We love morals until they come to us with mountainous melancholy and grim overcharged rebuke: then we so
gladly prefer intellect, the light-maker,' or beauty, he might
have added. He tells us of an oration in which 'P. pleased the
Boston people by railing at Goethe . . . because Goethe was
not a New England Calvinist,' and remarks that 'our lovers
of greatness and goodness after a local type and standard'
need to enlarge their vision, and that a man like Goethe, a
lover of truth and perceiver of it, is an 'incomparably more
helpful ally to religion than ten thousand lukewarm church-

members who keep all the traditions and leave a tithe of their
estates to establish them.' A moral narrowness and sterility
of this kind he felt to be inseparable from goodness when it
stands unsupported by truth and beauty. For an exemplar
of the highest form of goodness he turns once more to Milton,
whose object, he says, was to teach, but who poured into his
doctrine a sublime sense of beauty ('his giant imagination')
and a lofty sense of truth ('the stores of his intellect'). He
quotes the familiar words of the young Milton fired with
thirst for the supernal:

For whatever the Deity may have bestowed upon me in other
respects, he has certainly inspired me, if any ever were inspired,
with a passion for the good and fair. Nor did Ceres, according to
the fable, ever seek her daughter Persephone with such unceasing
solicitude as I have sought this τοῦ καλοῦ ἰδέαν, this perfect model
of the beautiful in all forms and appearances of things.

Here was no half-man or third-man, but a man of integrity
in the best sense, aspiring as a whole. That perfect model
which Milton glimpsed with the aid of imagination and in
accordance with which he endeavored to shape his life was at
the same time ethical and beautiful. 'Among so many con-
trivances as the world has seen to make holiness ugly, in
Milton at least it was so pure a flame that the foremost impression his character makes is that of elegance.'

In art as in life, the moral is inseparable from the beautiful.
The grand style in sculpture Emerson finds 'as admonitory
and provoking to good life as Marcus Antoninus. I was in
the Athenæum, and looked at the Apollo, and saw that he
did not drink much port wine.' In another passage, employing the Platonic idealism in a modified form, he explains his
admiration of Greek sculpture by saying that it was 'made
after a high and severe pattern made by men in whom the
moral law inhered. The Jove, the Apollo, and the Phidian
works are related to Virtue.' He observes in still another
passage the unhappy contrast between the purity and sever-

ity of these ideal forms and the frivolity and grossness of the modern spectators in the museums. A high wisdom is carved by Phidias, painted by Raphael, written by Shakspere. He points out that Shakspere was 'deeply indebted to the traditional morality.' Even when genius disowns the moral sense and lives loosely, it never confuses moral distinctions, as 'such fry as Beaumont and Fletcher, and Massinger, do continually,' since true genius and moral insight are of necessity proportionate. And always they are fused, not collateral. The sculptor, the painter, the poet, like Nature herself, refrain from drawing the moral. An explicit statement, a direct inculcation of the moral — this, for Emerson, is the heresy of the didactic, the perversion of the true relation of beauty and goodness. Shakspere is moral, 'not of set purpose, but by "elevating the soul to a nobler pitch,"' a saying equivalent, Emerson suggests, 'to Aristotle's maxim, "We are purified by pity and terror."' Without aiming at morality, all great art emancipates us from the egoistic self and elevates us to that universal self wherein the fair and the good are one and indistinguishable.

Thus, while the apostle of Art for art's sake is an unwitting traitor to his goddess, confining her to a single province, a Platonist like Emerson is her truest friend and worshiper, revealing her all-embracing beauty. So it would seem, at least; but actually, like Plato himself, Emerson ends by preferring that other goddess Virtue, who is the same and yet other, the supreme aspect of deity. Positing beauty as an ultimate, Emerson yet habitually refers us to 'its source in perfect goodness.' Conceding that beauty draws us toward that source, he yet prefers the more direct approach of virtue —

... the golden key
Which opes the palace of eternity.

That is the master key, the golden one; beauty is after all but silver. 'Wherever the sentiment of right comes in, it takes precedence of everything else.' In poetry itself it is supreme. Quantitative excellence, the ability to explicate his vision, the poet must have, and above it qualitative excellence, 'a vision fit for such a faculty'; and consequently, says Emerson, 'when we speak of Poet in the great sense, we seem to be driven to such examples as Ezekiel and Saint John and Menu with their moral burdens; and all those we commonly call Poets become rhymesters and poetasters by their side.' In another passage he states the opinion that 'the true poetry which mankind craves is that Moral Poem of which Jesus chanted to the ages stanzas so celestial.' And Emerson makes an end of the matter by concluding in all candor that the highest value of poetry is to subdue man 'to order and virtue,' and that 'the whole use in literature is the moral.'

For Plato, with his conception of art as an imitation at three removes from reality, the condemnation of poetry was natural enough; for Emerson, however, who follows the Neo-Platonists in regarding poetry as a symbolic presentment of reality, it was, to say the least, unnecessary. He had good grounds for the assertion that, since the highest beauty carries along with it in its aspiration the highest truth and goodness, it offers the supreme vision of reality. He accepts the reason, but not the conclusion. If we ask why it was that he stopped short of the conclusion, we shall find, I think, that the most obvious explanation is also the fundamental one, namely, that he inherited not a little of the exaggerated ethicism in which the New England mind had been steeped for two hundred years, that his ancestry offers to the view a kind of apostolic succession, that he himself had been a minister in the Unitarian Church, and that, though alienated from the church by the romantic or Transcendental spirit of the times, he remained to the end a lay preacher, the friend and aider of those who would live in the spirit. Segregating himself from the refracting influences of society, seeking the comparative solitude of his Concord study and the pine groves, he liked to regard himself as the scholar or Man Thinking; but his thinking was mainly, so he admits, a pious reception, as his lectures and writings were an endeavor to transmit piety to others.

§8

Certain it is that Emerson made valiant efforts to surpass the æsthetic limits of his heritage and environment and to do the fullest justice to the arts. In this departure from the local tradition of New England, he was encouraged most of all, apparently, by the example of the author of 'Wilhelm Meister,' a work that he was reading as early as 1830. Three years later, following the footsteps of Goethe in Sicily and Italy, he conned the words of his master as a sort of index to the worth of the art before him. Though 'unused to theatres,' he even ventured repeatedly to attend the opera, more dazzled than won, however, despite his experimental docility. The ballet he witnessed with the mingled feelings of a romantic Puritan, as a journal entry indicates. Quoting Goethe as laughing 'at those who force every work of art into the narrow circle of their own prejudices and cannot admire a picture as a picture, and a tune as a tune,' he asseverates that he was himself 'willing to look at this as a ballet, and to see that it was admirable, but I could not help feeling the while that it were better for mankind if there were no such dancers.' 'I have since learned God's decision on the same,' he adds, 'in the fact that all the *ballerine* are nearly idiotic.' [1] Through many years he sought to subscribe to the romantic

[1] Years later, when Fanny Elssler danced in Boston, he was still mindful of Goethe, in the spirit of whom he remarked, 'It is a great satisfaction to see the best in each kind, and as a good student of the world, I desire to let pass nothing that is excellent in its own kind unseen, unheard.' (*Journals*, 1841.) This is his conclusion to a two-page description and criticism of the performance, one page being devoted to æsthetic and the other to moral considerations. He is not now so sure of God's decision on the same; indeed, if anything, suspects divine approval, since 'such surpassing grace must rest on some occult foundations of inward harmony.'

enthusiasm for music, although the effort was as hard for
him as the attempt to laugh. Instead of responding to
music's cry of 'Away! away!' he soberly gropes for a meaning. 'Not having an ear for music, I speculate on the song
and guess what it is saying to other people; what it should
say to me. It is Universal and seems to hint at communication more general than speech, more general than music also.'
What it *should* say, not what it does say; it *seems* to hint, but
does not hint; no, the art of music, though Universal, was
not for Emerson, not even for Emerson the Romantic. Nor
could he experience rightly the significance of painting. It is
true that he remarks, while in Florence, that a man must
come thither to understand the powers of this art, and that
he himself, after making the rounds of the galleries, 'was
well-nigh "dazzled and drunk with beauty."' It is also true
that in subsequent years he was glad to inspect engravings
of the Italian masters brought by friends; but at no time
were there signs of his having acquired more than a rudimentary understanding of design and color.

Architecture and sculpture, however, appealed to him
more. In Sicily the churches caused him to hope that ere
long those in New England would be similarly adorned. In
Rome, Saint Peter's produced perhaps the strongest æsthetic
impression of his tour, drawing him back again and again.
'What a temple!' he exclaims:

When night was settling down upon it and a long religious procession moved through a part of the church, I got an idea of its
immensity such as I had not before. You walk about on its ample,
marble pavement as you would on a common, so free are you of
your neighbors; and throngs of people are lost upon it. And what
beautiful lights and shades on its mighty gilded arches and vaults
and far windows and brave columns, and its rich-clad priests that
look as if they were the pictures come down from the walls and
walking.

Thence we came out (I was walking with two painters, Cranch
and Alexander) under the moon and saw the planet shine upon the

finest fountain in the world, and upon all the stone saints on the piazza and the great church itself. This was a spectacle which only Rome can boast — how faëry beautiful! An Arabian Night's tale.

A few days later, after witnessing the illumination of the church with torches instead of moonlight, he summed up his impressions by saying that Saint Peter's is 'the sublime of the beautiful' and remarking simply, 'I love Saint Peter's church. It grieves me to think that after a few days I shall see it no more.' And from Florence, where the churches seem bare and poor, he looks back: 'Ah! ah! for Saint Peter's, which I can never more behold.' Yet by the time he reaches Milan he concludes that architecture is but an imitation of that sublimer architecture which exists in the soul, that 'one act of benevolence is better than a cathedral.' 'So do your duty, yours,' he adds, ingeniously finding authority for this end of the matter in a citation from no other than Goethe.

As for sculpture, Emerson valued highly 'such perceptions of the dignity or grace of the human frame as the student of art owes to the remains of Phidias, to the Apollo, the Jove, the paintings and statues of Michael Angelo, and the works of Canova. There are now in Italy, both on canvas and in marble, forms and faces which the imagination is enriched by contemplating. Goethe says that he is but half himself who has never seen the Juno in the Rondanini Palace at Rome. Seeing these works true to human nature and yet super-human, "we feel that we are greater than we know."' The idealistic grandeur of the Greeks was within the view of Emerson, though he was easily capable of remarking, in a tone unconsciously patronizing, 'The Jove of Phidias pleases me well' — Gad, it had better! Carlyle might have exclaimed but for his own Calvinistic aloofness from the plastic arts. Michael Angelo, however, won Emerson's warmest interest, as sculptor, painter, architect, and man. It is significant that in 1835, fresh from his sojourn in Europe, Emerson chose the Italian artist as the subject of a lecture before the Society for the Diffusion of Useful Knowledge.[1] It is significant also that copies of Angelo's works hung upon his study walls, and that he resisted the attempt of his friend Ward to prove to him, with engravings as evidence in the debate, 'that Raphael was greater than Angelo, great as Shakspere.' This was in 1839, when Emerson's choice of men of the First Class was: Phidias, Jesus, Angelo, and Shakspere. Although this choice is amply favorable to the fine arts, Emerson at once alters it by saying that if he 'must sift more sternly still,' his list will read simply: Jesus and Shakspere.

The summary impression left by a review of the attitude of Emerson toward the fine arts is that he sought with more earnestness than success to translate his theoretical approval into practical faith and knowledge. He confesses that he was 'ignorant enough . . . to wish to go to Europe only to see three or four persons' — not with the object of overcoming the limits of his culture. Instead of finding in Italy, like Goethe, '*einen zweiten Geburtstag, eine wahre Wiedergeburt*,' he admits that he is essentially unaltered, that he is a *Doppelgänger* (his giant going with him wherever he goes), and, charitably regarding his defect as a virtue, announces that travel is 'a fool's paradise.' The coachmen and the beggars are too much for him, nipping all sentiment in the bud. 'I was very glad,' he admits, 'to see no more antiquities, but to get home as fast as I could' — i.e., to dine with Mr. Rogers and some pleasant gentlemen. He goes north to Paris, and there, in the prime of manhood, he shrinks from the city's gay zest for life: 'Pray what brought you here, grave sir? the moving Boulevard seems to say.' Everywhere he is an alien:

Cœlum non animam mutant qui trans mare currunt.

---

[1] Published in the *North American Review* in 1837. He gave a series of six lectures on Biography, a kind of fore-study of *Representative Men*. The first lecture was on the tests of Great Men (possibly the original of his essay on the Uses of Great Men), and the first of his heroes was Michael Angelo. The lectures of his friend Carlyle on Heroes were delivered five years later.

As for the *beaux arts*, he concludes that they were 'born in Europe and will not cross the ocean, I fear,' and in his own case the fear was not wholly groundless.

Yet if Emerson's æsthetic sensibility did not extend far beyond literature, it was much livelier than is commonly supposed within literature. No other writer, Mr. Brownell has said, is so perennially young; and to be perennially young certainly implies the continuance of the lyrical impulse, of the love of beauty and poetry. Various critics have indicated plainly enough that Emerson was susceptible to what is termed 'pure poetry.'[1] He himself remarks that, for each painter, ten poets speak to him, and in a certain mood he could even assert that a dozen lines of true poetry are 'worth all the old trumpery Plutarchs and Platos and Bacons of the world.' This surprising declaration he set down in his journal, not in early youth, but at the mature age of forty-five; and nearly twenty years after, he was still capable of saying that 'when visions of my books come over me, as I sit writing, when the remembrance of some poet comes, I accept it with pure joy, and quit my thinking, as sad lumbering work; and hasten to my little heaven, if it is then accessible, as angels might.' If the reference to angels is a little suspicious, we may remind ourselves of that more earthy sentence in his essay on 'Books,' 'A man's library is a sort of harem.' Taking a practical turn, this affection prompted him to write abundantly on literature and to give many lectures (never printed) on English writers, including a single series of ten lectures on English literature. According to his son, the ministerial Emerson, having left the pulpit, cherished a desire to hold a chair of Literature in some New England college — to relinquish service as a prophet of the soul in favor of service as a teacher of 'correct taste.' As a Professor of Literature in Harvard College, Emerson would not have been

---

[1] For example, O. W. Firkins, *Ralph Waldo Emerson*, pp. 232–33, and Stuart Sherman, *Americans*, p. 106 fol.

among the scholars, 'for they are dead and dry,' he says; nor among the humanitarians, who 'trample on letters and poetry.' He would have been, rather, something of a humanist, in the proper sense of that term, absorbed in demonstrating how poetry imaginatively reveals the human law. He would have been strong where strength is rarest — in the perception of essentials, and in the power to make others perceive them. We may suppose that he would have been stronger here than his professorial friend Lowell. At the same time he would have been immeasurably inferior to Lowell in scholarship, as is obvious, and relatively deficient in human feeling, as is not quite so obvious. For, after all, whatever his æsthetic response to nature and to literary art, Emerson was wanting in emotional energy.[1] The passion of the spirit he experienced with a pure strength hard to match in modern times, but the passion of finite humanity burned pallidly within him and consequently failed of outward expression, either in action or in letters. If he had deep feeling, it was too promptly repressed or metamorphosed into the life of the spirit. He complains, with singular insight, that Americans have no passions, but only appetites; but he himself has neither. He passed at one step from the life of the senses to the life of the spirit, virtually omitting that vast intervening realm of the human emotions which is the main content of ordinary life and of literature.

This is the central deficiency in Emerson, and explains most of his more specific deficiencies. This is the reason why his efforts to enter into the point of view of the plastic arts were frustrate. This is the reason why, unlike Carlyle, he gave little more than a formal recognition to the genius of Goethe. This is the reason why, with all his delight in Shakspere, he nevertheless condemns him as *only* the master

---

[1] 'He was somewhat thin on the physiological side'; he 'clipped and pruned' the 'free luxuriance' of his genius, according to Walt Whitman, a disciple who revered him beyond any other contemporary and who said, 'I don't think I could honestly describe anything as a defect in Emerson.'

of revels to mankind. And this is the reason, though he did
not know it, why he finally banishes from his ideal common-
wealth all the poets and artists.

His own reason for banishing them, to be sure, is quite
different. A true book, he holds, is an organic expression of
ideal Nature, issuing through the agency of one mind from
the Universal Mind. To the Universal Mind each of us has
direct access; why, then, do we seek in books indirect access
to it? Because it chances that so much of the time we seek
inspiration in vain:

We go musing into the vault of day and night; no constellation
shines, no muse descends, the stars are white points, the roses,
brick-colored leaves, and frogs pipe, mice cheep, and wagons creak
along the road. We return to the house and take up Plutarch or
Augustine, and read a few sentences or pages, and lo! the air swims
with life, secrets of magnanimity and grandeur invite us on every
hand, life is made up of them.

Such is the virtue that resides in a good book. It has accomplished our high purpose for us; a transmutation or dis-
tillation of life into truth, it draws us into that religious frame
of mind which renders ordinary experience insignificant. To
obtain the virtue of the book we must yield to it; yet that,
again, is precisely what we must not do! The law of the book
is, 'that it should be first, that I should give way to it; I, who
have no right to give way, and, if I would be tranquil and
divine again, I must dismiss the book.' For no book, no dis-
tillation, is quite perfect and final; some distortion there
must always be; and always our guide is liable to become our
tyrant. 'The literature of every nation will bear me witness.
The English dramatic poets,' for example, 'have Shaksperized
now for two hundred years.' A wise reader will therefore
guard himself with periods of solitary thought, to the end of
self-recovery. He will use to the utmost his own unaided
vision, and resort to books only in his 'idle times,' in the
hours when his own vision is dim and inactive. He will read

poetry 'because a symbol always stimulates the mind.' He will seek the 'spermatic' books, such as Plato, Plotinus, and Plutarch. On the bended knee he will read the Bibles of the nations — the Vedas, the Upanishads, the sayings of Confucius. 'The office of poetry I supposed was Tyrtæan — consoling, indemnifying; and of the Uranian, deifying or imparadising.' The right function of art, Emerson constantly insists, is religious.

Yet in the very loftiness of the function of art lies the ground of its inferiority. For not only are all books imperfect, and all pictures and statues 'cripples and monsters'; they are also means rather than ends, and their highest function is to render themselves functionless! Comparing books with crutches, Emerson deems them proper only for the feeble and lame; employed by the strong, they 'weaken the muscular power, and become necessary aids.' Therefore, in proportion as the feeble and lame become strong, they should forego the aid of art and avail themselves of their own latent strength — 'the God dwells within.' As the books of the nursery are outgrown, then those of our youth, and then many of our later books, so perchance even 'Homer and Milton will be tin pans yet.' So eager is Emerson to show that books are merely initial that he ventures to disparage them even in his address at the opening of the Concord Free Public Library, observing that their 'costliest benefit' is to 'set us free from themselves; for they wake the imagination and the sentiment, — and in their inspirations we dispense with books.' The benefit is indeed costly. 'It pleases the great soul' — so the oracle speaks in another passage — 'that literature, art, persons, space, time should be undervalued.' Why undervalued rather than justly valued? This disparagement of the concrete, he goes on to declare, is made in no braggart spirit, 'but only in the spirit of a child who says, I am but a child, but I am heir of all.' One suspects, however, that a child who says that, is something of a braggart, and that in Emerson himself there is something of the spiritual braggart, something of romantic pride vitiating at times the simplicity and serenity of his insight.

The proper material for spiritual living, he insisted without end, is not art but life itself. For example, writing from Rome, he reports that art evokes in him only an evanescent and superficial emotion: 'It yields in me to the interest the most ordinary companion inspires.' Again, after conceding in his journal that 'some of the sweetest hours of life, on retrospect, will be found to have been spent with books,' he retorts: 'Yes; but the sweetness was your own. Had you walked, or hoed, or swum, or sailed, or kept school, in the same hours, it would have endeared those employments and conditions.' Elsewhere in his journal he wonders that we should prefer 'some "Lincoln bell"' of the poet to the bell of our own experience; he, for his part, will find his Lincolnshire 'in the next pasture, and the "bell" in the first thrush that sings.' [1] 'Retreat upon your own spontaneous emotions,' he advises himself and all men; dubious advice for himself, who needed more culture rather than more self-culture, and palpably false advice for the ordinary man, who usually retreats, in a sense not Emerson's, when he relies upon his own spontaneous emotions. And again, he represents the poet as saying, 'I am not a man to read books, but one receiving that which books are written to report.' As usual, the assertion is too broad, since observation easily shows that the poet needs a preliminary discipline in books of many kinds and especially an intimate acquaintance with the traditions of his art. What Emerson here says of the poet, he frequently says of men in general: let them be their own poets, let them perceive with their own eyes that life is not prosaic but poetic, that ugliness is but beauty unperceived, that common experience

[1] The preference of the blithe song of the throstle to the art-song of the poet — the doctrine, 'Let Nature be your teacher' — the advice, 'quit your books' — came to Emerson in part, of course, from his beloved Wordsworth.

may contain all that art has ever revealed and all that it may hereafter reveal, that 'the Law' — the supreme beauty and truth and goodness — speaks with highest potency in ourselves. If men would but trust to their own undeveloped powers and thus advance toward complete humanity, how soon would they pass beyond literature, 'imitative expression,' to spiritual living, beyond the means and toward the end.

When Emerson thus disposes of all the arts, including poetry, on the ground that they are at best initial, preliminary, propædeutic to spiritual living, he makes it difficult for the spiritually-minded critic to answer him on equally high ground. But, for that matter, all the seekers after the supreme, such as the author of the 'Imitation' and Jesus himself, are difficult to answer. If the moral sentiment within us responds gladly to their teaching of the spiritual life, which is high and hard, we cannot defend with much conviction that which is lower and easier. Nor will it suffice to assert that the high and hard includes the lower and easier and thus satisfies our thirst for totality. It is instructive to find that even Emerson, unremitting though he was in his quest of the spiritual, felt these difficulties:

'Seek ye first the kingdom of God, and all these things shall be added unto you.' What! Art? Hamlets? Ballads?
The life is more than meat and the body than raiment.

There is the question, and there is the answer. Dear to us is the hope that the men of religion will offer us all that we hunger for, but always our experience is that they leave us incompletely satisfied. Our deep need of beauty they affront by their neglect of it. If beauty is less than virtue, it is none the less more than meat and raiment; art, Hamlets, ballads we must have, nor shall they be termed fleshly. Speculating on a possible reconciliation of art and religion, Emerson expresses in his poem 'The Problem' his discontent with the professional man of religion, and in his journal his discontent with the professional poet ('The poetic gift we want, but not the poetic profession'), and in his essay on Shakspere he calls for a new type of man, the poet-priest, a whole man made up of these two half men who would answer all our needs. This organic fusion of art and religion stirs the imagination, and pleases us far better than Emerson's other solution of the problem — the rejection of art in favor of religion. Yet it, too, is an impossible solution, if by impossible we mean that which has never been and hence is likely never to be. The ideal of the poet-priest can only be approximated, and therefore — we may find the words in Emerson again — 'we shall cease to look in men for completeness, and shall content ourselves with their social and delegated quality.' We must put up with the priests, and with the poets; with religion, and with art.

Thus Emerson is really leading us nowhere when he dismisses art as merely initial, or when he proposes a union of art and religion.

If then we ask, finally, why it is that his discussion of the relation of art to life leaves us in the end unresponsive, why, with an insight probably unsurpassed in modern times into the higher services of art, Emerson yet makes us feel that he was rarely quite at home in the province of art, we must conclude, I think, that it is because his cast of mind was dominantly priestly rather than poetic, mystical rather than æsthetic. He is full of impetuous exaltations, of sudden raptures that carry him far aloft and beyond sight of the familiar terrain of man's life. Beneath his mysticism there is little articulated thought — such thought as Plato's or even Plotinus's — to sustain and direct it. He rises on the wings of faith, not from their high tableland of the mind, but from the flats of daily experience. Even when he lives with us, with home and kindred and nature and art, he is never in the current of the human affections but outside of them, contemplating them, on the verge of transcending them. ⌐He is always pluming his wings, not for an epic flight, but for a mystical ascension to the Highest, where the ways of God do not even need justification, and where the ways of men are forgotten. That absorbed interest in the ways of men — in their actions, thoughts, sensations, passions — which the æsthetic point of view presupposes, was, after all, wanting in Emerson, notwithstanding his resolutions to be a student of the world. He preferred his Plato and his Jesus to his ballads and his Hamlets, and preferred them so markedly that he never quite understood what the ballad-makers and the master of revels had accomplished. Sifting great men to ascertain the constitution of the First Class, he reduced the number sternly to two, Jesus and Shakspere. Logically he should have reduced the number to one, Jesus, and then have substituted for Him that Oneself whose praises his disciple Whitman was confusedly to sing.

CHAPTER III

LOWELL

§1

In no other American of the nineteenth century has the critical spirit manifested itself so comprehensively as in James Russell Lowell. Despite the fact that he leaves an impression of comparative superficiality and futility — shortcomings to which we are keenly sensitive to-day, perhaps because they are our own — he must still be regarded as our most distinguished literary critic. While there is far more of original vigor in both Poe and Emerson (and in Whitman, as will appear), he was free of the special purposes that limited their achievement as critics. The bulk of Poe's work was journalism, book-reviewing, ephemeral commentary on the books of the day; Emerson, at the other extreme, characteristically chose for his literary essays themes that are timeless; Lowell, however, attempted rounded portraits and estimates of so many authors of the past that he virtually wrote a critical history of literature from Dante to his own age.[1] As this contrast might imply, Poe read little outside his times; Emerson read widely but transcendentally;

---

[1] For convenient reference I will arrange his subjects in chronological order: 1. Dante (*Prose Works*, vol. IV); 2. Chaucer (III); 3. Don Quixote (VI); 4. Spenser (IV); 5. Marlowe (VII); 6. Shakspere Once More (III); 7. Shakspere's *Richard III* (VII); 8. Beaumont and Fletcher (VII); 9. Webster (VII); 10. Chapman (VII); 11. Massinger and Ford (VII); 12. Milton (IV); 13. Milton's *Areopagitica* (VII); 14. Walton (VII); 15. Dryden (III); 16. Pope (IV); 17. Rousseau (II); 18. Fielding (VI); 19. Gray (VII); 20. Lessing (II); 21. Wordsworth (IV); 22. Wordsworth (VI); 23. Coleridge (VI); 24. Keats (I); 25. Landor, Some Letters of (VII); 26. Carlyle (II); 27. Swinburne's Tragedies (II); 28. Percival, Life and Letters of (II); 29. Emerson the Lecturer (I); 30. Thoreau (I). (In this list I have disregarded *Lowell's Early Prose Writings, The Function of the Poet and Other Essays*, and *Letters of James Russell Lowell*.) An edition of Lowell's literary essays, thus arranged, would render a service to lovers of books.

while Lowell was a good deal of the detached scholar. Again, Poe in his most memorable work was concerned with technique; Emerson, as Lowell phrases it, with 'the profounder ethics of art'; and Lowell himself with both. Poe extolled beauty and fought the heresy of the didactic; Emerson, though eager for beauty, could not long lay aside his ministerial function; it remained for Lowell to mediate, with fair success, between the two. Poe and Emerson were at their best in critical theory; Lowell, wanting their turn for speculation, excelled in practice. Poe and Emerson have certain æsthetic doctrines associated with their names; but the name of Lowell suggests nothing of the kind, suggests, rather, gusto and flashes of insight, the free play of feeling and intelligence.

From what has just been said — that æsthetic doctrines are so inconspicuous in Lowell, and that he excelled in practice rather than theory — it might reasonably be inferred that he was an impressionist, that the center of interest in his essays is the man himself, a delightful personality, blending such qualities as warmth of sympathy, infectious enthusiasm, an active imagination and fancy, irrepressible wit and humor, fundamental sanity and common sense. In substantiation of this inference, it might be urged that we read his literary essays much as we read his charming letters — for their personal qualities — and that if we subtracted these personal qualities the essays would dissolve into nothingness, while in the case of Poe and Emerson the skeleton of ideas would remain. At a glance, one has reason to say of Lowell: his criteria are negligible, the man is all, he was an impressionist.

Such, I say, is the conclusion to which we are quickly drawn if we follow what Poe, with his one-track mind, somewhat haughtily termed ratiocination, or what Emerson, with his trackless mind, disparaged as mere logic or understanding. Yet surely the weakness of logic resides less in the thing itself than in the ease of its abuse by those who, indulging an emotional bias, disregard important facts and arrive at a predetermined conclusion. In the present instance, the important facts are twofold. In the first place is the obvious fact that the impressionist is not a critic without criteria, but a critic who refuses to delimit his criteria by deliberate formulation and application. To call Lowell an impressionist is not to dispose of his criteria. In the second place, a thorough scrutiny of Lowell's criticism would show that his criteria, far from being negligible, are really distinct and impressive. It could probably be demonstrated, indeed, that his weakness was the very reverse of that which is commonly alleged; that, instead of having insignificant criteria and effective personal qualities, he possessed a set of controlling ideas that wanted only the impetus of great personal qualities to make them in the highest degree significant and useful.

This is a large claim, necessitating a careful study both of his theory of criticism and literary art, and of his personal endowment and attainment.

§2

Books and the Man — in the commerce of the two lies the whole story of criticism. While Emerson defined the scholar or critic as Man Thinking, and, though a great reader, never lost himself in his books, Lowell might almost have defined the critic as Man Reading, since his habitual occupation was so much more passive than active, receptive than creative. In his commerce with books, Lowell's imports far exceeded his exports. From childhood to old age he read voraciously, in the fine library of his father, in the library of Harvard College, and in his own accumulating collection of books. Not long before his death he came to the conclusion that 'the problem of the scholar was formerly how to acquire books; for us it is how to get rid of them.' He spoke of Cotton Mather as book-suffocated, an epithet that perhaps describes himself quite as justly. From the greatest of English Puritans

he selected, with unconscious irony, the following motto for
one of his 'Elizabethan Dramatists':

> ... Who reads
> Incessantly, and to his reading brings not
> A spirit and judgment equal or superior,
> .   .   .   .
> Uncertain and unsettled still remains,
> Deep versed in books and shallow in himself.

As a professor of literature, aware of the *gründliche* Germans,
he read with a kind of monastic zeal; but even then, as well as
before and after, he must have been largely an epicurean
browser. In one of his essays he tells of his magical hours in
the old library in Harvard Hall, where he read undisturbed
save by the sun, which drew him to a north or south window
according to the season, and by his conscience, which re-
proached his truancy from the tasks of the day. 'It was the
merest browsing, no doubt, as Johnson called it, but how
delightful it was!' Though I do not know just what he refers
to in Johnson or Boswell, I do know that 'His Majesty having
observed to him that he supposed he must have read a great
deal; Johnson answered, that he thought more than he read'
— a quotation quite as damaging to Lowell as the above
motto from Milton. He was under no delusion as to his intellectual indolence. From his own experience he realized that
the profusion of books makes men 'depend on their shelves
rather than on their brains; it has supplanted a strenuous
habit of thinking with a loose indolence of reading which
relaxes the muscular fiber of the mind.' In his 'Moosehead
Journal' he confesses 'how tyrannical the habit of reading is,
and what shifts we make to escape thinking.' His weakness
in this regard is but one instance of the fact that his enthusiasms were far greater than his strenuosities — a fact, one
suspects, even in his moral nature, in which ideals counted for
more than standards. However that may be, his literary
essays, despite fluency of style, are inferior to Emerson's

in fundamental brain-work, in the 'mere logic' of the brain
as well as in its bolder movements.   There is scant evidence
that he really exerted himself to overcome the tendency he
deplored, though one might find some suggestion of his effort, and his defeat, in his definition of man as 'the only
animal that thinks he is thinking when he is merely ruminat-
ing'!

Intellectually indolent, Lowell was attracted to impres-
sionism. Although in his best years he appealed to standards, he was always, late and early, something of an impressionist. As late as 1883, speaking of Fielding, he affirmed the
vanity of seeking to weigh a man's work by fixed standards,
'when each of us stamps his own weights, and warrants the
impartiality of his own scales.' More than once he urges
skepticism as a primary attribute of the critic, meaning an
independence of tradition: a self-reliance that he himself
practiced most markedly, as one would expect, in his early
romantic criticism written under the influence of Charles
Lamb. Thus, he praised the Elizabethan poets for having no
creed, for knowing nothing of '"established principles" —
which seem, indeed, to be little better than scarecrows set
up by one half of the world for the other half to pelt with
mud. They knew that to be a slave in one thing is to be a
slave in all. . . . Freedom is the only law which genius knows.'
There being no established principles, the critic is to record
his 'impressions, which may be valuable or not, according
to the greater or less ductility of the senses on which they
are made. Charles Lamb, for instance, came to the old
English dramatists with the feeling of a discoverer. He
brought with him an alert curiosity, and everything was
delightful simply because it was strange. . . . He had the
great advantage . . . of not thinking it needful to make them
square with any Westminster Catechism of æsthetics.' Here
is that 'very air of a Columbus' which Browning observed
in the young American critic, and which clung to him even

in his maturity. Whatever else he may have become, he remained in large measure the discoverer, the adventurer in the realms of gold, full of zest and waywardness, recording impressions on senses not a little remarkable for ductility. As an impressionist of the romantic and not of our realistic age, he was concerned with the culling of beauties. 'I string together a few at random,' he says, a few being seventeen, but 'I shall excuse myself from giving any instances' of the author's faults. Instead of regarding quotations as a documentation and illumination of purposeful discourse, he tended to look upon himself as a kind of showman, displaying this, that, and the other, with comments expressing his own pleasure in the objects. Thus, in a comment on Spenser that promises to develop into purposeful discourse, he suddenly breaks off with the remark, 'But I am keeping my readers from the sweetest idealization that love ever wrought,' and reprints two entire pages of the 'Faërie Queene' which could presumably be found in any edition of that poem. Having skipped this long quotation, the reader is proudly asked whether 'there is any passage in any poet' — stimulating challenge to an unread audience! — 'that so ripples and sparkles with simple delight?' We like it, adds the showman, because — well, because we like similar things in Sidney and Dante; and presently he is heading toward another long quotation with the information that Ben Jonson spent a whole night 'looking to his great toe.' Nor is he nonplused when a fine exhibit is suddenly missing, but quite equal to the occasion, as when, in an essay on winter writers, he turns to the 'excellent snow scenery in Judd's "Margaret," but some one has confiscated my copy of that admirable book, and, perhaps, Homer's picture of a snow-storm is the best yet,' and so offers that instead.

Delightful, yes, these divagations, but at the same time indicative of an irresponsibility of mood that vitiates high achievement. We shall concede to him, as he concedes to

Walton, a genius for rambling; but we must also hold against him, as he does *not* hold against Lessing, the tendency of his thoughts 'to want connection.' When he tells us that enthusiasm has led him astray from his purpose, we cannot but doubt of the purpose itself: Was it really clear to him? Was it a serious purpose? Was it a purpose at all or an assortment of velleities? Of the three processes that enter into a serious purpose, namely, acquisition, organization, and explication, only the first interested him. We should have known, without his express statement, that he was capable of vast drudgery in acquisition but impatient in communication; significantly, he wholly omits from his statement the intermediate step of mental organization, the process of thinking the chaos of impressions into a luminous coherence. Even as an impressionist, he fell short of the ideal, which is surely not to express the first or second but rather the final impression resulting from repeated and protracted reflection. For the ideal impressionist is not intellectually indolent, but by hard thinking integrates his intuitions into a final impression and achieves a firm unity, and is never content, as Lowell sometimes was, with a mere congeries of intuitions. Wanting the command of wholes, he relied upon the parts; he expressed wonderfully the fragmentary intuitions that came to him during his reading or writing, as a single instance will show. It is the well-known remark that 'Pope's proverbial verse,

"True wit is Nature to advantage drest,"

unpleasantly suggests Nature under the hands of a ladies'-maid.' This is perfect insight, perfect criticism of not only a verse but an entire age of European culture. Deriving his intuition from the word 'drest,' Lowell perceives that lady's-maids are indeed eminently desirable for the adornment of social manners, but that when they bestow their art upon the great Mother, upon all that is sublime in *Natura naturans*,

they surpass their charming province.[1] Perhaps this expresses
quite as much as Arnold's elegant recognition that the age of
social life and manners, of prose and reason, was after all
'indispensable,' or as much as Carlyle's eloquent mouthings
over 'the putrid Eighteenth Century, such an Ocean of
sordid nothingness, shams, and scandalous hypocrisies as
never weltered in the world before.' Yet Lowell introduces
his remark almost parenthetically; it is a 'happy thought,'
a sudden flash that illuminates, and while he was always
capable of vivid coruscations he proceeded most of the time
in a soft-fluttering illumination that reminds one of what is
called heat lightning. If to succeed be to burn steadily, as
Pater has it, with a hard, gemlike flame, to maintain a state
of ecstasy, Lowell was a most inadequate impressionist.

But it is time to say plainly that Lowell was not content to
be an impressionist; that, on the contrary, he strove to possess himself of universal principles of criticism. While we may
say of his work, as of that of most modern critics, that it man-
ifests various impressionistic tendencies — recurrent skepticism, random expression of intuitions, complaisance with
a rambling mood as if it were a kind of wise passiveness —
it is clear that by the time he entered upon his most successful activity he had already formulated a set of criteria. 'Subjective criticism' he held to be 'as untrustworthy as it is
fascinating.' In the very passage I have quoted, in which he
praises Lamb as an impressionist, Lowell asserts that 'unless
we admit certain principles as fixed beyond question, we
shall be able to render no adequate judgment, but only to
record our impressions.' Impressions, to be sure, we must
have, fresh and keen as our faculties permit; for if we lack
'the capacity to admire' we cannot do justice to an author's
strongest side — cannot 'measure' him fairly, which is our

[1] To be just to Pope we should remember that, three verses above, he extolls
'The naked Nature and the living Grace'
and that he is the author of that other proverbial verse:
'And snatch a Grace beyond the Reach of Art.'

real object. A critic like Leigh Hunt has the 'feminine temperament' that gives 'acute perceptions at the expense of judgment.' While granting that the feminine virtue of openness to impressions is indispensable, Lowell is certain as a *man* can be that the sovereign virtue of a fertile criticism is judgment or measurement.

Rejecting subjective criticism as untrustworthy, he found his standards in three forms of supposedly objective criticism, viz., historical, æsthetic, and didactic criticism.[1]

When Lowell speaks of 'that breadth which comes only of thorough knowledge and sympathy,' he refers to the two indispensable preliminaries of judgment — vivid impressions and historical understanding. Comparatively neglected before the Romantic Movement, they had been well exemplified in Europe before Lowell came to his task, but in America he himself was the first distinguished critic-scholar adequately to indicate their importance. If he may be regarded as the forerunner of the impressionistic critics who to-day abound outside the universities, he may with better reason be viewed as the chief American ancestor of the historical critics and scholars who abound within the universities. Poe had neither the learning nor the flexibility implied in the historical approach; Emerson sensed in a general way the relation

[1] Lowell had no real leaning to the kind of criticism termed 'expressionistic.' It is true that he quoted approvingly, from one of its alleged prophets, a passage regarded by J. E. Spingarn as containing the essence of the expressionist system. Goethe, he says, contrasts 'a destructive criticism and a productive.' For the former, the critic 'has only to set up in his mind any standard, any model, however narrow,' and damn a work that does not conform. 'Productive criticism is a great deal more difficult; it asks, What did the author propose to himself? Is what he proposes reasonable and comprehensible? and how far has he succeeded in carrying it out?' (III, 67.) But this is a summary of the expressionistic position only if one misrepresents Goethe by omitting the second of his three questions, as Mr. Spingarn does in *Creative Criticism*, p. 20. Restoring the question in his translation of *Goethe's Literary Essays*, Mr. Spingarn renders it, 'Was his plan reasonable and sensible?' To ask this question is to invite all those hordes of intellectualistic and moralistic criteria which are forever breaking, like barbarian hosts, upon the beautifully simple empire of Croce and his lieutenants.

of an author to his times, as when he pointed out how heavily indebted Shakspere was; it remained for Lowell to state more clearly the nature of historical criticism, to exemplify it in studies of a series of great writers, and to demonstrate its value as a preparation for literary criticism in its highest form.

Historical criticism, he pointed out, measures an author 'relatively to his position in the literary history of his country and the conditions of his generation.' Although an author's positive merit is to be measured by a higher standard, 'a perfectly fair judgment' must indeed consider not only 'what he was, but what, under the given circumstances, it was possible for him to be.' While it is not essential that we should *explain* him by means of his circumstances,[1] it is essential that we should *understand* him by these means. Warning us of the danger of falling into anachronism, understanding requires us to win our way back to the author's generation. It is true that 'the principles of art are immutable,' but it is also true that 'their application must accommodate itself to the material supplied to them by the time and by the national character and traditions.' Behind this conception lies, as Lowell knew, the idea of the organic — the idea that literature is not a manufacture but a growth. The creative artist dooms himself to relative failure if he merely copies models instead of letting the 'genetic principle' of his land and time work through him; and, similarly, the critic who does not seek to understand the genetic principle in the writers of the past is incapable of a complete criticism. By study and imagination the critic must be able to *expatriate* himself; he will not commit the error, for example, of judging Rousseau 'after our blunt English fashion' and condemning him 'on the finding of a jury of average householders.' He must be able likewise to *ex-temporate* himself; instead of misrepre-

---

[1] Acquainted with the pseudo-science of Taine, Lowell was influenced more by earlier critics, especially Goethe.

senting the Puritans of New England, he will make it his
business to become 'contemporary with, and therefore able
to understand' them.

Nowhere has Lowell so clearly exemplified the nature and
value of historical criticism as in his attitude toward the
eighteenth century, the literature of which meant so little
to Poe, Emerson, Whitman, and the Romantics generally.
With becoming diffidence he recognized that a thorough-
going extemporation was necessary for the understanding of
Pope. 'I was brought up in the old superstition that he was
the greatest poet that ever lived'; then, as the romantic
revolt developed in America, came an 'ardent desire for
smashing the idols I had been brought up to worship. . . .
There was a time when I could not read Pope.' Lowell always retained, as he had reason to do, a measure of disap-
probation of 'the classicism of red heels and periwigs,' of
'the lullaby seesaw of the couplet,' of a poetry so remote from
the simple that 'everybody ceremoniously took a bushel-
basket to bring a wren's nest to market in.' He was justified
in preferring his Dante and Chaucer. Yet he managed to deal
with the literature of that alien age more justly, on the whole,
than any other romantic critic. He loved his 'Dear Dr.
Johnson,' 'gruff old Ursa Major,' and he was one of the first
to discover the real Fielding and to discredit the traditional
view of the man; but the most instructive example is his
return to Pope. He came to perceive that 'it is a school-boy
blunder in criticism to deny one kind of perfection because it
is not another'; that Pope had unquestionably achieved one
kind of perfection, the representation of conventional life,
as Chaucer had represented actual life, Spenser imaginative
life, Shakspere ideal life, and Milton interior life; and that he
had written 'one perfect work,' unsurpassed 'for wit, fancy,
invention, keeping,' and for power of 'pure entertainment,'
viz., 'The Rape of the Lock.' How did Lowell attain this
conclusion? Through historical understanding and historical

judgment. 'Pope,' he argues, 'had one of the prime qualities
of a great poet in exactly answering the intellectual needs of
the age in which he lived, and in reflecting its lineaments.'
In the hands of Pope the artificial style was not mechanical
but 'living and powerful, because he used it to express artificial modes of thinking and an artificial state of society.'
Under the given circumstances, it was not possible for Pope
to achieve the modes of perfection that we have in Chaucer,
or Spenser, or Shakspere, or Milton. He used, as every successful artist must, the materials offered him in his own time,
and used them supremely well. He is the greatest of English
poets in his own kind — this is the verdict of historical criticism, and it is very different from the old superstition that
Pope was the greatest poet who ever lived.

The verdicts of historical criticism, however, while final
within their jurisdiction, are not the ultimate verdicts of
literary claims. That Pope reached perfection in his special
department does not mean to Lowell that he was a greater
writer than those who fell somewhat short of perfection in
higher departments. In a comprehensive estimate of a writer
we must estimate also the department chosen for him by the
time-spirit. 'Is the department of Milton,' for example, 'no
higher than that of Butler?' This is a question which common sense requires us to ask, and which historical criticism
is incompetent to answer. While historical criticism has indeed a certain objectivity in forcing the critic to apply standards more authoritative than his personal likes and dislikes,
it none the less falls short of an ultimate verdict. If impressionistic criticism is relative to the critic, historical criticism
is relative to the age, and an absolute criticism is yet to
seek.

Speaking of Dante, Lowell says that in the end a poet must
be judged by his poetic qualities, and that 'he must be judged
by them absolutely, with reference, that is, to the highest
standard, and not relatively to the fashions and opportunities

of the age in which he lived.' Passing beyond the domain of
historical criticism, we must endeavor to plant ourselves 'on
the æsthetic point of view' — as British critics have rarely
done. For example, Wordsworth, says Lowell to a British
audience, 'has too commonly been estimated rather as
philosopher or teacher than as poet. The value of what he
said has had more influence with the jury than the way in
which he said it. There are various methods of criticism, but
I think we should all agree that literary work is to be judged
from the purely literary point of view.' Lowell means, I take
it, from the purely æsthetic point of view. When we rise
above the fascinations of impressionistic and the learning of
historical criticism and seek to estimate the absolute value
of a work of art, the questions that confront us are of a higher
mood: Is it in truth a work of art, and why? To what extent
is it beautiful or ugly — what quantity or degree of beauty
does it possess? Such are the questions that Lowell, as we
shall see, feels that he must ask and attempt to answer. But
they are not all. 'I believe we should judge a book,' he says,
'rather by its total effect than by the adequacy of special
parts, and is not this effect moral as well as æsthetic?' For,
observing that a work of art has effects on man's moral as
well as his æsthetic nature, and reasoning, like Aristotle,
from effects to causes, Lowell maintains that it possesses
ethical qualities, excellent or inferior, and that these ethical
qualities must play a coefficient part, along with æsthetic
qualities, in the determination of value. By way of illustration he points to the 'Chanson de Roland,' which is 'certainly not to be named with the "Iliad" for purely literary
charms' but is 'equipped with the same moral qualities' that
we respond to in Homer. To employ again terms I have
found useful, we may say that the 'Chanson' is distinguished
for its *quality* rather than its *quantity* of beauty, whereas the
'Iliad' is distinguished for both. Nor does Lowell merely
place the two — quality and quantity — side by side as

parallel considerations in the criticism of poem or poet; they
should be brought into relation in a 'comparative criticism'
that 'teaches us that moral and æsthetic defects are more
nearly related than is commonly supposed.' It teaches us
that 'faults of style and of thought' (and, correspondingly,
merits) are not fortuitous, but have 'their root in character
and temperament' and have 'their necessary relation to, and
dependence on, each other.'

Such, then, is Lowell's comprehensive vision of the task
of the critic. It involves sensitiveness to impressions, historical understanding, and an æsthetic-ethical judgment. Upon
these he bases his placement of the great authors — a habit
of his more naïve than dogmatic — ranking Homer, Æschylus, Dante, and Shakspere as the four supreme poets, and
Wordsworth as 'fifth in the succession of the great English
Poets.' Of Donne he said that he 'wrote more profound
verses than any other English poet save one only' — not
telling us whom he meant by the one. It must be admitted
that Lowell was a little childish in his love of superlatives.
But it must also be admitted (to apply a superlative to
Lowell himself) that beneath all his surface caprices lies a
literary creed, æsthetic and moral, that is the most representative of man's artistic experience through the ages yet attained in America. This creed has never been given sufficiently serious attention, presumably because Lowell, with
his genius for rambling, formulated it only in fragments. It
will be our task to put the fragments together.

§3

The unifying principle in the artistic and literary creed of
Lowell lies in his attempt to use the best ideas offered by the
two great critical traditions, the classic and the romantic.
His favorite examples, however, he found neither in the
ancient world nor in the nineteenth century, but in the
Middle Ages and the Renaissance, Dante, Chaucer, Shak-

spere, Cervantes, Calderon, and other of the early 'moderns.'[1]

In one of his essays he assures us that he is not going to renew the Battle of the Books; yet he did repeatedly renew it, fighting sometimes on one side, sometimes on the other, sometimes viewing the battle from the safe vantage-point of a neutral, and giving in the end the impression of a struggle waged inconclusively within his own mind. At one time it is a question of taste, not to be authoritatively settled; at another, it appears that both the ancients and the moderns are necessary, to clarify each other; now it is plain that the moderns have the better of it, giving us examples of form and the grand style in addition to their own special excellences; and again it is just as plain that the ancients are victorious, speaking to us with a clearer voice than that of any living language, through a literature 'rammed with life' and 'as contemporary with to-day as with the ears it first enraptured.' The key to this confusion in strategy is doubtless to be found in Lowell's reaction from the tyrannical 'formula which prescribed the Greek and Latin Classics as the canonical books of that infallible Church of Culture outside of which there could be no salvation.' 'I was a great while emancipating myself,' he says, from this formula — 'indeed, I am not sure that I have wholly emancipated myself even yet' (this as late as 1889). Having the Protestantism of the Protestant religion, Lowell balks at receiving anything on authority; truth itself, on these terms, ranks as superstition. That on the whole he regarded the supremacy of the ancients to be truth is the final impression left by a consideration of the drift of all his passages bearing on the Battle of the Books. Even in his address to the Modern Language Association, as

[1] Such moderns had also been the center of interest to the Schlegel brothers, who presented them as examples of the *romantisch*, of *eine eigentümlich moderne, nicht nach den Mustern des Altertums gebildete Poesie*. To Lowell, however, they were examples of principles that appear in both ancient and modern literature and must appear in all literature that is 'classic' in the sense of 'best.'

a teacher speaking to teachers, he confides his pleasure that
his grandson is 'taking kindly to his Homer,' for 'I had rather
he should choose Greek than any modern tongue,' a language
that taxes the sinews of the climber but leads him at last to
the summits; while in favor of the modern languages he
merely concedes that it may be prudent to allow them as
avenues to literature in the case of minds 'of softer fibre, and
less eager of emprise' than the commendable grandson
aforesaid.

While Lowell with a characteristic inner disunion gave his
heart to the older moderns and his head to the ancient
Greeks, within the sphere of art his recognition of the supremacy of the Greeks was almost constant. His most
serious discontent with their art (stated but once, I believe)
is that their tragic agents 'seem to be commonly rather types
than individuals,' wanting 'that exquisite analysis of complex motives' which reached its height in Cervantes and
Shakspere; yet while this is so, he observes in the same
passage, it is likewise true that the simplicity of Greek
tragedy 'is by no means that of expression, but of form
merely.' And in respect to form — 'to those laws of grace,
of proportion, of design' — he remarks in the same essay
(that on Shakspere, one of his best) — in respect to form,
which he holds to be virtually synonymous with art, he asserts that its laws are 'more clearly to be deduced from the
eminent examples of Greek literature than from any other
source.' He goes on to say:

It is the Greeks who must furnish us with our standard of comparison. Their stamp is upon all the allowed measures and weights
of æsthetic criticism. . . . The model is not there to be copied merely
[Lowell repeatedly condemns the modern antique], but that the
study of it may lead us insensibly to the same processes of thought
by which its purity of outline and harmony of parts were attained,
and enable us to feel that strength is consistent with repose, that
multiplicity is not abundance, that grace is but a more refined form
of power, and that a thought is none the less profound that the

limpidity of its expression allows us to measure it at a glance. To be possessed with this conviction gives us at least a determinate point of view, and enables us to appeal a case of taste to a court of final adjudicature, whose decisions are guided by immutable principles.

To the Greeks Lowell was indebted for the principles or qualities that constantly guided his æsthetic criticism: *unity, design, proportion, clearness, economy, power, control, repose, sanity, impersonality,* all of which are involved in the conception of self-subsistent form. Among nineteenth-century English critics we think of Matthew Arnold as almost solitary in urging impressively the claims of form as understood by the Greeks; but Lowell was a more frequent champion, who lacked impressiveness largely because his doctrine on this subject as on all subjects was set forth somewhat in the manner of *obiter dicta*, which is to say that he himself was deplorably wanting in that sense of design that he includes among his immutable principles. He preaches the gospel of form the more strenuously because as Anglo-Saxons 'we care nothing about Art,' and because romanticism led to a criticism 'which regards parts rather than wholes, which dwells on the beauty of passages.' Passages, he says, are good only 'when they lead to something, when they are necessary parts of the building, but they are not good to dwell in.' Thus, Carlyle is an ineffective humorist because of his indifference to form, whereas Cervantes 'had been trained to authorship in a school where form predominated over substance, and the most convincing proof of the supremacy of art at the highest period of Greek literature is to be found in Aristophanes.' Fine passages do not make fine literature, nor do 'admiring italics' constitute criticism. In the pseudoclassical eighteenth century, which had nearly all the classical qualities except *power*, as romanticism later had power but was deficient in the rest, Lowell praised writers like Pope and Gray for keeping alive for us the tradition that writing *was* an art; nor did he hesitate to put in the forefront of one of his definitions of form a term dear to pseudo-classicism but anathema to romanticism, the term 'decorum': form, he says, is 'the artistic sense of decorum controlling the coördination of parts and ensuring their harmonious subservience to a common end.' And it was for not keeping decorum that he was all but ready to hang William Wordsworth, acquitting him at last only on the plea of a divine insanity.

When speaking of decorum, Lowell is not thinking of an arbitrary standard of propriety and elegance as the grand masterpiece to observe, but of 'a higher or organic unity.' He makes much of that contrast between organic and mechanical form adumbrated by the ancients and brought to clearness by A. W. Schlegel, Coleridge, and Emerson. Emerson himself he attacks for violating the law of life:

> Roots, wood, bark, and leaves singly perfect may be,
> But, clapt hodge-podge together, they don't make a tree.

One of Lowell's most explicit statements of the contrast is the following passage, written quite in the manner of Aristotle, on the requirement of organic unity in the drama:

In a play we not only expect a succession of scenes, but that each scene should lead, by a logic more or less stringent, if not to the next, at any rate to something that is to follow, and that all should contribute their fraction of impulse towards the inevitable catastrophe. That is to say, the structure should be organic, with a necessary and harmonious connection and relation of parts, and not merely mechanical, with an arbitrary or haphazard joining of one part to another. It is in the former sense alone that any production can be called a work of art.

This use of a biological analogy, he goes on to remark, legitimately implies a principle of *life* or *soul* in a work of art, and elsewhere he reminds us of the Platonic enthusiasm of Spenser for the idea that 'Soul is form, and doth the body make.' The thought-and-emotion — the intuition of our latter-day expressionists — grows into bodily form, as in 'Hamlet,' for example, in which the character of the Prince

was 'the ovum out of which the whole organism was hatched.'
From the inner life proceed even the rhythm — whether
verse or prose — and the very words themselves. 'He who is
thoroughly possessed of his thought, who imaginatively conceives an idea or image, becomes master of the word that shall
most amply and fitly utter it' — hence it was that Shakspere
was not constrained to blot his manuscripts, his language
being not the vehicle of his thought but 'its very flesh and
blood.' It follows that translation is essentially impossible,
for we soon discover 'not only that there is a best way, but
that it is the only way.' The line from Pope about wit and
nature, while itself, as Lowell might have remarked, a capital
instance of organic expression, misrepresents the true concept
of form, which 'is not a garment, but a body.' The creative
idea and the form created 'cannot be divided without endangering the lives of both.' For idea and form, substance
and expression, matter and style, meaning and music, thought
and word, are not two things but merely two aspects of one
thing. We may discover a similar correlation between a
writer's experience of life and his artistic product. Behind
the product lies, or should lie, the writer's experience, 'because nothing that has not been living experience can become
living expression'; and behind his personal experience of life,
furthermore, there lies 'the collective thought, the faith, the
desire of a nation or a race,' which is 'the cumulative result
of many ages, is something organic, and is wiser and stronger
than any single person, and will make a great statesman or a
great poet out of any man who can entirely surrender himself to it.' Thus it appears that the organic principle is active
in the entire functioning of a poet, from the message given
him to communicate to the means of expression; and thus
does Lowell repeat, in less mystical language, what we have
already found in Emerson.

Form, then, is Lowell's primary criterion of a work of art,
sometimes conceived in its structural effect, sometimes in its

organic cause. So far he may be termed an Aristotelian, an exponent of the 'Poetics' and of romantic critical theory that amplified Aristotle's conception of a work of art as an organism. We may next observe that he again follows Aristotle in requiring not merely organic form but *ideal* form, 'that sense of ideal form which made the Greeks masters in art to all succeeding generations.' Twice in his essay on Shakspere he defines art essentially in the Greek way, once as 'that ideal representation of the great passions' and elsewhere as 'Nature as it is ideally reproduced through the imagination.' We are here treading on dangerous ground, inasmuch as modern romanticism, while eagerly availing itself of the words *ideal* and *imagination*, has robbed them of their old meaning without offering a definite new meaning (or, at least, a new meaning that the ancients could have accepted). Other passages in Lowell, however, make it quite clear that his own sense of the ideal is substantially that of the Greeks. He agrees with Aristotle as to the relation of poetry and history, asserting that 'the proper object of poetry' is ideal nature, and that history, 'far from being ideal,' is 'still farther from an exclusive interest in those heroic or typical figures which answer all the wants of the epic and the drama.' 'Do we know as much of any authentic Danish prince as of Hamlet?' 'Truth to nature,' he concludes, 'can be reached ideally, never historically.' Again, he agrees with Aristotle as to the relation of the ideal and the actual, when he writes: 'The true ideal is not opposed to the real [actual], nor is it any artificial heightening thereof, but lies *in* it'; although in some passages his conception of the ideal is akin rather to Plato's. Here we may pause, for it is to this ideality that Lowell assigns the signal excellencies of not only the Greeks but also the greatest of English poets — it is the secret of Shakspere's supremacy and permanence.

Precisely what, then, in Lowell's mind, is the relation of the actual, the real, and the ideal? 'Am I wrong,' he asks, 'in using the word *realities?* wrong in insisting on the distinction between the real and the actual? in assuming for the ideal an existence as absolute and self subsistent as that which appeals to our senses, nay, so often cheats them, in the matter of fact?' In the type of writer whom he depreciates as 'the so-called realist,' we do not find 'the facts of life' but merely 'the accidental and transitory phenomena' of life. Whereas the Greeks in their tragic art removed everything in some degree from 'the plane of the actual and the trivial,' showing nothing that 'could be met in the streets,' 'we barbarians, on the other hand, take delight precisely in that. We admire the novels of Trollope and the groups of Rogers because, as we say, they are so *real*, while it is only because they are so matter-of-fact, so exactly on the level with our own trivial and prosaic apprehensions.' Even on the occasion of the unveiling of the bust of Fielding, Lowell fully expresses what might be called his conscientious scruples with regard to realism. Fielding, he concedes with damnatory parentheses, 'has the merit, whatever it may be, of inventing the realistic novel, as it is called'; and for the praise of Fielding he is driven to a contrast between him and 'some French so-called realists for whose title-pages I should be inclined to borrow an inscription from the old tavern-signs, "Entertainment for Man — and Beast."' For if Fielding painted vice 'as a figure in the social landscape, . . . he at least does not paint the landscape as a mere background for the naked nymph,' nor does he fail to indicate the consequences of sin upon the fortunes of his characters. In his blunt way he wrote with a serious moral purpose, and his deficiency lies rather in his literary creed, which calls for exactitude, not for truth, the actual, not the real. From the same point of view Lowell deprecates also the detailed exactitude of 'what is called pre-Raphaelite on canvas and in verse,' a mode of art which gives an 'uncomfortable feeling of *costume*' and a merely cluttered landscape, instead of that sense of reality everywhere present in a true pre-Raphaelite like Dante.

'The real and abiding facts,' then, we are to seek, not as the realist and naturalist affirm, in the transitory phenomena of life, but in 'those everlasting realities of the mind which seem unreal only because they lie beyond the horizon of the every-day world.' Not even Spenser, with a Platonism that carries him far from the actual, transports us to a world of unreality — 'it is only a world of unrealism. It is from pots and pans and stocks and futile gossip and inch-long politics that he emancipates us.' The right use of the actual life surrounding an author, as the examples of Homer, Dante, Shakspere, and Goethe suffice to show in all the great ages of literature, is not to rest content with depiction of it but to 'levy' upon it for images and illustrations in the service of a higher reality.

Thus, while ideality involves a certain remotion from actuality, it at the same time *uses* the actual by drawing upon it in order to envisage and represent types of human nature. The true ideal, we have already quoted Lowell as saying, lies *in* the actual. To take a crucial instance, that of the poet Chaucer, a close observer of manners who held the mirror to contemporary life, we perceive that he 'reflected life in its large sense as the life of *men*, from the knight to the ploughman — the life of every day as it is made up of that curious compound of human nature with manners.' In contrast with a poet like Crabbe, who scatters rather than deepens 'the impression of reality,' and makes us 'feel as if every man were a species by himself,' a poet like Chaucer, 'never forgetting the essential sameness of human nature,' gives not only the individuality of each character but his type, which 'will continue contemporary and familiar forever.' 'So wide,' Lowell concludes, 'is the difference between knowing a great many men and that knowledge of human nature which comes of sympathetic insight and not of observation.' Or, to return to the case of Fielding, we must admit that, great as was his genius, it was a genius 'incapable of that ecstasy of conception' which 'produces figures that are typical without loss of characteristic individuality, as if they were drawn, not from what we call real life, but from the very source of life itself.'

§4

Now, the faculty that perceives the essential type and disengages it from accidental particulars, and then reclothes it with fitting particulars through an ecstasy of conception, is the imagination. Although the Greeks exemplified this and all other workings of the faculty of imagination, they did not use the term itself for any of its higher manifestations. From romantic theorists, Coleridge most of all, Lowell derived a theory of the imagination that runs everywhere through his writings. This was true of Emerson likewise, only whereas Emerson preferred to speak transcendentally of the Reason (a synonym used sparingly by Lowell) and suffused his doctrine with not a little of the Coleridgean moonshine, Lowell made a comparatively successful effort to lay hold of the term with his Understanding and to distinguish with clearness and consistency the various offices of Imagination. Noting carefully all his important passages on the subject, we shall discover, I think, no fundamental contradictions of the following summary.

Imagination is a faculty that operates in three ways. First, there is a *spiritual imagination,* a power of intuitive insight indispensable for great art yet not specifically æsthetic; secondly, there is a *plastic imagination,* a creative power of shaping materials into organic unity, which is the primary æsthetic imagination; and thirdly, there is an *expressive imagination,* a power of realizing or representing the parts of the whole, which is the secondary æsthetic imagination.

Imagination is, first of all, 'the spiritual eye.'[1] Lowell is perhaps quite as insistent as Coleridge and Carlyle and Emerson on the insufficiency of the Understanding, without sharing, however, their inclination to brush it hastily aside. While invariably suspicious of cloud castles, he readily concedes that Coleridge was 'a main influence in showing the English mind how it could emancipate itself from the vulgarizing tyranny of common sense, and teaching it to recognize in the imagination an important factor not only in the happiness but in the destiny of man.' Thus does he describe the spiritual influence of the stimulating mind that, in 'The Friend' and 'Aids to Reflection,' addressed itself to all that lay deepest and unexpressed in the young men of England and America. In his literary essays, however, Lowell is of course not concerned with the direct use of spiritual imagination, the highest reach of human power, but with its indirect use in literary art. It appears, for instance, in the brave translunary things of Donne that 'open vistas for the imagination through the blind wall of the senses,' and among modern English poets it appears most signally in Wordsworth, who, notwithstanding the most egregious artistic weaknesses, 'seems to have caught and fixed forever in immutable grace the most evanescent and intangible of our intuitions, the very ripple-marks on the remotest shores of being.' In his enthusiasm for 'the incomparable Odes to Duty and on Immortality,' Lowell was at one with Emerson and the other Transcendentalists. And yet he could not forget that it was only in height and depth that Wordsworth excelled and not also in breadth, that his was 'a piecemeal insight,' a receptive or feminine imagination; and consequently he refused to allow him 'a place beside the few great poets who exalt men's minds, and give a right direction and safe outlet to their passions through the

---

[1] According to Coleridge, the Reason, as opposed to the Understanding, is 'an organ bearing the same relation to spiritual objects . . . as the eye bears to material and contingent *phenomena*.' (*The Friend*, 144, ed. Shedd.)

imagination, while insensibly helping them toward balance of character and serenity of judgment by stimulating their sense of proportion, form, and the nice adjustment of means to ends.' He is not with Shakspere; he is not even with Spenser. He could give us only momentary vistas of that ampler realm which the great poets disclose to us — 'not the world of abstraction and nonentity, as some conceive, but a world formed out of chaos by a sense of the beauty that is in man and the earth on which he dwells. It is the realm of Might-be, our haven of refuge from the shortcomings and disillusions of life. It is, to quote Spenser, who knew it well —

"The world's sweet inn from care and wearisome turmoil."'

Divine glimpses Wordsworth could give us of a world more truly real than the world of appearance, but he had not the masculine, creative energy needed to give shape and clarity to that world and make it habitable. He could not reach to the ultimate effect of idealization, which is the creation of a whole world superior to our own (better, in Aristotle's sense) because freed from embarrassing accident and rendered in its pure type.

Thus, in its ultimate reaches the spiritual imagination can shape a typical cosmos, an approximation to the type intended by nature. This is the achievement, for example, of Dante, 'the highest spiritual nature that has expressed itself in rhythmical form,' who 'has shown us the way by which that country far beyond the stars may be reached, may become the habitual dwelling-place and fortress of our nature.'

But the Ineffable is not alone the goal of the spiritual imagination: it has likewise its less aspiring but invaluable aim of envisaging the constitution of man rather than the secret order of the cosmos, and man in his total humanity rather than pure spirituality. Such is the imagination of Homer and the Greeks generally, and of Shakspere and Cervantes among the moderns — an humanistic or ethical imagination, dwelling upon the ethos or permanent elements in human nature, which resolves the many men into certain types of man. It is the function of this imagination to mark 'the outlines and boundaries of character, not by arbitrary lines drawn at this angle or that, according to the whim of the tracer, but by those mountain-ranges of human nature which divide man from man.' Alcestis and Antigone, Hamlet and Cordelia, Don Quixote and Sancho Panza are not persons whom we have seen, but persons whom we might see if we were so fortunate, not persons 'who have been,' but persons who 'might have been.' Superior to all such types is the 'type of what is highest in human nature'; rising supreme over all mountain-ranges of character is the grand form of the loftiest mountain. Whereas Emerson centers his gaze upon this absolute ideal as seen from the plain of the commonplace, seeking to possess it in ecstatic contemplation, Lowell is content to pursue it by the arduous way that leads from range to range toward the summit. Between men as they are and ideal Man are those many-formed types which constitute the chief substance of enduring literature. Lovers of outlines and boundaries, the Greeks delineated these types, and the comprehensive intellect of Shakspere, adding an 'exquisite analysis of complex motives,' revealed them with unexampled truth and variety. If Dante, master of the human soul, showed best the capacities of spiritual imagination, Shakspere, master of men, excelled all other poets in humanistic or ethical imagination.

Imagination, in these activities, is for Lowell the main instrument in the attainment of understanding of life, and of the happiness that springs from understanding. It was consequently natural for him to tend to measure a work of art by the vitality of its ethical or spiritual insight. This would determine its quality of beauty, and quality, he everywhere implies, is the *final* and highest consideration. Explicitly, however, he insists again and again that the *initial* and inescapable consideration in a work of art is quantity, that is, its degree of beauty rather than its kind, since it is this which determines whether indeed it may be called a work of art at all. Accordingly, his primary criterion, as we have already observed, is that of form. Form being the *sine qua non* of art, Lowell maintains that first among all the functions of the imagination is form-giving. Imagination is from this point of view to be defined as 'the faculty that shapes, gives unity of design and balanced gravitation of parts'; it is a faculty that 'looks before and after' (connecting beginning, middle, and end, as Aristotle would say); and the seat of this presiding faculty 'is in the higher reason' — reason, as Wordsworth phrases it, 'in its most exalted mood.' Of imagination thus conceived as a shaping or creative faculty, Wordsworth himself was 'wholly void,' for though he owned a rich quarry he could not build a poem. As his 'insight' was 'piecemeal,' so was his 'utterance.' Approaching, at his finest, the majesty of Milton, he ever lapsed into the diffuse and commonplace. And not only Wordsworth, foremost of the English romantic poets, but virtually all modern writers in Europe and America, Lowell rated as wanting in this *sine qua non* of art because they neglected the whole in their concern for expressive parts; Matthew Arnold's own indictment of modern poetry is not more sweeping. Not occasionally but in nearly every essay that he wrote, Lowell demands of his subjects that they reveal the presence of 'the plastic imagination, the shaping faculty,' 'that shaping imagination which is the highest [primary, rather] criterion of a poet.'

Yet expressive parts are, of course, needed to constitute the whole, and although modern criticism makes too much of them, they must be provided for in an adequate æsthetic. Subordinate to the plastic imagination, then, as means are subordinate to an end, the expressive imagination nevertheless plays an essential rôle. It provides the images, the feelings, the concepts, the rhythms, the words that will fitly represent what the writer wishes to convey. Shakspere has this excellence with all the rest, finding in that teeming mind of his the vehicle for communicating his every intention. A writer like Carlyle, on the other hand, has the power of expression without the plastic sense, stimulating us endlessly without leading us toward any large and luminous object. Lowell might as well have instanced himself as an example; for assuredly his merit as an artist is the modern merit of brilliant piecemeal insight and utterance, both in his poems and in his essays, and his defect is the absence of the shaping faculty and the higher spiritual imagination that makes a cosmos out of chaos. In his capacity of literary critic, however, he did not rest content, as Poe constantly and Emerson sometimes inclined to do, with the judgment of others in accordance with his own merits and defects, but frankly invoked standards that would depreciate himself along with his contemporaries. This argues a disinterestedness and a breadth as rare as they are admirable.

It remains to say that all these kinds of imagination, spiritual, plastic, and expressive — corresponding nearly with the vision, the faculty divine, and the accomplishment of verse required of the poet by Wordsworth — must be authenticated by other human faculties. Possibly having in mind another phrase of Wordsworth's, 'emotion recollected in tranquillity,' Lowell speaks of profound poetry as 'very passion of very soul sobered by afterthought and embodied in eternal types by imagination.' Before passion is fit to be embodied, it must be worked upon by the mind in its reflective and contemplative activity, which deepens and enriches while it tranquillizes, and, melting away the dross of egoism, begets 'that concurring instinct of all the faculties which is the self-forgetting passion of the entire man.' The essence of this selfless passion is not the superficial excitement of the emotions, nor even the 'fine madness' of the soul, but that 'something even finer than that fine madness,' viz., 'the

imperturbable sanity' that characterizes the great poets.
This Lowell everywhere insists upon, under a variety of
names: 'reserve,' 'restraint,' 'sobriety,' 'repose,' and the like.
In his enthusiasm for imagination, which in his day had only
recently been made the central term in literary criticism, and
had not yet fallen into the limbo of the trite where it now
dwells not without hope of restoration, Lowell contrived to
maintain his critical equilibrium by steadily insisting upon
the ineluctible claims of its 'less showy and more substantial
allies.' 'There must be wisdom,' he writes, 'as well as wit,
sense no less than imagination, judgment in equal measure
with fancy, and the fiery rocket must be bound fast to the
poor wooden stick that gives it guidance if it would mount
and draw all eyes.' The image, to be sure, is romantically
derogatory to the allies, making them only a poor wooden
stick; yet, after all, the stick that gives guidance is indispensable for right aspiration toward the heavens. A more
ordinary but juster image appears in the essay on Percival,
whose verse 'carries every inch of canvas that diction and
sentiment can crowd, but the craft is leaky, and we miss that
deep-grasping keel of reason which alone can steady and give
direction.' The most enlightening example, however, is that
of Dante, who in his 'Vita Nuova' enables us to see in some
sort 'how, from being the slave of his imaginative faculty, he
rose by self-culture and force of will to that mastery of it
which is art.' For Dante attained the harmony of his faculties, imaginative, moral, and intellectual, essential to his
great poetic achievement, and his aspiration toward the
heavens was not a flight into the inane but a steady climb 'to
that supersensual region where the true, the good, and the
beautiful blend in the white light of God.' Platonist by nature, Aristotelian by training, and the very avatar of the
Christian idea, 'his feet keep closely to the narrow path of
dialectics, because he believed it the safest, while his eyes
are fixed on the stars.' Allowing no 'divorce between the

intellect and the soul in its highest sense,' he makes 'reason and intuition work together to the same end of spiritual perfection.' Though of aspiration all compact, he will not, like so many moderns, trust himself to the thin air without guidance, but will follow the leading of reason till it can lead no more:

> What Reason seeth here
> Myself [Virgil] can tell thee; beyond that await
> For Beatrice, since 'tis a work of Faith.

These are lines quoted by Lowell himself; and they may be taken to have expressed for him his conviction that in literature no less than in life the value of imagination, the aspiring and creative power, is determined by its relation to reason, the power of guidance.

§5

In the foregoing attempt to summarize with some degree of system Lowell's innumerable brief discussions of form and of imagination, we have repeatedly touched upon but never formulated his position in regard to the immemorial problem of the function of literature. Possibly the problem itself received its final statement in the well-worn words of Horace: Should poetry, should literature, instruct or delight, or instruct and delight at the same time? How did Lowell deal with this question?

His attitude is surprisingly definite and consistent; and it is an attitude that forbids our continuing to set him down as a Puritan whose didacticism was ill concealed with romantic gusto and random insight. We have too often accepted as truth his satiric portrait of himself in 'A Fable for Critics,' forgetting that it is a portrait of the immature Lowell, still in his twenties, still burdened with the *isms* of his sentimental and Transcendental period, not the Lowell who returned from Europe a few years later with a larger vision of the values of life. There is not only self-condemnation but also prophecy in his recognition that

The top of the hill he will ne'er come nigh reaching
  Till he learns the distinction 'twixt singing and preaching.

He *saw* the distinction in 1848; he *learned* it a few years later
under the tutelage of European experience and an inner compulsion; he exemplified it well enough in the best of his later
poetry; and he stated it in its significant nuances in his literary criticism.

'The first duty of the Muse,' he says with ample candor,
'is to be delightful.' While this is not the whole duty of the
poet, it is his primary and fundamental obligation, just as the
plastic imagination, while not the only kind of imagination, is
the first kind that we look for in his work. A poem is an
æsthetic, not a moral or intellectual performance; its special
concern is with beauty, not with goodness or truth. Lowell
plainly enough denounces 'that invasion of the æsthetic by
the moral' and by the intellectual, 'which has confused art
by dividing its allegiance.' In a passage in which he is apparently combating the didactic tendencies of Arnold's conception of the grand style, of culture, and of the value of
poetry, he deplores a recent disposition 'to value literature
and even poetry for their usefulness as courses of moral philosophy or metaphysics, or as exercises to put and keep the
mental muscles in training.' Elsewhere, he complains of
Wordsworth that he regarded poetry 'as an exercise rather
of the intellect than as a nepenthe of the imagination.'
Lowell also tells us that late in life he re-read the whole of
the 'Arabian Nights' 'with as much pleasure as when I was a
boy, perhaps with more. For it appears to me that it is the
business of all imaginative literature to offer us a sanctuary
from the world of the newspapers, in which we have to live,
whether we will or no.' He thus allows ample room for what
he terms 'literature as holiday,' literature 'as a charmer of
leisure,' literature suited to 'our hours of relaxation.' He was
well aware, like Aristotle long before him, of a merely recre-
ative function of literature; and he was equally well aware, as

Aristotle had been, of a higher function, in which the principle of pleasure reappears, so to speak, on a higher plane, in vital relation with moral and intellectual values. It is the function of imaginative literature not only to give mere pleasure (πρὸς ἡδονήν), but also to give rational enjoyment (πρὸς διαγωγήν): not only to give the pleasure of pastime which prepares us for work, but also to give what might better be called happiness, an end and not a means, a serious working of the soul and not a sportive activity. If it is necessary to relate to some tradition Lowell's view of the end of literature, let us refrain from the facile and false assumption that he was a 'Puritan' (as was Milton for that matter) and instead label him an 'Aristotelian.' In a dozen passages he protests, as outspokenly as Poe, against the heresy of the didactic involved in the deliberate teaching of morals through literature — it is gravel in strawberries and cream. The primary object in tragedy, for example, 'is not to inculcate a formal moral'; and yet the moral is there, for, 'representing life, it teaches, like life, by indirection.' From Shakspere we may no doubt derive many lessons, as he himself very likely realized, 'but I do not believe that he wrote his plays with any such didactic purpose. . . . He did not mean his great tragedies for scarecrows. . . . He loves the hawk-nature as well as the hen-nature; and if he is unequaled in anything, it is in that sunny breadth of view, that impregnability of reason, that looks down on all ranks and conditions of men, all fortune and misfortune, with the equal eye of the artist.' If this is the morality of the most comprehensive of intellects, what shall we say of the morality of the highest spiritual nature, Dante? Is it possible to reconcile the 'Divine Comedy,' with the idea that the primary function of art is to delight and not to teach?

Lowell is exceptionally systematic in his approach to the answer. A poet, he says, must not be judged historically, relatively to his age; but absolutely, according to the ar-

tistic qualities of his work and according to the man's
genius and his vision. 'We may reckon up pretty exactly,'
says Lowell, 'a man's advantages and defects as an artist;
these he has in common with others, and they are to be
measured by a recognized standard.' The quantity of beauty,
we might say, can be measured with fair accuracy. But the
quality eludes our makeshift instruments: 'there is something
in his *genius* that is incalculable.' If we compare say Æschylus and Euripides, we cannot but feel that 'the latter, though
in some respects a better dramatist, was an infinitely lighter
weight. Æschylus stirs something in us far deeper than the
sources of mere pleasurable excitement.' Instead of mere
pleasure, he gives us happiness, rousing that which is 'most
sacred in us.' For 'the man behind the verse is far greater
than the verse itself.' And so of Dante: it is not for his purely
æsthetic excellence, 'but it is for his power of inspiring and
sustaining, it is because they find in him a spur to noble
aims, a secure refuge in that defeat which the present always
seems, that they prize Dante who know and love him best.
He is not merely a great poet, but an influence, part of the
soul's resources in time of trouble.' The qualification of
beauty is here determined by the romantic conception of
genius and personality. But in the next paragraph, the culminating one in the long essay on Dante, emphasis shifts
from the man to his vision, from the idiosyncratic to the universal. 'All great poets have their message to deliver us,
from something higher than they. . . . In the company of the
epic poets there was a place left for whoever should embody
the Christian idea of a triumphant life, outwardly all defeat,
inwardly victorious, who should make us partakers of that
cup of sorrow in which all are communicants with Christ.'
And Dante has done this. If the normal method of the poets,
even of the great poets, is to teach like life by indirection,
nevertheless the high cunning of Dante showed that it is
possible to combine 'poesy with doctrine' without loss of

power in either, but rather enhancement. While Emerson, impatient of the labor of removing the historical barriers to an understanding of the 'Divine Comedy,' never paid due homage to Dante, but looked to the future for his type of the poet-priest, Lowell by dint of 'twenty years of assiduous study' (as he himself tells us) arrived at the conclusion that the type had been for once realized, and not merely fore-shadowed, in Dante himself.

If Lowell found his highest happiness in Dante, his debt to some of the other 'moderns' was not much less. In the more strictly modern ages, from Milton down to his own time, he found, to be sure, nothing that stirred the whole of his nature to passion, and he gave excellent reasons for not being stirred deeply.[1] Toward the ancients, at the other extreme chronologically, his prevailing attitude was one of admira-tion rather than love, an attitude that would probably not have been reversed if he had bestowed twenty years of study to the Greeks. In the halfway moderns, however, above all in Dante, Cervantes, Calderon, and Shakspere, he found the function of literature achieved with a warmth of energy that kindled his utmost enthusiasm. Conceding the supremacy of the Greeks in respect to form, and consequently in respect to imagination in its plastic activity, he held that the best of the moderns had a sufficient sense of form along with a rich-ness of ethical and spiritual imagination wanting in the an-cients. This was true even of Calderon, 'with his tropical warmth and vigor of production,' who won a place close to Lowell's heart (see, for instance, 'The Nightingale in the Study'), but who, because he was *Spanish* rather than broadly human, could not be ranked critically with Cervantes and the others. In 'Don Quixote' the imagination of Cer-vantes is not so much Spanish as 'universal and cosmopoli-

[1] Most of these reasons have been brought together and interpreted by Harry Hayden Clark in an article on 'Lowell's Criticism of Romantic Literature.' (*Publications of the Modern Language Association*, XLI [1926], pp. 209–28).

tan'; his book is 'a *human* book in the fullest sense of the word,' next to Shakspere in innate understanding of human nature, in the power of embodying 'generic types rather than individuals,' so that 'Don Quixote and Sancho, like the men and women of Shakspere, are the contemporaries of every generation.' These two characters, 'who together make a complete man,' Lowell found specially significant for consideration of latter-day generations of quixotic romanticists, since, as Coleridge has it, Don Quixote is Reason without common sense, while Sancho is common sense without Reason — both are vital to the integrity of man. The criticism of modern romanticism suggested by Cervantes attracted Lowell the more because it was conveyed in a humorous and satiric vein kindred to his own, a vein, moreover, 'thoroughly good-natured,' unembittered by the experience of life, sweet and fresh despite a large acquaintance with misfortune and disenchantment, as if 'the notion of *Weltschmerz*, or the misery of living and acting in this beautiful world,' had never occurred to him.

As for Shakspere 'once more' — 'that divine apparition known to mortals as Shakspere,' as Lowell styles him even in his late years — the romantic critics were right, he maintains, in regarding him as a great artist, though it is not for his plastic and expressive imagination that we love him, but rather for his serene and comprehensive humanity. Like Chaucer, Shakspere delights 'in the pageantry of the actual world,' and, unlike Dante, essentially holds to 'the moral of worldly wisdom,' so that his genius is human rather than spiritual; and yet he lifted the human to a plane higher than the actual by means of his typifying or idealizing imagination. Men and women as we know them reappear in his plays shorn of all that is accidental and meaningless, and stand revealed as enduring types of what men and women essentially are. Dante, writing an epic on *Man* instead of a man, had left *men* for Shakspere: and Shakspere gladly took them for his theme, not chance individuals but broad types of men, creating beneath the summit of Dante and above the plain of everyday humanity a vast plateau region where the air is fresh and clear — 'how serene and high he seems,' how grandly he rises above 'our self-exploiting nineteenth century, with its melancholy liver-complaint'! As free as Cervantes of egoistic *Weltschmerz,* he elevates us to the region of the eternally human, of *das ewig Weibliche* and *das ewig Männliche.* To know Shakspere is to know life itself, and in that knowledge to be happy. Only the *destiny* of man remains obscure, and for a vision of that we must climb with Dante, as Lowell unweariedly did, toward the summit and the vision beatific.

§6

And now, finally, we may proceed to formulate succinctly the conception of literary art and its functions that we have studied in the foregoing pages:

Literature is the ideal representation of human nature. Each literary work must have first of all a self-contained form, possessing such qualities as unity, design, proportion, clearness, power, economy, control, repose, sanity, impersonality. This form is organic; that is, the structure is determined from within by the 'soul' or animating conception, and the conception in turn is organic, proceeding from the writer's personal experience and cultural heritage. The faculty that images the whole and the necessary and harmonious relation of the parts is the plastic imagination. Form must be not only organic but ideal; that is, it must embody the real that resides in the actual. The faculty that images the ideal is the spiritual imagination. When the spiritual imagination acts in its ordinary capacity, representing the perdurable types of human nature, and in so doing achieves an elevated breadth, it may be termed the humanistic or ethical imagination. When it acts in its extraordinary capacity, revealing the life of the soul itself, and in so doing achieves height if

*need be at the expense of breadth, it is the ultimate spiritual
imagination. Of this ultimate spiritual imagination, two kinds
may be distinguished: an inferior kind that expresses momentary
intuitions, and a superior kind that transforms the entire chaos
of experience into a vision of the cosmos. In all its activities,
the imagination must be guided by other human faculties, most
of all by reason.*

*Form determines quantitatively the beauty of a given work of
art; spiritual imagination, guided by reason, determines it
qualitatively. In the 'possible unity' of the greatest degree and
the finest kind of beauty, we may conceive of the perfect work of
art.*

*The function of a work of art is to give delight. Of delight
there are two general grades: first, the delight of recreation, when
the more serious faculties are resting with a view to future working and the sportive faculties are free to confer charm upon
leisure; and secondly, the joyful exercise of the higher faculties,
or perhaps of all the faculties of mind and spirit working in
harmony and so producing happiness rather than mere pleasure.
For the fulfillment of both grades of delight, excellence of form is
requisite; but the higher grade demands in addition moral or
spiritual excellence — the contagion of a fine personality or the
inspiration of an ideal vision of life.*

From the test of a summary Lowell's literary creed issues
triumphant. If it were possible for us to lay aside our
memory of the personality of Lowell and of the weaknesses of
his essays, and to concentrate our minds solely upon the
system of ideas outlined above, we should certainly be drawn
to the conclusion that we have here the sanest and most comprehensive conception of literature formed in America prior
to the twentieth century. Laying aside also our twentieth-
century predilections (if we have them) for various limited
kinds of art denominated realistic, we are bound to admit the
impressiveness of a creed that offers justification, at one and
the same time, for Æschylus, for Aristophanes, for the 'Ara-

bian Nights,' for Dante, for Chaucer, for Cervantes, for Shakspere, for Milton, and for Wordsworth. As Aristotle based his
'Poetics' upon the attainment of the writers before his day,
so did Lowell seek his principles in the achievement of an immensely rich past. In so doing, moreover, he was saved from
vagueness by the soundness of his discrimination, which for-
bade his accepting as really excellent everything that happened to be historically necessary. It was easy for him, in his
romantic age, to reject the claims of the literature of pseudo-
classicism; it was not easy but difficult and admirable for him
to deplore the drift of romanticism itself: its tendency to
sentimentalism rather than true passion, to egoism rather
than impersonality, to excitement rather than repose, to unreality rather than a higher reality, to concern for parts
rather than for wholes. Nor did he find room for modern
realism, arising in his time and still on trial in ours, since in
practice it violated his standards of moral truth and made
undue concessions to the spirit and method of science. Banishing from his more serious thought pseudo-classicism,
romanticism, and realism, he founded his creed upon the examples of classical art and the masterpieces of the Middle
Ages and the Renaissance. Within these ample limits, he had
before him virtually all of the greatest writers of Greek,
Italian, Spanish, and English literature. Despite his personal lukewarmness toward the ancients, he believed that he
must concede their preëminence in the first essentials of art.
As the leading humanist of the renaissance of New England,
he made it his twofold task to belittle the specious attrac-
tions of the recent moderns, and to establish the high claims
of those halfway moderns or halfway ancients, from Dante
to Milton, whom the American public had not rightly valued.
From the romanticism that resounded about him in his early
manhood, he derived chiefly a part of his terminology, notably the term 'imagination,' which he used with romantic
frequency and unromantic caution. The result of his entire

procedure (doubtless in the main an unconscious one) was a conception of literature that one would find it perilous to assail, unless with the weapons of a skepticism that logically destroys itself along with everything else. Lowell's creed is almost the unwritten constitution of the republic of letters.

Why is it, then, as we acknowledged at the beginning, that the critical essays of Lowell leave an impression of comparative superficiality and futility? The answer is inescapable: it is not his creed that is weak, but the man himself. Lowell is a capital instance of the fact that it is possible to think both rightly and feebly, just as it is possible to think both wrongly and energetically. Most men of distinction do the latter, espousing with fanatical ardor the errors or the half-truths of their age, exploiting the potentialities of the special tendencies everywhere current round them. Heedless of the fact that in the higher interests of humanity truth is not cumulative as in science, they are hoodwinked by the provincialism of their time and easily convinced that their partial truths are the whole truth. Loyal only to their age, they are rewarded by their age, and also by posterity, on the ground that they have made a distinctive contribution. And so they have; though it is a contribution to truth and not truth itself. A small part of the truth they see steadily, but they do not see steadily the whole or even a large portion of the whole. Such men of distinction were Poe and Whitman. On the other hand, there are occasionally a few men who attain distinction through a vital valuation of their own age and a vital revaluation of tradition, a few men who make all truth their province and who have power sufficient to effect a conquest and settlement of a very large part of the truth. The best modern example is Goethe; the best example in American letters is Emerson. Related with this class are many who share the same impulse but who are far less distinguished because they want the power of conquest. Of limited endowment, they lack the vitality which is the first requisite for greatness, and for which no such qualities as sanity and comprehensiveness are really compensatory. They are neither small tyrants, like the first class, nor great leaders, like the second, but useful lieutenants of the great leaders. Such a man was Lowell.

Poet, scholar, teacher, critic, essayist, editor, abolitionist, patriot, ambassador to the Old World; possessing an extraordinary assortment of qualities — sensuousness, emotionality, imagination and fancy, facility of expression, moral earnestness, common sense and logic, wit and humor — Lowell stood forth among his contemporaries because of his accomplished versatility rather than because of high attainment. Once or twice, as in the 'Biglow Papers' and the Harvard 'Commemoration Ode,' he was able to fuse most of his powers in adequate expression, but the rest of the time he was a man of parts, a man of shreds. Capable of growth — more capable than Poe or even Emerson — he was unhappily incapable of self-mastery, no part of his nature being strong enough to force the rest into submission. Nor did he find help in the age in which he lived, which suffered his own difficulties writ large. Born in 1819, he came to maturity a little too late to accompany the central impulse of the romantic spirit, and also too early to adjust himself to the expansive democracy and scientific standards of the next age. Less sensitive to the positive elements of his time than to its transitional movement, he felt himself carried restlessly backward and forward.[1] A disillusioned romanticist, aspiring to a more adequate vision of reality, he found in the rising spirit of science less help than hindrance, and at the same time was unable really to vitalize, like Goethe, the tradition of humanism. 'The struggle of Goethe's whole life,' said Lowell, 'was to emancipate himself from Germany, and fill his lungs with a more universal air.' And this was equally the struggle of

[1] Walt Whitman, born in the same year, drew his powers together slowly but effectually, having inner reservoirs far deeper than Lowell's and a singular abandonment to the emotional currents of the age.

Lowell himself — to rise above the place and age in which he lived and to breathe the air that gives perennial life to the master-spirits. But alas! in his case it was the struggle of a half-man.

Through his youth and early manhood he was immersed in a sentimental romanticism from which he never wholly freed himself. Those were the years of 'The Band,' of imitation of Keats and Lamb, of enthusiasm for beauty and liberty, of oscillation between joy and melancholy, of personal revelations from God and the cocked pistol at the forehead. By the year 1849, when the fanatical tendency of the abolition movement repelled him, Lowell definitely began to move in another direction. When he went abroad two years later, his object was not that of Emerson, to think and hold converse with thinkers, but to lay himself open to European culture. After his return his bookishness grew upon him, and in the winter of 1854–55 he delivered a course of lectures in Boston that virtually decided his appointment at Harvard. Lowell the poet and reformer was now Lowell the scholar and critic. As the humanists of the Renaissance had restored the classical world, so did Lowell now bring to his countrymen Dante and the Renaissance — not the European romanticism of his own century, which he more and more regarded as wanting in substance and reality. And yet, despite his increasing aversion from sentimentalism, introspection, egoism, and pseudo-idealism; despite his skeptical turn of mind, his common sense, his wit and satire, his Puritanic moral fervor, and his admiration of the serenity and impersonality of the masters of literature, he remained powerless to dwell at ease in the ampler air that he had reached. Even in his maturity he bore the burden of a sentimental temperament and of romantic enthusiasms that he could not intellectually approve. Neither his skepticism, abetted by the scientific drift of his age, nor that Puritan conscience that he tells us he inherited from his forbears, could eradicate the sentimentalism that he honestly professed he abhorred. The very frequency of his condemnation of it in others is indicative of his own inclination to it. It was his favorite obsession, giving him self-distrust but also insight. In two whole essays, that on the poetaster Percival and that on Rousseau and the Sentimentalists, he exerted himself to analyze the type, with such success that his description is one of the most telling that we have in English. Though his estimate of Rousseau wavers, and though his other subject was a man of straw, Lowell in these two essays disports brilliantly over the whole field of modern sentimentalism. The theme fascinated him not merely because it afforded an opportunity to contrast the 'liver-complaint' of modern writers with the health of the older, but also because it enabled him indirectly to describe his own symptoms and his own modes of alleviation. When, for instance, he declares that 'Percival was led to the writing of verse by a sentimental desire of the mind, and not by that concurring instinct of all the faculties which is a self-forgetting passion of the whole man,' he bears witness to his own want of integrity. Again, Lowell airs his own problem when, in the following passage, he accounts for 'a class of authors too numerous in these latter days':

In Europe the natural growth of a world ill at ease with itself and still nervous with the frightful palpitation of the French Revolution, they are but feeble exotics in our healthier air. Without faith or hope, and deprived of that outward support in the habitual procession of events and in the authoritative limitations of thought which in ordinary times gives steadiness to feeble and timid intellects, they are turned inward, and forced, like Hudibras's sword,

'To eat into themselves, for lack
Of other things to hew and hack.'

Compelled to find within them that stay which had hitherto been supplied by creeds and institutions, they learned to attribute to their own consciousness a grandeur which belongs of right only to the mind of the human race, slowly endeavoring after an equilibrium between its desires and the external conditions under which they are attainable. Hence that exaggeration of the individual, and depreciation of the social man, which has become the cant of modern literature. Abundance of such phenomena accompanied the rise of what was called Romanticism in Germany and France, reacting to some extent even upon England, and consequently upon America. The smaller poets erected themselves into a kind of guild, to which all were admitted who gave proof of a certain feebleness of character which rendered them superior to their grosser fellow-men. It was a society of cripples undertaking to teach the new generation how to walk.

Such were the teachers of Lowell's youth, though in the healthier air of a pioneer nation. Instead of looking to the vague promise of the unexhausted West as contrasted with the hopelessness of a decrepit Europe, Lowell was dominated with the purpose of attaching himself to the secular mind of the human race and thus becoming in the best sense a social man. More even than Emerson he rested upon the mind of the past; more than Emerson he looked to the typical Poet or Seer of an elder time as to one who sang 'with blood-warm truth':

> His soul was led by the eternal law;
> There was in him no hope of fame, no passion,
> But with calm, godlike eyes he only saw.

These lines are from an early poem, the 'Ode' of 1842, an extraordinary confusion of romantic wonder and humanitarianism with humanistic aspiration — a confusion, it must be admitted, from which he never fully extricated himself. Released and happy while he sat at the feet of his few masters, 'beholding true being, but hardly' (like the soul in Plato's 'Phædrus'), he soon weakened and drooped, when left to himself, and sank to the inferior realm of opinion and discord. Unable to complete his conversion, he experienced a secret *penchant* for the things that he spurned, and found himself engaged in a whole series of conflicts that he could not resolve. Head and heart, reason and imagination, classic and romantic, ancients and moderns, aristocracy and democracy,

humanism and humanitarianism, religion and science were
engaged in inconclusive warfare within him. Keen of wit, he
was inclined at times to witness this warfare from the vantage point of irony. Fundamentally in earnest, he was oftener
inclined to join one side or the other, or to propose an in-
glorious compromise (symbolized by the title of his poem
'Pessimoptimism'). For the most part, however, his mastering desire was to escape the scene of conflict and take
refuge in the realm of outward action, or in friendship, or in
nature, or in the reading of books. Living in

This age that blots out life with question-marks,

he could secure himself from his inner tumult in one after
another of these asylums of the spirit, and there attain at
least the illusion of life.[1]

It is significant that the essay on Dryden is one of the
most discerning that he wrote. Observing that Southey was
in some respects similar to Dryden, Lowell leaves it for us to
observe that he himself was still more akin to Dryden, both
in his endowment of qualities and in the difficulties imposed
upon him by his epoch. 'Singularly interesting' to him was
this vacillating poet-critic of a transitional epoch hostile to
'earnest convictions.' When he says that 'it is the weight
of the whole man, not of one or the other limb of him, that we
want,' he calls to mind himself equally with his subject. He
reminds us of himself when he reports Congreve's remark
that Dryden's life was 'variety and not of a piece'; when he
notes in Dryden 'that inequality and even incongruousness
in his writing which makes one revise one's judgment at
every tenth page'; when he observes that Dryden tended to

---

[1] In *Nature in American Literature*, pp. 158–70, I have described in some detail Lowell's confusion and his modes of escape — especially his escape through
days of 'right Chaucer' with outward nature. Most of the phenomena of his
inner life he himself expressed, in their intricate lineaments, in 'The Cathedral,'
first published in 1870, a poem of about eight hundred lines which Lowell said
'wrote itself.'

skepticism and was also given to flashes of intuitive insight;
when he remarks that Dryden's taste was not 'the result of
instinct' but rather 'the slow result of reflection,' surely a
fact in his *own* emphasis on classical form; when he suspects
the self-consciousness of Dryden in the lines on Antony —

> Quick to observe, and full of sharp remorse,
> He censures eagerly his own misdeeds,
> Judging himself with malice to himself;

and when he justly declares that 'there are continual glimpses
of something in him greater than he, hints of possibilities
finer than anything he has done.' Likewise, when he describes the age into which Dryden was born, Lowell in effect
describes the environment in which he (with poor Percival)
happened to pass his days. 'It may be conjectured,' he says,
'that Dryden's Puritan associations may have stood in the
way of his more properly poetic culture,' just as he believed
that the Puritan spirit may have stood in his own way. The
fact that Lowell was living too late to experience the full
flush of the romantic faith is paralleled with the fact that
Dryden was too late to feel the firm support of the Renaissance, the movement in his time being 'a downward one,
from faith to skepticism, . . . away from those springs of imagination and faith at which they of the last age had slaked
the thirst or renewed the vigor of their souls.' Admirably did
Lowell state the large problem that confronted both himself
and Dryden:

All ages are, in some sense, ages of transition; but there are times
when the transition is more marked, more rapid; and it is, perhaps,
an ill fortune for a man of letters to arrive at maturity during such
a period, still more to represent in himself the change that is going
on. . . . Unless, like Goethe, he be of a singularly uncontemporaneous nature, capable of being *tutta in sè romita*, and of running
parallel with his time rather than being sucked into its current, he
will be thwarted in that harmonious development of native force
which has so much to do with its steady and successful application.
Dryden suffered, no doubt, in this way.

And so did Lowell, even more. To be uncontemporaneous
like Goethe, to rise to a region above the turmoil of the day,
was the high ambition that impelled him after his first resi-
dence in the scenes of European culture, and that lends to his
writings on the great authors not merely a romantic enthusiasm but also an accent of genuine exaltation. His full realization of this ambition was thwarted, however, partly because
his native force was inadequate, and partly because he was
sucked into the current of his times. At the most we may
venture to say of him, as Dryden said of a poet that Lowell
loved, that 'he is a perpetual fountain of good sense,' a
fountain not unmixed with the waters of Helicon; or to declare that Dryden's praise was also Lowell's — that 'amid
the rickety sentiment looming big through misty phrase
which marks so much of modern literature, to read him is as
bracing as a northwest wind.' At the least we may class him,
as he classed Dryden, among those who impregnate rather
than invent, among those 'brokers of thought' who perform a
great if secondary office in literature.

CHAPTER IV

WHITMAN

§1

THE importance of Walt Whitman as a literary critic has never been rightly recognized. He was not, to be sure, a professional critic like Poe or Lowell; he did not concern himself, except casually, with reviewing contemporary books and writing rounded estimates of authors. In the field of what might be termed applied criticism — the application of criteria to particular works or writers — he regarded himself, with excess of modesty, as the 'hell of a critic.' When told that Burroughs thought him a rather considerable critic in his own way, he remarked, 'If I am it must be in an intuitive fashion: but I guess I am not.' This also is less than the truth, if by 'intuitive' he meant impressionistic, since it is certain that he both reflected much on all the authors that interested him from Homer to Carlyle, and applied to them a set of criteria to which he was singularly faithful from his journalistic days to his oracular old age in Camden. Yet, if he was not a professional critic, a writer on men and books, he was nevertheless one of the most important critics that America has produced, because of the theory of literature that he formulated. It will be well for us to remember, in studying this theory, that Aristotle attained his supreme position in the history of criticism, and likewise Wordsworth his prominent place in modern English criticism, by virtue of a few pages of speculation on the nature of poetry. Whitman is a critic in the same sense in which Wordsworth is a critic. Both Wordsworth and Whitman concerned themselves with the theory of poetry; both were primarily interested in the relation of poetry to contemporary life; both illustrated their

theory with collections of poems — 'Lyrical Ballads' and
'Leaves of Grass' — which made but a slight impression
upon the public of the time, but which were destined to be
viewed later as turning-points in literary history; and both
set forth their theory, awkwardly yet memorably, in a series
of prefaces or similar compositions.[1]

In philosophical speculation such as Whitman attempted,
writing without logical method is assuredly an awkwardness,
frequently an exasperating awkwardness. In a late essay on
American poetry, Whitman blandly informs us that he has
'gossip'd about it all, ... taking the privilege of rambling
wherever the talk carried me.' Another essay on American
literature he wrote in response to an invitation from the
editor of the 'North American Review' on condition that he
be permitted to 'put down some mélanged cogitations regarding the matter.' This essay belongs to his last years,
when invalidism rendered sustained thought impossible, but
'mélanged cogitations' quite as aptly characterizes his first
preface to 'Leaves of Grass,' published nearly half a century
before. While it would be gratuitous to point out here that
Whitman's verse strongly resembles the prose of that preface, it is worth remarking that the prose resembles the
verse. As a critic, Whitman announced his theory with the
same bald affirmations, the same cataloguing method, the
same fragmentary phrasing set off with the same rows of
periods, that he had employed with better reason in his
ejaculatory verse. Not content with defying the traditions
of English verse, he defied also the traditions of English
prose. Only, whereas he always approved his choice of verse
form, he later drew closer to normal prose — in 'Democratic
Vistas,' for example, which conventional rhetoricians might

---

[1] With the prose of Walt Whitman may be included *Notes on Walt Whitman
as Poet and Person*, a work ostensibly by John Burroughs, who in 1920 conceded,
'I have no doubt that half the book is his.' (Barrus, *Life and Letters of John Burroughs*, I, 129.) In the present chapter, however, I have not seen fit to draw
upon this ambiguous work.

read with a lenient eye on the ground that the writer showed a decent regard for syntax and the organization of material. To placate the rhetoricians is not in itself a very important matter, but to make one's self clear is, as Whitman came to realize; in 'Democratic Vistas' he therefore made a sturdy effort to explain rather than to hint. Taken as a whole, however, his critical speculation is a mass of mélanged cogitations that is intelligible mainly because one may say of it, as Whitman said of his poems, that it had from the beginning to the end the advantage of being constructed 'from a central and unitary principle.' If the critical thought of Whitman had undergone great changes, we should probably have found it unprofitable to seek to reformulate it in our own terms; happily for the interpreter, however, he did have a 'thought at the center' to which he steadfastly adhered. Repetition, in his case, in large measure accomplished the task that usually belongs to clear articulation. Despite what he termed his 'damned ill-regulated mind,' he made it possible for us to restate the articles of his creed.

Before attempting to do this, however, we must survey Whitman's equipment for the tasks of literary criticism.

This equipment included originality, in the sense of power independent rather than derived, certainly a requisite for great criticism no less than for great creation. In his emotional and imaginative endowment Whitman was, beyond question, impressively massive, and this endowment was served by his sound physical organization, especially by his senses, which were more exquisitely responsive than those of any other American writer. It is impossible to doubt, at this late date, his intense moral earnestness, his passion for living and inducing others to live what he conceived to be a more abundant life, though it is easy to question the soundness of his ethical assumptions. In the realm of ideas, he was remarkably susceptible to the modes of thought current in his time, to which he added perhaps nothing by revitalizing the thought of the past. He was certainly not notable for humor, for common sense, for reasoning power — three of the critic's most valued servants. Wanting these ancillary powers, his mind habitually sought *abandon* — either a richly charged reverie or the sudden stab of ecstasy. These enchantments he secured by merging himself in external nature or in the pageantry of humanity, passing at a leap from the observation of particulars to the sense of totality.

While an immediate experience of life was always his foremost concern, Whitman was also eager to 'absorb' all that he could derive from the arts. In general, painting did not much interest him, although he testified that he could not stand before a Millet picture with his hat on. Music, however, he regarded, in conformity with the romantic faith, as the most spiritual of the arts; and he contrived to hear far more of it, and to learn much more of its terminology, than any of the other great Romantics in American literature.[1] His 'musical passion,' as he terms it, followed his passion for the theater. 'As a boy or young man I had seen (reading them carefully the day beforehand) quite all Shakspere's acting dramas, play'd wonderfully well.' Vividly did he remember Booth, Hamblin, Clarke, Forrest, Scott, Placide, Sheridan Knowles, Charlotte Cushman, Fanny Kemble. He first saw Edwin Booth in Payne's 'Brutus,' 'which affected me for weeks'; and after seeing him in various Shaksperian rôles concluded that the genius of Booth was 'one of the grandest revelations of my life, a lesson of artistic expression. The words "fire," "energy," "*abandon*," found in him unprecedented meanings.'[2] In the drama, as in music, Whit-

---

[1] A. B. Kelley, *The Major American Romantic Writers' Knowledge and Use of the Art of Music*, a dissertation, University of North Carolina, 1928.

[2] At the same time it was Whitman's custom to scan the audience as 'rigidly' as the play itself: 'The emotional nature of the whole mass arous'd by the power and magnetism of as mighty mimes as ever trod the stage — the whole crowded auditorium, and what seeth'd in it, and flush'd from its faces and eyes, to me as much a part of the show as any.'

man's experience was far more extensive than that of Poe, Emerson, and Lowell.

The extent of Whitman's reading of books, inevitably the largest item in the equipment of a literary critic, has never been accurately measured. Late in life he acknowledged, 'I am not a constitutional reader,' which appears to have been true of him; yet in Emerson's opinion he was 'a copious book man,' which also appears to have been true. We may accept again, his own statement that he could never 'study' and had scant liking for books requiring 'close application — the observance of rules of logic'; but we must also accept his statement that he often read books that did not particularly interest him, 'because of an end beyond the book.' He had plenty of curiosity, plenty of the modern passion for exact knowledge. Concerning himself with the human body, he gave himself this advice: 'Read the latest and best anatomical works. . . . Study the anatomical plates — also casts and figures in the collections of design.' Or, concerning himself with man's past, he felt that he should 'See to Roman history. I discover that I need a thorough posting up in what Rome and the Romans were.' As the foreign words in 'Leaves of Grass' might suggest, he knew no language save his own; but he was wise enough not to make a virtue of ignorance — specifically in the case of German, 'the one foreign language I am sorry I did not go into when I was young.' In his early years he read (unlike his New England forerunners) 'cartloads' of novels good and bad, 'a most important formative element in my education.' Early, too, he read the Bible, the works of Shakspere, and Homer, large portions of which he knew by heart and 'spouted' outdoors while training for oratory. As a newspaper editor he secured, and often reviewed, the new books of his age and new editions of old books,[1] expressing his indebtedness to them for assistance 'in a thousand invisible

[1] E. Holloway gives a list of one hundred volumes that Whitman noticed or reviewed in the *Eagle* alone, *Uncollected Poetry and Prose*, I, 127–29 *n*.

but potent ways.' In his old age, if one may judge from countless references in Traubel's Boswellian record, he solaced his depression not with light reading but with the substantial pabulum that had always attracted him, including, against medical advice, some of Carlyle's works and Froude's life.[1]

The most impressive evidence of the extent of Whitman's reading can be secured only by gathering and classifying the references to books and authors scattered throughout his writings. This I have done; here, however, I can present only the main conclusions, together with enough of his judgments to indicate the nature of his applied criticism.

Since the purpose at the heart of 'Leaves of Grass' was essentially evangelical, it is not surprising that the book that Whitman quoted or referred to more often than any other is the Bible. As his notebooks show, he thought of himself, while preparing to write his book, as a Christ reborn 'in New York and San Francisco.' No model of greatness could satisfy him 'except Christ; he alone brings the perfumed bread, ever vivifying to me, ever fresh and plenty, ever welcome and to spare.' Already, too, he was coupling the two ancient religions, Hebrew and Greek: 'Yes, Christ was large and Homer was great.' By 1860 he was thinking earnestly of these 'two religious platforms' — 'the classic masterpiece of virtue,' the reasoning Greek, and 'the Jew the Christ, the Consolator,' type of love and purity — both of which he would keep, adding 'a third religion' that should include what they omit. Probably there was no extended period of his life when he did not frequently read the Bible; and, like the New England Transcendentalists, he read also in the 'Scriptures' of other peoples, especially of the Hindoos and the Chinese. Easily

---

[1] The books named by Whitman himself as among those at hand at this time are as follows: the Bible, Homer, Shakspere, Scott, Emerson, Ticknor's *Spanish Literature*, John Carlyle's *Dante*, Felton's *Greece*, George Sand's *Consuelo*, 'a very choice little Epictetus, some novels, the latest foreign and American monthlies, quarterlies, and so on.'

foremost among his Greeks was Homer, whom he read, often out of doors, in his early years, and apparently returned to again and again. Next to Homer were the dramatists, Æschylus and Sophocles, and, less prominently, Euripides and Aristophanes. He probably knew little of Plato save the dialogues on the life and death of Socrates. He little more than mentions Pindar, Demosthenes, Pythagoras, and Plutarch. In his Camden house was a nook devoted to translations from the Greek and classical works by modern scholars. In his old age he repeatedly opened Symonds's 'Greek Poets' and Grote's 'History,' and expressed a desire to learn more of Greek music and painting. In these last years, too, he was warmly interested in Epictetus, who had also been an early favorite — 'I think even at sixteen.' On the whole, these facts seem to indicate, if not wide learning in Greek culture, at least an eager interest, and, in the case of Homer, a more or less ardent devotion. Whitman was doubtless speaking his own mind when in an address in 1851 he said that 'it refreshes the soul to bring up again one of that glorious and manly and beautiful nation, with his sandals, his flowing drapery, his noble and natural attitudes and the serene composure of his features. There the artist appetite is gratified; and there all ages have longed to turn as to one of the most perfect ideals of man.'

Although at one time Whitman was reading freely in a translation of Virgil, he had scant interest in Roman civilization and literature. Of the Middle Ages he again knew little: a few ballads, some Chaucer, the 'Nibelungenlied' (inclined thither by Carlyle, very likely), and Dante, to whom he was indifferent. Modern French literature he thought had the virtue of not being Puritanical. For his knowledge of it he relied largely on magazine articles and other forms of hearsay; but he saw a performance of 'Athalie' and read a few authors, notably Rousseau, Hugo, and Taine. Like the New-Englanders he felt himself drawn to the Germans by all that he read or heard of their philosophy and *belles-lettres*. Though he came to Wagner's music too late to understand the comparisons people liked to make between that grandiose art and his own poetry, he followed thoughtfully the expositors of the Kant-to-Hegel philosophy, since it seemed a corroboration in the abstract of what he had been creating in the concrete. He followed Carlyle and Emerson in their high estimate of the importance of Goethe: in 1846 he reviewed a translation of 'Dichtung und Wahrheit,' giving also three columns of extracts from it in his newspaper; later he read Lewes's life, and frequently referred to Goethe's personality and writings. Other German writers who interested him were Richter, the Schlegels, and above all the emancipated Heine. Like Emerson he was attracted to Swedenborg, whose followers he sometimes joined in their meetings. Of the Russian authors, the only one whom he seriously sought to estimate was Tolstoy, and that was late in life.

In English literature during and since the Renaissance, Whitman's reading was large and his preferences were marked. Shakspere is second only to the Bible in the number of his quotations and references.[1] I have already given, for what it may be worth, Whitman's statement that in his early years he had read and seen on the stage all of Shakspere's acting dramas. Many passages in them he knew by heart and loved to recite to his patient friends or still more patient Nature. He was perhaps rather well acquainted with the history of Shakspere criticism, and wasted not a little time in following the Baconian controversy. For Milton he had an aversion; contenting himself, for example, in a review of a new edition of the poems, with a circumspect consideration of the format of the volumes. There is good reason to believe that he found 'The Pilgrim's Progress' fascinating, and he read with care Macaulay's essay on Bunyan.[2] It is amusing to

[1] Holloway, *op. cit.*, I, xxiv.

[2] I have in preparation an article, 'The New Pilgrim's Progress,' on the de-

note that he was repelled by the egotism of Dr. Johnson, whom he damned with the sentence: 'His soul was a bad one.' Although naturally cold to the unimpassioned poets of the age before the French Revolution, he loved Burns, and early and late read 'Ossian' — of which he was probably the last important devotee.

Aside from Shakspere, the English writers that Whitman knew best were naturally those of his own century. Coleridge he held to be 'in some respects . . . above all poets . . . — he was like Adam in Paradise, and almost as free from artificiality.' This opinion Whitman expressed in an early review of 'Biographia Literaria,' a book for the few who can appreciate its 'fascinating subtleties,' among whom he implicitly classes himself. Wordsworth he looked upon as a lost leader, a man who showed his lack of true sympathy for men and women by coming out for kingcraft, obedience, and the like; yet in ranking him with Bryant and Longfellow he intended, as we shall see, to concede his greatness. His own favorite among all the British romanticists was, however, Walter Scott. In one of his last prefaces he wrote: 'Along in my sixteenth year I had become the possessor of a stout, well-cramm'd one thousand page octavo volume (I have it yet) containing Walter Scott's poetry entire — an inexhaustible mine and treasury of poetic forage (especially the endless forests and jungles of notes) — has been so to me for fifty years, and remains so to this day.' He read thoroughly, he said, all the poems, and over and over again the ballads of the Border Minstrelsy. He was also charmed by the novels, the 'chief pleasure' of his old age, especially 'The Antiquary' and 'The Heart of Midlothian.' He was 'permeated' with Scott as with Shakspere, despite his frequent disparagement of them as anti-democratic. Byron's egotism he found magnetic but lurid and introverted. He read Keats as one of the

velopment of Whitman's idea of life as a pilgrimage, for which he was indebted mainly to Bunyan and to Hawthorne ('The Celestial Railroad').

'pleasantest' of modern poets, and did not care for Shelley. Apparently next to Shakspere and Scott he esteemed Tennyson, whom he regarded as a kind of modern Shakspere, manly, original, 'nature's own' despite an obvious polish and sophistication; for if, as Burroughs said, 'His glove is a glove of silk,' at the same time 'the hand is a hand of iron.' The best work of Tennyson he held to be 'The Idylls of the King,' notwithstanding its remoteness from democratic America. When Tennyson was elevated to the peerage, Whitman (unlike his friend Harned) still proclaimed his faith in him.

His faith in Carlyle was equally great. In the 1840's he was reading and reviewing 'Sartor Resartus,' 'Heroes,' 'The French Revolution,' 'Past and Present,' and 'Chartism.' At first disapproving of the style, he presently came under its spell; and from the beginning he was inclined to regard Carlyle as fundamentally a democrat, one of his own camp, despite his alienation from common humanity. He was indebted to Carlyle not only as a powerful critic of modern civilization, but also as the writer who introduced the Germans to him as well as to his elders. He invariably took up cudgels for Carlyle, one of the two writers (the other was Emerson) who came to occupy his serious thought in old age. In his last years he was reading Froude's life, the Goethe-Carlyle and Emerson-Carlyle correspondence, the letters of Mrs. Carlyle, etc., and it even pleased him to imagine a visit from Carlyle — 'in this room talking.' Perhaps the best measure of his warm admiration, however, is his reception of Carlyle's opinion of the author of 'Leaves of Grass,' 'the fellow who thinks he must be a big man because he lives in a big country.' Traubel reports that Whitman was highly amused, and exploded in quiet chuckles. On another occasion, when asked whether Carlyle had made any bows in his direction, Whitman laughed and replied: 'Not one; I was outside to Carlyle: he could not divine what I was up to: I think I was no more to Carlyle than any other disturber of the peace.' It was not often that Whitman rated highly those who did not recognize him as a prophet of the soul.

To Matthew Arnold he was, as he said, constitutionally antipathetic, reading him with weariness. As Arnold reproved Carlyle, so did he reprove Arnold with carrying coals to Newcastle, the world being already surfeited with elegance, propriety, criticism, analysis. He sought to hoist Arnold with his own petard by labeling him a 'Philistine,' a term that must have impressed him in the Heine essay, the only one that he applauded. Among the Victorian novelists, Whitman knew early and well Charles Dickens, who furnished the occasion for one of his first lucubrations on democracy in literature, but for whom his enthusiasm seems to have waned later. Thackeray he apparently never liked; George Eliot he read in old age 'with great assiduity.' He knew at least the core of the argument of Mill on Liberty; and he was deeply interested in Darwin, both as a man of Emersonian sweetness and as the expounder of an epochal scientific theory.

More concerned, however, with the New World's contribution to culture, Whitman read carefully our own writers. Though he once acknowledged that the attempt to rank authors in order of value is an unprofitable procedure, he certainly worried his mind often with the hierarchy of the American *literati*. His placing of the poet Bryant 'among the first in the world,' in an editorial written in 1846, is curious yet not wholly inexplicable; but it is difficult to understand why as late as 1888 he held Bryant to be supreme among the writers of America. He describes Bryant as trained in the classic school of Dryden and Pope and greater than either of those poets; as a follower and equal of Wordsworth; as being comparatively indifferent to 'Leaves of Grass'; — but clearly these are not arguments strongly in Bryant's favor. 'For reasons,' he wrote in his essay on 'Old Poets,' 'I have been gradually tending to give the file-leading place for

American native poesy to W. C. B.'; but precisely what the controlling reasons were cannot be considered here. Fenimore Cooper, like Scott, used to stir him up 'clarionlike,' and he still could read him with enthusiasm in those long years at Camden. Poe he imitated in his own early tales, but he maintained that not until his last years did he esteem the melodious expressions of morbidity by which Poe won a mansion in the 'poetic area.'

Of Emerson, as personal friend and 'Master,' as lecturer and poet and essayist, as type of the American and of man, Whitman had so much to say that there is room here for only the barest summary. Sixteen years younger than Emerson, he attained mature self-expression at the time when Emerson was the spiritual spokesman of America. 'Master he was, for me, then,' and master he remained after the disciple had also become a master. In his loyalty Whitman never forgot the seal of approval that Emerson had unhesitatingly fixed upon 'Leaves of Grass'; and although doubts as to Emerson's later attitude became an 'old question' in the inner circle at Camden, Whitman could never think of his first great friend without gratitude and unstinted admiration, and spoke of him oftener than of any other writer. He held that Emerson was in some respects 'ultimate,' that he would probably be 'eternally useful,' that he was 'a star of the first, the very first, magnitude maybe.' Such claims he never made for Bryant, even when he inconsistently ranked Emerson below that poet. When at the close of 1888 Traubel spoke doubtfully of Bryant, Whitman replied that, while he regarded him highly, 'all in all Emerson is way, far, above all others: not one to share his glory,' and this was his prevailing judgment. Where he might have attacked, he defended Emerson: Emerson was not hurt by his bookish learning, was not narrowly moral, was not wanting in democracy. If any abatement had to be made, it was likely to be followed by 'But I hate to allow anything that qualifies Emerson.'

Of Thoreau he complained that his love of nature was too bookish and that he held common humanity in disdain; but one trait drew him, the man's 'lawlessness' — 'his going his own absolute road let hell blaze all it chooses.' A welcome example of this independence was reported to him by Emerson: 'Henry carried your book around Concord like a red flag — defiantly, challenging the plentiful current opposition there!' Among the Cambridge and Boston writers, Whitman responded only to Longfellow, 'poet of melody, courtesy, deference,' an invaluable 'counteractant' in materialistic America. Lowell he regarded as a builder, not a grower of verses. In Whittier, 'pretty lean and ascetic,' he nevertheless found genuineness and moral energy, and to him he gave a place in the quadrumvirate of American poets — Bryant, Emerson, Longfellow, and Whittier — about whose order of precedence he was so sorely puzzled.

It goes without saying that this record of Whitman's acquaintance with books omits a number of authors that he mentioned but did not carefully read, and a large number that he read but did not mention. Even so, the sum is large, especially when we consider that Whitman has never been regarded as a bookman. Indeed, there is ground for suspecting that he was in fact, like virtually all great poets, a good deal of the bookman, and that he has misled us through his own boast that he belonged to the future rather than to the past. The more we learn of his years of apprenticeship, the more certain it becomes that he developed in the usual manner, by eager reading and mainly unconscious imitation, as well as by direct experience of life and self-expression. Remembering, perhaps, Emerson's warning (in 'Representative Men') that 'the greatest genius is the most indebted man,' Whitman informs us, in his poems, that his preparation had been elaborate, though he was doubtless unaware of the extent of his preparation through books. At all events, it is clear that, in so far as reading prepares a writer for critical speculation and appraisal, Whitman was far better equipped for his task than has ordinarily been realized. He was better equipped than Poe, probably in quantity of reading, quite certainly in quality. Devoted to Homer, the Bible, and Shakspere, to Scott and Tennyson, to Carlyle and Emerson, he had access to the two ancient traditions, the Greek and the Hebraic, and the two newer traditions, the feudal and the democratic. Most of his deliberate thinking concerned these traditions, in terms of which he drew up the articles of his literary creed.

That creed is as follows:

There are many kinds of literature, because each age interprets life in its own special way; and each kind has its validity. Yet there is a best kind, not as yet realized. Broadly speaking, all the past kinds are expressions of feudalism and superstition. By virtue of the law of progress, the new age now dawning, the age of democracy and science, will be the best, and its literature will be the best. Therefore it is impossible to formulate the characteristics of the best literature on the basis of any literature already produced. Looking to the future rather than the past, the critic must be a revolutionary and a prophet. In formulating the new theory, such a critic will be guided by the characteristics of the age, as they are coming to clearness in America. These characteristics are, in the first place, Democracy, which is faith in the common man, belief in the greatness of spiritual individuality; and, in the second place, Science, which is faith in nature, belief in the glory of the physical. From these two is now being born a new religion, greater than either the Greek or the Hebrew. The function of the literature of the future will be to bring on the new age and eventually to give it full expression. And its law of expression must be natural — organic. The mode of expression suited to the régime of feudalism is becoming anachronistic, and we must now envisage a new mode suited to the régime of Democracy and Science.

§ 2

In the explication of Whitman's creed, we may conveniently begin with the idea that the law of expression must be organic. Already familiar to us through its prominence in Emerson and Lowell, this idea is frequently indicated and everywhere implied in the speculation of Whitman from the 1855 Preface onward. Reviewing 'Heroes and Hero-Worship' in 1846, he had objected:

No great writer achieves anything worthy of him, by inventing merely a new *style*. Style in writing, is much as a dress in society; sensible people will conform to the prevalent mode, as it is not of infinite importance anyhow, and can always be so varied as to fit one's peculiar way, convenience, or circumstance.

This might have been said by Alexander Pope, who had admirably set forth and exemplified the pseudo-classical theory that art is nature well dressed. By 1855, however, as the frontispiece portrait of his book suffices to show, Whitman decided that it was of considerable importance *not* to conform to the prevalent mode of dress; and, as the poems show, he had decided to invent a new style of writing, more radically novel than Carlyle's. For style, he had come to believe, is not the dress of thought but its expression, is not a shaping from without but a shaping from within, is not mechanical but organic. 'Nothing is finer,' he now felt, 'than silent defiance advancing from new free forms. . . . The cleanest expression is that which finds no sphere worthy of itself and makes one.' Thus, to the silent defiance of the poems he added the outspoken defiance of his Preface. The poetic principle, the essence of beauty, consists not in rhyme or uniformity or ornament, but 'comes from beautiful blood and a beautiful brain':

The greatest poet . . . is the channel of thoughts and things without increase or diminution, and is the free channel of himself. He swears to his art, I will not be meddlesome, I will not have in my writing any elegance or effect or originality to hang in the way be-

tween me and the rest like curtains. I will have nothing hang in the
way, not the richest curtains. What I tell I tell for precisely what
it is. Let who may exalt or startle or fascinate or soothe I will have
purposes as health or heat or snow has and be as regardless of
observation.

The poet must not stand in his own way, must not tamper
with the spontaneous unfolding of what is pressing outward
to birth and growth, is not to compose his poem (not even 'a
shred'), but let it proceed unhindered from his own composition. 'Who troubles himself about his ornaments or fluency
is lost'; apparently all that the poet can rightly do is to trust
that in him 'the greatnesses are in conjunction' — that he
himself is a true poem, as Milton said, and an index to reality.
For it is the function of the poet 'to indicate the path between reality' and the human soul. When we perceive the
beauty of simple reality, we have no use for distortion, the
grotesque, artificial ornament, romance itself. Only 'those
ornaments can be allowed that conform to the perfect facts
of the open air and that flow out of the nature of the work and
come irrepressibly from it and are necessary to the comple-
tion of the work.' Indeed, 'most works are most beautiful
without ornament,' leading 'to first principles' by the simplest and most natural means.

To be organic is to be natural: true poems will happen like
events in nature, will develop like growing plants. Obedient
to 'the free growth of metrical laws,' they will 'bud from them
as unerringly and loosely as lilacs or roses on a bush, and
take shapes as compact as the shapes of chestnuts and or-
anges and melons and pears.' The finest utterance will ever
be, like nature, simple. 'The art of art, the glory of expression and the sunshine of the light of letters is simplicity. . . .
To speak in literature with the perfect rectitude and insou-
ciance of the movements of animals and the unimpeachable-
ness of the sentiment of trees in the woods and grass by the
roadside [cf. the title 'Leaves of Grass'] is the flawless tri-

umph of art.' To do that is to make what we call a work of art but might better term a work of nature; for in effect it is an addition to the works of nature, and may henceforth be contemplated by men with the same satisfaction with which they contemplate 'the flight of the graygull over the bay or the mettlesome action of the blood horse or the tall leaning of sunflowers on their stock or the appearance of the sun journeying through heaven.' Accordingly, we have here a capital criterion of artistic excellence; we may ask of a work of art, Has it the same kind of existence that we see in nature — does nature accept it as a foster-child? And this question Whitman was wont to frame in its most naïve form: What impression does a poem produce when it is read out of doors and tallied with nature? In his first Preface (from which I have been quoting exclusively) he proposed that the reader undertake to 'read these leaves in the open air every season of every year,' and in time he had some reason to think well of his suggestion, since in 1888 he reported, apropos of a pocket edition, 'I am nearly always successful with the reader in the open air.' Most indoor reading he then pronounced a 'disease,' to which he acknowledged that he himself was not immune despite his habit of seeking in nature the 'last deciding tests.' Yet there were times when, with the inconstancy of the Transcendental lover of nature, he entertained a quite other mode of thought. Thus, one winter day at the sea-beach, contemplating the monotonous spread of sea and sand, and emotionally stirred as never by poems and music, he experiences doubt as to the actual source of his feelings: 'Let me be fair,' he says, 'perhaps it is because I have read those poems and heard that music.' Again, there is his marginal comment on the following sentence from an article in 'Graham's Magazine': 'The mountains, rivers, forests and the elements that gird them round about would be only blank conditions of matter if the mind did not fling its own divinity around them.' His comment is, 'This I think is one of the most indicative sentences I ever read.' No doubt it was; and it is also indicative of his own mental confusion in proposing that, because a poem should be organic rather than mechanical, it should be measured by its similarity to the gray-gull, the blood horse, the sunflower, and the sun. But his amplest recognition of the relation of poetry to man and to nature occurs in his article on 'Poetry To-day in America' (1881), in which he says plainly enough: 'The rule and demesne of poetry will always be not the exterior, but interior; not the macrocosm, but microcosm; not Nature, but Man.'

On the whole, however, it was in the phenomena of nature that he sought support for his doctrine of the organic principle in art. Holding that the antinomy of art and nature must be broken down, that the truly artistic is after all the truly natural, Whitman frankly based his æsthetic in the conception of a natural organism, and even sought to elicit from the life of nature the more definite principles that animate works of art. These animating principles he found to be chiefly two: power and delicacy. Thus, on the winter day at the beach, the ocean impressed him with its two qualities, in a sense opposites, of grim power and subtle delicacy. Again and again these are the qualities that he emphasized in nature, and consequently in art. Apparently he concluded that a work of art would be perfect if it reconciled these opposites.

He was ever looking for power, strength, energy. Speaking, for instance, of Carlyle — the 'rugged, mountainous, volcanic' Carlyle — he announced: 'It is time the English-speaking peoples had some true idea about the verteber of genius, namely power.' The 'last and highest beauty,' he says elsewhere, is strength, 'tallying our race, as it were, with giant, gnarl'd, enduring trees, or monoliths of separate hardiest rocks.' He is suspicious of culture because it jeopardizes the natural in man, reducing and clipping away 'the simply good and healthy and brave parts of him, . . . like the border-

ing of box in a garden.' Doubtless 'you can cultivate corn
and roses and orchards — but who shall cultivate the mountain peaks, the ocean, and the tumbling gorgeousness of the
clouds?' To these sublimities must we look if we would preserve our measure of 'fertility and power'; and to them did
Whitman himself look. As a writer, it came to him, he tells
us, 'that instead of any special lyrical or epical or literary
attempt, the sea-shore should be an invisible *influence*, a per-
vading gauge and tally for me, in my composition.' Applying
to current art this prime law of power ('dearest of all to the
sense of the artist'), Whitman declared that the outstanding
fact in modern poetry was 'the almost total lack of first-
class power, and simple, natural health.' It was deplorably
wanting in American literature. It was wanting, if anything
was wanting, in Emerson, who needed it to round out his
qualities of sureness, highness, delicacy. It was wanting in
the literature of England, except for Carlyle. Modern English literature with Carlyle left out 'would be like an army
with no artillery. The show were still a gay and rich one —
Byron, Scott, Tennyson, and many more — horsemen and
rapid infantry and banners flying — but the last heavy roar
so dear to the ear of the train'd soldier, and that settles fate
and victory, would be lacking.' In another place Whitman
crystallized this comparison in a single phrase, '*Power*, so important in poetry and war'; and elsewhere he related his
idea of power with the Darwinian idea of a struggle for existence.

Although Whitman in one of the above quotations speaks
of power as the highest quality of beauty, his many musings
on this subject indicate that he regarded it as the first essential rather than the highest. The highest is delicacy, subtlety, indefiniteness, suggestion, impalpability, atmosphere.
It is the last enchantment of nature, and likewise of man and
art. 'The final proof of song or personality,' he writes in his
last years, 'is a sort of matured, accreted, superb, evoluted,

almost divine, impalpable diffuseness and atmosphere or invisible magnetism, dissolving and embracing all — and not any special achievement of passion, pride [both of which involve the concept of power], metrical form, epigram, plot, thought, or what is call'd beauty.' Here we meet once more Poe's dogma of the indefinite, the old romantic unity of atmosphere. In another passage on this theme we encounter a number of familiar ideas:

Poetry . . . must leave dim escapes and outlets — must possess a certain fluid, aërial character, akin to space itself, obscure to those of little or no imagination, but indispensable to the highest purposes. Poetic style, when address'd to the Soul, is less definite form, outline, sculpture, and becomes vista, music, half-tints, and even less than half-tints. True, it may be architecture; but again it may be the forest wild-wood, or the best effects thereof, at twilight, the waving oaks and cedars in the wind, and the impalpable odor.

Here we have the romantic depreciation of definite form and consequently of the arts of sculpture and architecture, together with the romantic exaltation of the indefinite and consequently of the arts of painting and music. We have also the romantic standard of external nature, since the musician's effects of delicate suggestion and impalpability, equally the painter's effects of vista and nuance, are tallied, perhaps excelled, by the dim suggestions of Nature herself — the fluid air, the outlets of the heavenly spaces, the forest wild-wood provocative at twilight, the speaking of oaks and cedars in the wind, the odors charged with elusive expression. It was in this æsthetic faith that Whitman composed his poems, of which the leading characteristic, he says in 'A Backward Glance,' is *Suggestiveness*:

I round and finish little, if anything; and could not, consistently with my scheme. The reader will always have his or her part to do, just as much as I have had mine. I seek less to state or display any theme or thought, and more to bring you, reader, into the atmosphere of the theme or thought — there to pursue your own flight.[1]

Suggestiveness, furthermore, is to be a main æsthetic characteristic of the poetry of the future, which will be couched in 'a language fann'd by the breath of Nature, which leaps overhead, cares mostly for impetus and effects, . . . seldomer tells a thing than suggests or necessitates it.' Along with suggestiveness, the poetry of the future will have the complementary characteristic of power. Once, at least, Whitman brings the two side by side in the space of a single sentence, when he writes: 'The poetry of the future aims at the free expression of emotion (which means far, far more than appears at first)' — i.e., power, as understood above — 'and to arouse and initiate, more than to define or finish' — i.e., delicacy or suggestion.

To sum up, then, we are to deduce our æsthetic from the analogy of nature. The most beautiful and the most natural are identical. From 'the lesson of Nature' we learn that a work of art is properly an organism, the outward aspect of which is determined by the quality and purport of the life within. In the process of expression through development and externalization, the interior idea will obey the method of nature, the polar method of power and delicacy, exuberance and suggestion.

We have still to consider the relation of the organism to its environment. A creature in nature does not stand alone — neither does a creation of art. They express not only themselves but their surroundings; poems, says Whitman, 'grow of circumstances, and are evolutionary.' In his own poems and in his prose from the first Preface to 'A Backward Glance,' he shows again and again that his thought is filled with the controlling ideas of his time, with the ideas of historical relativity, of evolutionary development, of indefinite

---

[1] This carries to the extreme Emerson's doctrine of 'creative reading.' The poet, it appears, is a hinter, not a maker. It is the reader who makes, or mars.

progress. It is plain that he drew heavily upon not only his romantic predecessors but also his scientifically minded contemporaries.[1] It is just as plain that, being himself romantic in disposition, he interpreted very freely and uncritically the knowledge and speculation of his age.

In the Preface of 1855, the background of the thought is not only the romantic and Transcendental enthusiasm for the perfection of nature, the finality of the ego, the excellence of revolt and liberty, the value of life in the present, and the certainty of progress hereafter; these are fused with the scientific spirit of the age, which measured time and change after a new system, gave emphasis to the importance of environment, saw vividly the differences in life and thought in the successive periods of history, saw likewise the intimate continuity that links period with period, tended to believe in progress as a scientific law, and in general turned away from the spiritual to the natural law, scrutinizing the physical with a somewhat excited fascination. A single example of this fusion of the romantic and the scientific will suffice. It is the passage in which the romantic background is the spirit of revolt against the authority of the past and the desire for immediate life here and now — the same romantic background as that of the opening of Emerson's 'Nature,' 'Our age is retrospective. . . . Why should not we also enjoy an original relation to the universe?' A half generation later than Emerson, Whitman writes:

The direct trial of him who would be the greatest poet is to-day. If he does not flood himself with the immediate age as with vast oceanic tides . . . and if he does not attract his own land body and soul to himself and hang on its neck with incomparable love and

[1] The distinction between the romantic mind and the scientific mind is merely one of convenience. In Herder, for example, an initiator of the Romantic Movement, the dominant interests and assumptions of nineteenth-century science were already vital. Acquainted with the significance of Herder, Whitman came to maturity late enough to experience also the scientific temper as displayed in Victorian geology and biology and as applied to art by a writer like Taine.

plunge his semitic muscle into its merits and demerits . . . and if he be not himself the age transfigured . . . and if to him is not opened the eternity which gives similitude to all periods and locations and processes and animate and inanimate forms, and which is the bond of time, and rises up from its inconceivable vagueness and indefiniteness in the swimming shape of to-day, and is held by the ductile anchors of life, and makes the present spot the passage from what was to what shall be, and commits itself to the representation of this wave of an hour and this one of the sixty beautiful children of the wave — let him merge in the general run and wait his development . . . Still the final test of poems or any character or work remains. The prescient poet projects himself centuries ahead and judges performer or performance after the changes of time. Does it live through them? Does it still hold on untired? Will the same style and the direction of genius to similar points be satisfactory now? Has no new discovery in science or arrival at superior planes of thought and judgment and behaviour fixed him or his so that either can be looked down upon? [1]

This is a good instance of Whitman's preoccupation with time and change. Curiously, the passage also contains one of his clearest recognitions of the contrary principle of permanence, of that eternity which is the bond of all times, that similitude which underlies the seemingly disparate. But this principle, upon which Emerson had loved to focus all his thought, for the most part appears fitfully and parenthetically in the work of Whitman. He did not deeply concern himself with those elements in life and art which have usually been held to be universal and defiant of the march of time, but gave his imagination rather to those daughters of Time that Emerson described as 'marching single in an endless file.' Though they were all charmingly different, only one belonged to him, named To-day, or America. Like all her sisters, she was 'muffled and dumb,' but out of his incomparable love for her the poet could penetrate to her mystic meanings and fix them with words. Hereafter her image could live on enshrined

[1] The passage is reproduced without omission. The rows of periods are Whitman's.

in verse, giving delight and inspiration to countless men, till at length a new Day should arrive so different, perchance, that the image of To-day would be transcended. For time is obedient to the law of progress.

Out of this prevailing sense of relativity issued 'Leaves of Grass.' The Preface opens with a paragraph in which the Past, or Europe, is regarded as a 'corpse' slowly borne to its burial, and the second paragraph celebrates the vitality of the Present, or America. To-day, in this country, for the first time, man has a theme for a kind of poetic expression that *might* last forever. There have been many kinds in the past, each valid because faithfully reflecting the age, but hitherto there has been no age — and consequently no poetry — even approaching our own in richness of promise. In the profoundest sense, America is indeed the land of Opportunity. Here is Democracy, on a grand scale, and at a time when Science is enabling the poet to erect his structure on a solid foundation. These are the ultimate materials of poetry; we have reached the turning-point in history, are entering now the world's supreme age. Such was the faith that impelled Whitman to the writing of his book as a first expression of the new age — 'an utterance' (he said in 1876) 'adjusted to, perhaps born of, Democracy and Modern Science,' in which material and form are in organic correspondence:

As I have lived in fresh lands, inchoate, and in a revolutionary age, future-founding, I have felt to identify the points of that age, these lands, in my recitatives, altogether in my own way. Thus my form has strictly grown from my purports and facts, and is the analogy of them.

§3

The unifying idea in our analysis up to this point has been nature. *Ut natura poesis.* A poem should have the freedom and simplicity of the organisms of nature, and like them derive its form from the quality of the life within. It should be able to take its place in nature, and hence affect its readers as nature affects them. Its merit may be tested by reading it out of doors. This merit should include the complementary characteristics of nature, volume of power and delicacy of suggestion. While expressing the quality of the life within, it also expresses its special environment, which is verily part of its life: its own spirit is largely the time-spirit and the national spirit. Like a natural organism, it has a place in the historical or evolutionary scheme. Assuming that the idea of progress is subsumed in the idea of evolution, we may say that the poetry of the future will surpass that of the past. Hence, while we concede that 'Shakspere was the greatest of his kind,' we must add the question, 'But how about his kind?' A higher kind, democratic and scientific, will hereafter arise in America, the land of the future, where the evolutionary process will perhaps attain its end.

We have now to consider the function of the poet in a somewhat different light. It is not merely 'expression' — the registration of himself, his time, his land. It is also moral 'aidancy' — the prophetic forecast and furtherance of the higher state of human culture and poetic expression that we are approaching. For convenience, we may distinguish between the poet's natural function and his moral function, although it should be borne in mind that Whitman himself desired to minimize this dualistic contrast, believing that nature was essentially moral. 'Within the purposes of the kosmos,' he writes, 'and vivifying all meteorology, and all the congeries of the mineral, vegetable and animal worlds — all the physical growth and development of man, and all the history of the race in politics, religions, wars, etc., there is a moral purpose.'[1] Such is his teleological theory; though in practice it

[1] His occasional Emersonian sense of a dualistic contrast rather than unity may be instanced by the passage in *Democratic Vistas* in which the relation of the moral and natural is merely that of analogy. What Emerson liked to term the Moral Sentiment and what Whitman sometimes terms Conscience and here terms 'right, justice, truth,' 'has its analogy in the material universe,' in which

may well be questioned whether he did not make the moral natural rather than the natural moral. For our present object, it will suffice to observe that in his view the great writer is not only a great expresser but also a moral force.

While agreeing with the Romantics that music holds the loftiest place among the arts, Whitman believed that in fact 'the greatest art' in the modern world is literature, 'not only more eligible than all the other arts put together, but . . . the only general means of morally influencing the world.' He had no more patience than Emerson with the narrowly æsthetic view of literature — the 'æsthetic contagion' or 'beauty disease' — of which he spoke with the same animus that Poe had expended upon the heresy of the didactic. Morality he deemed 'the only real vitalization' of man's artistic impulse, because 'there is something greater' than both our science and our art, namely, 'the thought of God, merged in the thoughts of moral right.' Whoever contributes to this thought is 'dearest to humanity.' Like Arnold, like Emerson and many another modern, Whitman held that poetry would hereafter more and more do the work of religion, and that the ultimate criterion of literature is its religious quality. 'Standing on this ground — the last, the highest, only permanent ground — and sternly criticizing, from it, all works, either of the literary, or any art, we have peremptorily to dismiss every pretensive production, however fine its æsthetic or intellectual points, which violates and ignores, or even does not celebrate, the central divine idea of All.' Disparaging the intellectual element in the romantic fashion, and the æsthetic in the fashion loosely called Puritan, Whitman from 1855 onward conceived the poet as 'a seer,' a revealer of the divine idea. The greatness of a poet is measured by the depth of his ethic and spiritual insight. 'Poems of the depth, as distinguished from those of the surface,' are written only by poets

there is something that 'holds together this world, and every object upon it, and carries its dynamics on forever sure and safe.'

who live by the faith that they express. Thus, the organic principle rules on the moral as well as on the natural plane. When Whitman says that the poet 'does not moralize or make applications to morals,' he is referring merely to such morals as conformed to the narrowness and cant of his contemporaries; for everywhere he makes abundantly clear his belief that the poet is, above all, in the highest sense, a moralist, not only in the sense that he achieves an ethical result, but also in the sense that he possesses, consciously or unconsciously, an 'ethic purpose.' In Whitman himself, this ethical purpose was assuredly conscious. The proof lies plain to view in his own affirmations in his early prose writings, in his 1855 Preface, in his 1872 Preface, and in 'A Backward Glance.' Present in him from the beginning of his plan, this ethical purpose grew clearer and clearer in his mind. 'Ever since what might be call'd thought, or the budding of thought, fairly began in my youthful mind, I had had a desire to attempt some worthy record of that entire faith and acceptance ("to justify the ways of God to man" is Milton's well-known and ambitious phrase) which is the foundation of moral America.' How worthy the result at last appeared in his eyes and those of his disciples, is adequately expressed in his bald self-endorsement, 'I think the "Leaves" the most religious among books.'

§ 4

Believing that great literature is an organic expression of its age and nation, and at the same time is dominated by an ethical and spiritual purpose, Whitman discerned in his own land and time neither expressers nor prophets. Living, as he conceived, between the two vast eras of history, the aristocratic and the democratic, he regarded the former as dead and the latter as powerless to be born. Only a divine *literatus* could breathe life into the new body politic that was being framed in this New World. He aspired to be this *literatus.* Only a great critic could effect the necessary 're-adjustment of the whole theory and nature of poetry.' He set out to be this critic. And it may plausibly be argued, more than three quarters of a century after the publication of his book, that in large measure he achieved his high aims. Surpassing all other American authors in influence, he is read, imitated, quoted, by hosts of contemporary writers. Whether his work has attained its maximum effect or is still to extend its conquests, it would be venturesome to say; but there is no question that Whitman has become an example and an authority. Amply confident of his own ultimate success, he was nevertheless capable of remarking with modesty, '"Democratic art" will have to wait long before it is satisfactorily formulated and defined — if it ever is.' It was not his desire, any more than it was Emerson's, to establish a dispensation in life or art as tyrannical as that he had overthrown. As 'seer,' as 'national expresser,' he used what power and insight he possessed, willing that future bards and critics should exemplify and formulate the new art more adequately.

He realized, moreover, that his task of construction was inherited rather than novel. With a larger historical perspective than one would expect of him, he came to think of the nineteenth century as 'ripening into fruit the seeds of the two preceding centuries,' the 'germination even of the United States to-day dating back to, and in my opinion mainly founded on, the Elizabethan age in English history.' He saw that his enthusiasm for democracy in politics and letters had also animated the English poets of the epoch of the French Revolution, though unlike himself they had had the singular handicap of being Europeans. The Revolution itself he regarded as on the whole a terribly costly failure. Reviewing Hazlitt's 'Napoleon' (he had previously reviewed Carlyle's 'French Revolution') in January of the revolutionary year 1848, Whitman said:

We would rather at this moment over every kingdom on the continent of Europe, that *the people* should rise and enact the same prodigious destructions as those of the French Revolution, could they thus root out the kingcraft and priestcraft which are annually dwindling down humanity there to a lower and lower average. . . . When it is observed how deeply the fangs of that kingcraft are fixed — and how through-and-through the virus of that priestcraft is infused — it will make one come nigh to think that only some great retching of the social and political structure can achieve the blessed consummation.[1]

Hopes raised later in 1848 having been disappointed, Whitman turned with renewed enthusiasm to the American Revolution, not in his day a remote event. 'The old men, I remember as a boy, were always talking of American independence'; and he never forgot the veterans who survived and the memories that were recounted. What the French Revolution had briefly signified to the Lake poets of England, the American Revolution continually signified to Whitman: marked a fresh beginning in history, destined to lead to a train of consequences grand beyond imagining.

Having been successful, the American Revolution was in his view the proximate beginning of the future world-order. In the development of democratic culture in the United States, of necessity the first stage of 'preparation-strata' was political independence — the break with Europe, the compacts of the Declaration of Independence, the Federal Constitution. Not in 'old history — miracles — romances' but in these 'unquestion'd facts' did we have our foundation. The second stage, still in progress, he described as material independence — the achievement of prosperity, railways, labor-saving machines, organization of cities, etc. The third stage will be æsthetic and religious independence: 'The Third Stage, rising out of the previous ones, to make them and all

[1] Compare 'Years of the Modern,' *Drum-Taps*, 1865, in which Whitman prophesied a revolutionary war, 'a general divine war,' to make the world safe for democracy.

illustrious, I, now, for one, promulge, announcing a native expression-spirit, ... self-contain'd, different from others, ... to be evidenced by original authors and poets to come, ... and by a sublime and serious Religious Democracy sternly taking command, dissolving the old, sloughing off surfaces, and from its own interior and vital principles, reconstructing, democratizing society.' The goal, it will be perceived, lies far in the future, inasmuch as we have not yet attained the third stage of preparation. Our polity, with our material strength supporting it, is American; yet our standards in the æsthetic-religious realm are still European. 'How can we,' he asked, 'remain, divided, contradicting ourselves, this way?'

In his attempt to resolve this contradiction by showing how America must achieve her cultural independence, Whitman maintained that the first step must be destructive. Before we can build up an American culture, we must tear down the European structure that has been raised here on alien shores. Before we can have a New World, we must turn away in mind and heart from the Old World.

In his 1855 Preface, it will be remembered, Whitman begins with the premise that the past is dead and merely awaits burial; that, though it was no doubt 'fittest for its days,' it is not fit for our days; that its animating spirit 'has passed into the new life of the new forms.' The new forms of civilization have 'the best authority,' namely, the national soul. 'As if it were necessary to trot back generation after generation' to consult the old records! Evolving out of European stock a distinctive race, the very 'race of races,' America should be indebted to Europe only through the channel of immigration; while looking abroad for human materials, she must not imitate Europe's outworn culture.[1] Lumping Europe with

---

[1] Although this position was weakened by admissions in the later writings of Whitman, it cannot be said that he ever wholly abandoned it. See pages 226–27.

Asia, Whitman maintained that East is East and West is West, and that if the twain eventually met it would be through the Americanization of the world. America alone could effectively break away from the past and usher in the second great age of history, the democratic age, because America alone is a composite of many races and has an ideal physical theater for her great drama. 'Think, in comparison, of the petty environage and limited area of past or present Europe!' The immense geography and varied fluid population of the United States never failed to stir the imagination of Whitman and to fortify his belief that this country is self-sufficient. The fact that he explored the West and South in the prime of life and again later, whereas the author of 'English Traits' had twice traveled in Europe, signifies a fundamental cleavage between the two men in their conception of culture. Speaking in his last years of his lack of foreign travel, Whitman averred not only that 'Leaves of Grass' was a 'this-side book,' but that it 'had to be guarded against all counter-inspirations.'

While assured that he and his land must turn away from Europe and be true only to themselves, Whitman was none the less powerfully attracted by the feudal tradition. If he loved to prefigure the American future, he was also eager to dwell in imagination, in the romantic manner, upon old forgotten things and battles long ago. While he rejoiced he also lamented that the age of chivalry is gone:

The ages of steel and of contending armies, and the smoke of battle, and the neighing of the war horse, have passed away. — Knights go forth no more, clad in the brazen armor, to redress the wrongs or the injury of the weak. — Barons, with their long trains of esquires and men-at-arms, no more are seen abroad in search of opportunities to show their valor and gain booty. The time of the fluttering of pennants in the breeze, while 'ladies faire' look down upon a sort of feudal boxing match, is also departed.

Rather curiously did he link his condemnation and his admiration, as when he spoke of the 'gorgeous procession of European feudalism, with all its pomp and class-prejudices' or when he admitted that 'there is plenty of glamour about the most damnable crimes and hoggish meannesses, special and general, of the feudal and dynastic world over there, with its *personnel* of lords and queens and courts, so well-dress'd and handsome.' He was also inclined to admit with reluctance that only feudalism could produce the great personalities that were the final goal of his social theory — 'types of tallest, noblest personal character yet — strength and devotion and love better than elsewhere — invincible courage, generosity, aspiration, the spines of all' — here, indeed, 'feudalism is un-rivall'd.' Among the plays of Shakspere, he asserted that those which best display his distinctiveness and his glory are the historical plays, 'founded on the contests of English dynasties, and the French wars,' 'conceiv'd out of the full-est heat and pulse of European feudalism — personifying in unparallel'd ways the mediæval aristocracy, its towering spirit of ruthless and gigantic caste.' He loved their pag-eantry, color, vivid action, splendid personalities, so unlike the drab actualities of American life. Hard-pressed to meet so formidable a counter-inspiration, he took refuge in his friend O'Connor's suggestion that the 'barbarous and tumul-tuous gloom' of these dramas shows that Shakspere could not 'have sought to indoctrinate the age with the love of feudalism'; indeed the time might come, he thought, when we should look upon these plays as after all 'the first full *exposé* . . . of the political theory and results . . . which Amer-ica has come on earth to abnegate and replace.' Walter Scott and Tennyson, his two favorite modern English poets, Whit-man viewed as the natural successors of Shakspere. At length, feudalism has been 'dirg'd by Tennyson's sweet sad rhyme.' Rhyme, it is worth noting, he regarded as the 'fitting' type of verse for feudalism — 'venerable and heavenly forms of chiming versification' — but as unsuited to the genius of

American democracy and of the prairies and Rocky Mountains. While he admired Tennyson as the last great poet of feudalism, revealing afresh its perennial charm, he admired Carlyle as its great critic, revealing its fatal shortcomings:

I consider Carlyle's by far the most indignant comment or protest anent the fruits of feudalism to-day in Great Britain — the increasing poverty and degradation of the homeless, landless twenty millions, while a few thousands, or rather a few hundreds, possess the entire soil, the money, and the fat berths. Trade and shipping, and clubs and culture, and prestige, and guns, and a fine select class of gentry and aristocracy, with every modern improvement, cannot begin to salve or defend such stupendous hoggishness.

The feudal order, in society and politics, must go, nay, has already gone, its passing marked by the death of an American inaugurator of the new order — Abraham Lincoln.

Along with the feudal state, Whitman rejected the church. 'The aimless sleepwalking of the middle ages,' the basis of what has passed for religion through many centuries, will be definitely terminated by the light of modern science. 'With Science, the Old Theology of the East, long in its dotage, begins evidently to die and disappear.' As true knowledge dawns upon the human mind, 'The whole theory of the special and supernatural and all that was twined with it or educed out of it departs as in a dream.' Religion will be released from the bondage of the 'fables, crudities, and superstitions' that constitute the strongly entrenched Old Theology — the 'fossil theology of the mythic-materialistic, superstitious, untaught and credulous, fable-loving, primitive ages of humanity.' We shall cease to love fables and love reality; we shall give over superstition in favor of knowledge; we shall no longer look for the supernatural but for the natural; we shall seek no more for material evidences but for spiritual; we shall abandon the myth of a special creation in order to understand the divinity of all creation. For science, rightly conceived, is not a destroyer but a preserver and revealer.

Assuming that the new theology can be 'only beneficent,
Whitman contrasts it with the dangerous fanaticism that
accompanied the old doctrines, a fanaticism 'capable of devouring, remorseless, like fire and flame.' The old theology
lent itself to priestcraft, which is as bad as kingcraft. In an
editorial printed in 1847, Whitman conceives that 'each
popinjay priest of the mummery of the past is babbling his
alarm' at the resistless advance of the democratic spirit that
is to enable men to attain the development intended by God.
But as science will demolish the old theology, so will democracy cast down the priests:

> There will soon be no more priests. Their work is done. They
> may wait awhile . . . perhaps a generation or two . . . dropping
> off by degrees. A superior breed shall take their place . . . the
> gangs of kosmos and prophets en masse shall take their place. A
> new order shall arise and they shall be the priests of man, and every
> man shall be his own priest.

The average man is divine, and has but to recognize his self-
sufficiency in the perfect universe revealed by science. The
king and the priest are dead, long live the new king-priest!

The literature of feudalism Whitman likewise rejected.
While it is true that he loved Shakspere, Scott, and the
Arthurian Tennyson, whom he regarded as consummate expressions of the old order, he proclaimed that the time had
arrived when writers must seek inspiration in the new vision
of life and not in the conventions of a moribund romantic-
feudal literature. 'Romantic literature,' he asserted in
'Democratic Vistas,' has reached an *impasse*. Here in our
New World, in novel, tale, and drama, we are content with
'the same endless thread of tangled and superlative love-
story, inherited, apparently from the Amadises and Palmerins
of the 13th, 14th, and 15th centuries over there in Europe.'
The differences are merely external: 'The costumes and associations brought down to date, the seasoning hotter and
more varied, the dragons and ogres left out — but the *thing*, I

should say, has not advanced — is just as sensational, just as strain'd — remains about the same, nor more, nor less.' Equally obvious is the futility of our poetry: 'The accepted notion of a poet would appear to be a sort of male odalisque, singing or piano-playing a kind of spiced ideas, second-hand reminiscences, or toying late hours at entertainments, in rooms stifling with fashionable scent.' Looking back in 1881, Whitman declared that the 'flow of poetry for the last fifty or eighty years, and now at its height, has been and is (like the music) an expression of mere surface melody, and the triumph of technical art.' In attaining a certain virtuosity in respect to mechanics, we have also attained the 'twentieth remove from verities.' Content with the dregs of the feudal convention, we have forgotten that freshness, power, and truth are possible.[1]

There was, however, a second article in Whitman's indictment of the literature of the nineteenth century: it was (as Lowell was saying) morbid. Modern writers tend 'to turn everything to pathos, ennui, morbidity, dissatisfaction, death.' Instead of interpreting this tendency, in the romantic fashion, as an indication of profound spiritual aspiration, Whitman bluntly remarked, 'I call this thing in our modern literature delirium tremens.' It pleased him to mark the taint of morbidity in writer after writer. 'The basis of Burns's character,' for instance, 'with all its fun and manliness, was hypochondria, the blues.' The Immortality ode of Wordsworth, beneath its hopes and rejoicings, he classed as a poem of melancholy. He deplored the melancholy of Bryant, one of his idols, and of course that of Poe and of Hawthorne. The presence of this insanity in the wholesome air of America he attributed to the influence of the decadent Old World, picturing 'Europe, with all its glories,' as a 'vast abnormal ward or

---

[1] Several decades after the eighties, the same complaint was voiced by Edgar Lee Masters in 'Petit, the Poet':

> Tick, tick, tick, what little iambics,
> While Homer and Whitman roared in the pines.

hysterical sick-chamber.' Responsible for conventionalism — the reminiscent mood — Europe was also responsible for morbidness — the pessimistic mood. And the two moods, in Whitman's mind, were closely related, in regard to their cause and their possible remedy. 'Modern verse,' he observes, 'generally lacks quite altogether the modern, and is oftener possess'd in spirit with the past and feudal, dressed maybe in late fashions. For novels and plays often the plots and surfaces are contemporary — but the spirit, even the fun, is morbid and effete.' Our pessimism is, partly at least, the consequence of conventionalism based upon a dead past. Health does not come from death. The remedy must lie in a release of the spirit of life inherent in us as in all men, a reliance upon the time-spirit that cannot be suppressed without menace to spiritual health. This is a remedy that may be sought confidently, not by an exhausted Europe, but by an America whose immense vitality has never been used.

§ 5

From his time of apprenticeship to his last years at Camden, Whitman brooded over the thought which, as he says, the young Goethe derived from Herder, 'that really great poetry is always (like the Homeric or Biblical canticles) the result of a national spirit,' and the complementary thought that a national spirit is always the result of really great poetry. What does this signify for America?

I know not a land except ours that has not, to some extent, however small, made its title clear. The Scotch have their born ballads, subtly expressing their past and present, and expressing character. The Irish have theirs. England, Italy, France, Spain, theirs. What has America? With exhaustless mines of the richest ore of epic, lyric, tale, tune, picture, etc., in the Four-Years' War; with, indeed, I sometimes think, the richest masses of material ever afforded a nation, more variegated, and on a larger scale — the first sign of proportionate, native, imaginative Soul, and first-class works to match, is (I cannot too often repeat) so far wanting.

And yet, in the new world of the twentieth century, 'Can there be any doubt who the leader ought to be?' The next world-leader must be America, which Columbus discovered only in a physical sense. America is yet undiscovered in a spiritual sense.

Accepting the challenge of the unknown, Whitman set out to discover the native spirit, the genius, of America. This he attempted through the method of mariners and scholars, who seek the passage from the known to the unknown, though in his case the method involved two rash assumptions: first, that he understood Europe, the 'known,' and secondly, that 'unknown' America must be the opposite of Europe. Adopting these assumptions, he proceeded to disclose the secret of America in a series of antitheses, the validity of which he could test by comparing the America thus defined with the America of his direct observation.

One of these antitheses, already touched upon, is geographical. To the petty environment of the European nations Whitman opposes the grand theater that nature has given us in America — 'areas of amplitude rivaling the operations of the physical kosmos.' As he announced exultingly in his first Preface, 'The United States themselves are essentially the greatest poem.' The native poet will write down this poem in words, by identifying himself with the landscape of his country:

He incarnates its geography and natural life and rivers and lakes. Mississippi with annual freshets and changing chutes, Missouri and Columbia and Ohio and Saint Lawrence with the falls and beautiful masculine Hudson, do not embouchure where they spend themselves more than they embouchure into him. The blue breadth over the inland sea of Virginia and Maryland and the sea off Massachusetts and Maine and over Manhattan bay and over Champlain and Erie and over Ontario and Huron and Michigan and Superior, and over the Texan and Mexican and Floridian and Cuban seas and over the seas off California and Oregon, is not tallied by the blue breadth of the waters below more than the breadth of above and below is

tallied by him. When the long Atlantic coast stretches longer and
the Pacific coast stretches longer he easily stretches with them
north or south. He spans between them also from east to west and
reflects what is between them.[1]

As a poet of the Atlantic seaboard, Whitman naturally
loved to send his imagination to the West. Thus, writing as
early as 1846 on 'The New World and the Old,' he contrasted
the wretchedness of man on the shores of the Loire, the Seine,
the Garonne, and Bantry Bay with the happiness of man that
is possible beyond the Alleghanies:

Stretching between the Alleghany Mountains and the Pacific
Ocean, are millions on millions of uncultivated acres of land — long
rolling prairies — interminable savannahs, where the fat earth is
covered with grass reaching to a height unknown in our less prolific
north — forests, amid whose boughs nothing but silence reigns,
and the birds are not shy through fear of human kind — rich open-
ings by the side of rivers — trees and verdure making from year
to year their heavy deposits on the remains of the trees and verdure
that have decayed before them. The mind becomes lost in tracing
in imagination those hidden and boundless tracts of our territory —

> 'Where rolls the Oregon and hears no
> Sound save his own dashing.' [2]

The geography of the West plays an essential part in 'Leaves
of Grass,' as Whitman himself asserted in the plainest terms
after making a long journey to the prairies and the Rockies. 'I
have found the law of my own poems,' he said to himself with
unintentional and excessive irony upon contemplating the
'entire absence of art' in the mountains. In the end he inclined to find 'America's characteristic landscape' not in the

[1] Whitman's is a kind of geometrical geography: the figure that results from
his spans, east and west, north and south, above and below, is a cube. It appears to contain Mexico and Cuba; in other passages his imperialistic turn of
mind led him to include also, as logical parts of the country, Canada and the
Pacific Ocean with its islands. He witnessed the Mexican War, and died only
six years before the Spanish War.

[2] 'Thanatopsis.' There are also echoes, in the above passage, from 'The
Prairies' and 'A Forest Hymn.'

mountains, however, but in the 'less stunning' prairies and plains, which, broadly and silently unfolding, imprinted their image upon his senses — 'the æsthetic one most of all.' Matching on land the grandeur and monotony of the sky and ocean, freeing, soothing, nourishing to the soul, 'these interminable and stately prairies' seemed to him destined to be 'the home both of what I would call America's distinctive ideas and distinctive realities.' He almost thinks that the valley of the Mississippi is, or soon will be, the American Union, the dwelling place of a people at once the most peaceful and warlike, the most money-making and restless, in the world, and the inspiration of a literature that will at last speak for the nation. 'New England (the technically moral and schoolmaster region, as a cynical fellow I know calls it) and the three or four great Atlantic-coast cities, highly as they to-day suppose they dominate the whole, will have to haul in their horns.' If the future of the world belongs to America, the future of America belongs to the West.

A second antithesis that Whitman employed in his definition of America has to do with the social and political structure of the Old and the New World: to the feudalism of Europe, he opposes the democracy of America. Since feudalism is aristocratic, our democracy must be equalitarian. Since feudalism exalts the exceptional man, our democracy must exalt the common man.

Upon the idea of the common or average man Whitman bases his conception of a new social order and a new literature to express it. Holding that the aristocratic conception still prevailing was expressed by the literature of feudalism, he denounces that literature ('Shakspere included') as no less than 'poisonous' to 'the life-blood of democracy.' He cannot accept the 'favorite standard of the eminent writer' — meaning Carlyle — who so eloquently calls for 'the rule of the best men, the born heroes and captains of the race (as if such ever, or one time out of a hundred, get into the big places, elective or dynastic),' since this would still be an arbitrary rule rather than reliance upon 'the sterling common soil of the race.' [1] In 'Specimen Days' he recorded his opinion that this sterling common soil is peculiarly American:

Other lands have their vitality in a few, a class, but we have it in the bulk of the people. Our leading men are not of much account and never have been, but the average of the people is immense, beyond all history.

Nor could he accept the theory of that other influential British critic of society and literature, Matthew Arnold, enemy of numbers and philistines and exponent of the saving remnant. 'Arnold always gives you the notion that he hates to touch the dirt — the dirt is so dirty!' Yet truly, Whitman adds, 'everything comes out of the dirt — everything: everything comes out of the people, the everyday people, the people as you find them and leave them: not university people, not F.F.V. people: people, people, just people!' This must be the faith of America. It is idle for us to hope to rival the splendor of European aristocracy. Our principal, if not only, reason for being is to achieve 'an immense and distinctive commonalty over our vast and varied area, west and east, south and north — in fact, for the first time in history, a great, aggregated, real PEOPLE.' Herein must lie our superiority, and hence the inspiration of our literature. Down to our own times, 'Literature, strictly consider'd, has never recognized the People, and, whatever may be said, does not to-day.' To be sure, 'There is, in later literature, a treatment of benevolence, a charity business, rife enough it is true; but I know nothing more rare, even in this country, than a fit scientific estimate and reverent appreciation of the People.'

With this right estimate and appreciation Whitman concerned himself steadily, mingling with the middle class and lower class (the latter term I do not recall his ever using) and

[1] A main object in *Democratic Vistas* was to attack Carlyle's theory of a natural aristocracy.

observing their qualities of mind and character. Affection-
ately, with slow-moving eyes, he scrutinized 'our American
young men and working people — the firemen, the railroad
employés, the steamer and ferry men, the police, the con-
ductors, and drivers — the whole splendid average of native
stock, city and country.' Amid the 'interminable swarms'
of the cities, he experienced 'a singular awe,' and he declared
that in the current humanity of his beloved Manhattan could
be found 'the directest proof yet of successful Democracy.'
He looked with admiration upon the agricultural West, where
the frontier spirit of initiative scorned conventionalism, 'that
poison to the Democratic vitality.' The young men of a navy
training-ship that he visited satisfied him that the future of
America was safe; so did the soldiers in the hospitals during
the terrible war, with 'their decorum, their religious nature
and fortitude, and their sweet affection.' Repeatedly, and in
the main consistently, he described the average American
qualities. To begin with, the people are natural: free — fresh
— unconscious. 'There is that indescribable freshness and
unconsciousness about an illiterate person that humbles and
mocks the power of the noblest expressive power,' just as the
sea and prairies and sublime mountains mock the poet and
painter. Then, they have faith and pride. Faith 'pervades
the common people and preserves them . . . they never give
up believing and expecting and trusting,' and they have the
pride and dignity that come of optimism. They also have
good-nature, affection, comradeship, decorum, intelligence —
qualities that make for harmony in ordinary life. Finally, in
an emergency, they show the qualities of devotion and heroism, as in the case of the Civil War, when a tide of idealism
swept before it the materialism of the age and country. In
one of his last writings, Whitman reports that among these
and other qualities he has 'invariably found coming to the
front three prevailing personal traits, . . . Good-Nature,
Decorum, and Intelligence.' But the best indication of the

ground of his apostleship of the people is a rhapsodic catalogue of traits in his first Preface:

Their manners speech dress friendships — the freshness and
candor of their physiognomy — the picturesque looseness of their
carriage . . . their deathless attachment to freedom — their
aversion to anything indecorous or soft or mean — the practical
acknowledgment of the citizens of one state by the citizens of all
other states — the fierceness of their roused resentment — their
curiosity and welcome of novelty — their self-esteem and wonderful sympathy — their susceptibility to a slight — the air they have
of persons who never knew how it felt to stand in the presence of
superiors — the fluency of their speech — their delight in music,
the sure symptom of manly tenderness and native elegance of
soul . . . their good temper and open-handedness — the terrible
significance of their elections — the President's taking off his hat
to them not they to him

— these, he says, are poetry still unspoken and awaiting
gigantic treatment.[1]

In the definition of American culture, then, the first step
must be acceptance of the people or average humanity, upon
whom 'all the superstructures of the future are to permanently rest.' Turning now to these superstructures, we must
admit at once that the idea of the average will no longer
serve, but must give place to the opposite idea of the individual. In the society of the future we shall witness the solution of 'that paradox, the eligibility of the free and fully
developed individual with the paramount aggregate.' For the
divinity of the average is in the main latent rather than attained, and it can be attained only through the development
of the individual. Accordingly, inconsistent though it may at
first appear, 'the democratic averages of America' must in
the future display that high development of individuals that

[1] Not only personal observation, of course, determined this picture of the
average. Whitman absorbed many intellectual influences into his vision; for
example, the Emersonian optimism, gospel of self-reliance, and doctrine of the
unity of man. Like Emerson (and Wordsworth before him), Whitman conceived of the poet as a man speaking to men.

has characterized the European ideal of the past, those very
'ranges of heroism and loftiness with which Greek and feudal
poets endow'd their god-like or lordly born characters — indeed prouder and better based and with fuller ranges than
those.' Of the two elements or sexes of the democratic idea,
clashing but equally indispensable, the average and the individual, it is clear that the former is preparatory and the latter
final. Thus the goal of democratic civilization is the same as
that of any other civilization, namely, a 'rich, luxuriant,
varied personalism,' 'the pride and centripetal isolation of a
human being in himself.' The unfolding of the divinity latent
in the average is complete only when the idiocrasy of the individual has fully asserted itself. Democracy is superior to
other forms of society simply because it gives to all members
of the aggregate an unhindered opportunity for self-realiza-
tion. On a vast scale like nature's, it 'breaks up the limitless
fallows of humankind, and plants the seed, and gives fair
play.' In this growth of individuals, literature and the other
arts are of high service. That literature should recognize the
people is not enough; it must also furnish 'suggestions of personality' to aid men and women in their growth.

Conceding that modern science and democracy appear to
be 'endangering, perhaps eliminating' that personal and individual growth which is the true end of civilization, Whitman
made most earnest efforts to envisage a new human pattern,
'a typical personality of character, eligible to the uses of the
high average of men — and *not* restricted by conditions in-
eligible to the masses.' Believing that the feudal pattern of
the gentleman and the lady was becoming anachronistic, he
strove to imagine a pattern suited to an age of democracy.
Though sometimes showing his awareness of permanent elements in human nature, in none of his speculations did he
make them his central theme; instead, he devoted himself
eagerly to outlining the ethical traits that were to differentiate the future from the past, on the assumption that the

broad base of democracy would of itself assure due attention
to the universal traits. His controlling purpose was already
plain in the manuscript notebook dated 1847, on the first
page of which he wrote: 'True noble expanded American
Character is raised on a far more lasting and universal basis
than that of any of the characters of the "gentlemen" of
aristocratic life, or of novels, or under the European or Asian
forms of society or government.'

Realizing that to define the unformed future is the work of
a prophet and that a prophet has small use for 'doubts and
qualms,' Whitman launched forth on his task of framing a
new vision of man. Yet the realm in which he found himself
was not Chaos. Dim suggestions came to him from average
American humanity, whose qualities, set forth above, reappear in his ideal ethos. Plain hints came to him also from
modern science. To understand Whitman's conception of
man, it will be necessary to examine in some detail his
antithesis between the old ignorance and the new knowledge
and his antithesis between the superstitious religion of the
past and the scientifically based religion of the future.

§ 6

No idle singer of an empty day, Whitman accepted, along
with democracy, its 'twin' — science. 'Best gift of our age,'
'crowning glory' of the modern world, it marks the close of
the Dark Ages, of the long night in which man has lived in
ignorance and fear. It is the light of the world, 'a sun, mount-
ing, most illuminating, most glorious — surely never again to
set.' This light Whitman accepted without hesitation, endeavoring to 'absorb whatever science indicates.' Boldly he
stated, 'I have thoroughly adopted the conclusions of the
great Savans and Experimentalists of our time, and of the
last hundred years' — conclusions that reached him through
various channels, especially the newspapers and magazines,
if one may judge from the clippings that he marked and pre-

served. He kept reports of lectures on the 'Progress of Science' and on the 'Scientific Convention at Montreal,' articles on 'Comets, their History and Habits,' and other astronomical subjects, a description of 'Scenes on the Ocean Floor,' an exposition of the 'Origin of Coal,' an account of 'Lyell's Geological Tour' (1845) and one of 'A Second Visit to the United States by Sir Charles Lyell' (1849). He projected poems on 'the different branches of the Sciences' — a poem of arithmetic, a poem of astronomy, a poem of chemistry, a poem of geology. He planned also a poem of entomology, for which he was ambitious to 'get from Mr. Arkhurst the names of all insects.' He believed that science will hereafter be 'the only irrefragable basis for anything, verse included.' It is the 'father' of the best poetry and of the best religion. 'Faith, very old, now scared away by science, must be restored, brought back by the same power that caused her departure.' Our ideas 'of the unknown and of unreality' must be based upon the known and the real.

The known and the real are the sphere of science. Through the reasoning process, 'clear and passionless as crystal,' science demonstrates that 'law is the unshakable order of the universe.'

What has ever happened . . . what happens and whatever may or shall happen, the vital laws enclose all . . . they are sufficient for any case and for all cases . . . none to be hurried or retarded . . . any miracle of affairs or persons inadmissible in the vast clear scheme where every motion and every spear of grass and the frames and spirits of men and women and all that concerns them are unspeakably perfect miracles all referring to all and each distinct and in its place.

Science thus enjoins absolute acceptance of the universe. The passage quoted is from the 1855 Preface; and late in life, in 'A Backward Glance,' Whitman was still of the same mind, still convinced that the message of science to the poet is that every object is perfect, 'not only consider'd from the point of

view of all, but of each.' His controlling thought remained
the supposedly scientific idea that 'Whatever is is right.' [1]
When this thought was focused upon 'each,' some concrete
object, a blade of grass, a fish in the water, Whitman liked to
use the term 'miracle.' When, on the other hand, it was
directed upon the 'all' to which each object refers, he was
prone to use some such term as 'Kosmic Spirit.' For the poet,
he avers in his expansive way, 'must vocalize the vastness
and splendor and reality with which Scientism has invested
Man and the Universe (all that is called Creation), and must
henceforth launch Humanity into new orbits, consonant with
that vastness, splendor, and reality (unknown to old poems),
like new systems of orbs, balanced upon themselves, revolv-
ing in limitless space.' Instead of a poetry wedded to children's tales, mere amorousness, upholstery, and rhyme, we
must now have a poetry 'revivified by this tremendous in-
novation, the Kosmic Spirit.'

Now, in the perfect order of the universe, 'The law over all,
the law of laws, is the law of successions' — of evolution.
Although, in a late essay on Darwinism, Whitman suspected
that a yet higher law might arise as inquiry advanced, that
'in due time the evolution theory will have to abate its
vehemence, cannot be allow'd to dominate every thing else,
and will have to take its place as a segment of the circle,' yet
he more than once stated his belief that it was the greatest of
laws and as such he allowed it to permeate his thought from
his first Preface to the end of his life. In his first Preface he
heralds the science that has done away with the theory of
special creation, refers to the nebular hypothesis ('Our earth
gathered itself in a mass'), and sees with Lyell 'vast stretches

[1] This deistic dictum, which appears in a talk with Traubel, even impelled
Whitman to concede that the 'utterly incredible' 'facts' of the church must
somehow 'have a place' in the total scheme of things. It may be noted that the
naïve deism of Shaftesbury seems often a more congenial background for his
rhapsodic celebration of perfection than the Platonic-Transcendental doctrine
of the 'Each and All' that passed from Coleridge through Emerson to Whitman.

of time' and 'the slow formation of density' and 'the patient
upheaving of strata.' In his closing years, he spoke of evolution as the greatest law of nature, of himself as 'an evolution-
ist — not in the first place a *révolutionnaire,*' and of his 'Passage to India' as the 'essential ultimate me. . . . The burden
of it is evolution — the one thing escaping the other — the
unfolding of cosmic purposes.' Along with this belief in evolution he experienced at times the deterministic feeling that
'The whole matter has gone on, and exists to-day, probably
as it should have been, and should be.'

Accompanying Victorian science in respect to the idea of
evolution, Whitman went ahead of his age in his conception
of the human body and sex. In a period when eugenics was
not yet a fashionable topic of conversation, he asked, 'Will
the time hasten when fatherhood and motherhood shall become a science — and the noblest science?' Bored with the
emphasis on romantic love ('mere amorousness'), he welcomed the biological fact, hushed in society and books, that
men are fathers and women are mothers. He perceives that
sex, rejected, dispelled, is actually always immanent — 'the
root of roots: the life below the life.' To conventional repression he attributes 'most of the ill births, inefficient maturity,
snickering pruriency, and of that human pathologic evil and
morbidity which is, in my opinion, the keel and reason-why of
every evil and morbidity. Its scent, as of something sneaking,
furtive, mephitic, seems to lingeringly pervade all modern
literature, conversation, and manners.' [1] Where this conventional repression is absent, we find instead something almost
as bad, namely, sensual voluptuousness. This is the source of
'the wit, or what passes for wit, of masculine circles,' of the
'erotic stories and talk' in which men seek to 'express' rather
than repress. This second condition, however, is 'like a dis-

[1] Cf. Whitman's more general condemnation of the morbidity of modern
literature, pp. 190–92, above. Romantic love is a decadent part of a decadent
whole — the feudal convention.

ease which comes to the surface, and therefore less dangerous than a conceal'd one.' Having set forth these two conditions, Whitman continues: 'The time seems to me to have arrived, and America to be the place, for a new departure — a third point of view.' This we shall attain when we perceive, through the scientific spirit, 'that the sexual passion in itself, while normal and unperverted, is inherently legitimate, creditable, not necessarily an improper theme for poet, as confessedly not for scientist.' This is the point of view, he tells us, that prevented his yielding to the astute advice of Emerson that he should omit his Children of Adam in order to gain a hearing for the rest of his poetry. If to be modern is to be scientific, the modern poet must be scientific. Accordingly, Whitman endeavored to secure exact knowledge of sex, as of so many other subjects. As early as 1847 we find him reviewing a medical book, 'Woman, and Her Diseases, from the Cradle to the Grave': '"To the pure, all things are pure," is the not inappropriate motto of this work: and the mock delicacy that condemns the widest possible diffusion among females of such knowledge as is contained in this book, will receive from us no quarter.' Eight years later, in the Preface to his poems, he announced in all candor, 'The innocence and nakedness are resumed . . . they are neither modest nor immodest'; and in the poems themselves he aimed to speak like a new Adam who has tasted the fruits of modern science.

The modern poet must accept, then, unquestioningly, rejoicingly, that known and real physical order which has been described by scientific reason. Yet his highest theme is not to be the physical order, nor can he rest content with reason. Whitman perceives the tendency of the modern world to be 'essentially intellectual, infidelistic,' to be satisfied with 'pure compulsion or science'; that along 'with an extra development and acuteness of the intellectual faculties, there is a mark'd absence of the spiritual.' He concludes that it is only a 'half-way science' that 'scoffs at reminiscence of dryad and hamadryad,' that knowing a tree is less than 'affiliating a tree.' He concludes that 'When it comes to explaining absolute beginnings, ends,' it is doubtful, after all, whether 'evolution clears up the mystery any better than the philosophies that have preceded it.' 'Bring all the ... science of the world,' he cries, and I will 'baffle and humble it with one spear of grass.' [1] Nevertheless, impotent though it be before the ultimate interrogations, science renders possible at last, after the long reign of superstition, the *approach* to the answers. It is at once the destroyer of false and the upbuilder of true faith.

As beneficent destroyer, science has freed the modern poet from superstitions, crude fables, materialistic myths, devouring fanaticism, and false conceptions of sin, deformity, disease, and death. It has given the *coup de grâce* to the devil, the hell, and the notion of natural depravity that satisfied the lurid imagination of the Puritans. As upbuilder of faith, on the other hand, it has revealed the immensity, the splendor, the perfection, of that physical universe which is so significant a part of the All. It has prepared the way for a new and more inclusive theology — a theology that will throw 'the true arch over all teaching, all science' — that Science of God which is 'the supreme and final Science,' and of which the theme is 'the central divine idea of All,' or 'the physical, moral, and spiritual kosmos.' Accepting all that modern science tells us of the physical kosmos, we may proceed to the comprehension of the moral and spiritual kosmos. While conceding that the scientific reason discovers truth, Whitman is dominated with the thought, throughout his first 'Leaves of Grass,' that the soul is superior to reason and that it commands a superior order of knowledge: 'Whatever satisfies the soul,' he says, 'is truth.' This affirmation

[1] There is an interesting passage on the contributions and limits of natural science in Traubel, II, 168–69.

becomes more explicit in 'Democratic Vistas,' in which, quite in the Transcendental manner, he proclaims that material things are verily unmeaning when viewed in disconnection from the soul, and indeed derive from the soul whatever reality they may be said to have:

All the objective grandeurs of the world, for highest purposes, yield themselves up, and depend on mentality alone. Here, and here only, all balances, all rests. For the mind, which alone builds the permanent edifice, haughtily builds it to itself. By it, with what follows it, are convey'd to mortal sense the culminations of the materialistic, the known, and a prophecy of the unknown. To take expression, to incarnate, to endow a literature with grand and archetypal models — to fill with pride and love the utmost capacity, and to achieve spiritual meanings, and suggest the future — these, and these only, satisfy the soul. We must not say one word against real materials; but the wise know that they do not become real till touched by emotions, the mind. Did we call the latter imponderable? Ah, let us rather proclaim that the slightest song-tune, the countless ephemera of passions arous'd by orators and tale-tellers, are more dense, more weighty than the engines there in the great factories, or the granite blocks in their foundations. ... To the cry, now victorious — the cry of sense, science, flesh, incomes, farms, merchantise, logic, intellect, demonstrations, solid perpetuities, buildings of rock and iron, or even the facts of the shows of trees, earth, rocks, etc., fear not, my brethren, my sisters, to sound out with equally determin'd voice, that conviction brooding within the recesses of every envision'd soul — illusions! apparitions! figments all! [1]

§7

Having some knowledge of the materials that Whitman consciously used, we are now in a better position to understand what he means by the American Character of the

---

[1] A decade later, after the death of Carlyle, Whitman writes another confession of faith, in which he sketches the German metaphysic from Kant through Schelling to Hegel, 'the truest cosmical devotee or religioso.' He finds Hegel's formulas 'an essential and crowning justification of New World democracy,' and is puzzled to account for their appearance in the Old World. (*Prose Works*, I, 310–24.)

future as opposed to the European type of the past. From democracy he derived his acceptance of the average; there is a
marked resemblance between his picture of the actual average
American of the present and the ideal individual personality
of the future. It was essential that his 'basic model' be one
adapted 'for general use' — the average idealized to the
divine average. From science Whitman derived his acceptance of the physical universe, an integral part of which is
man, or rather man's body; so that he rejected asceticism
and all repression in favor of natural physical expression.
From the affirmations of the soul he derived his acceptance of
the spiritual universe, finding support in science: above the
halfway science that rests in the physical, he sought to throw
the arch of a science of God, a veracious theology. In sum,
his model of the new man in the New World, to be imitated
like Christ in Christian society or the gentleman in feudal
society, must be determined by the average, the physical,
and the divine.

The model thus imagined was the subject of 'Leaves of
Grass.' Identifying himself with the model, Whitman represented himself not so much as he was but rather as he would
be. His 'Myself' was not the *'moi seul'* of Rousseau, so that
he announced at the beginning, not that *'Je ne suis fait
comme aucun de ceux que j'ai vus,'* but that 'What I assume
you shall assume.' Despite what has been termed his exhibi-
tionism, his affinity was not so much with the Rousseau of
the 'Confessions' as with the Rousseau of, let us say, the
second 'Discourse,' who described the natural man or noble
savage as compounded of self-love and pity. In Whitman, a
century later, these elementary principles of the human soul
reappear in equal prominence though under various names,
the commonest of which are *pride* and *sympathy*.[1]

[1] 'Whitman,' says Emory Holloway, 'had imbibed not a little of Rousseau's
passion for the natural man.' (*Whitman*, 1926, p. 222.) While this is no doubt
true, the *direct* debt of Whitman to Rousseau was probably slight. His explicit
references to Rousseau are as follows. In 1846 he refers to 'the fascinating

The American Character will be marked, first, by a new pride. Although Whitman, in the years in which he was brooding over his book, regarded a 'haughty bearing' as 'that most contemptible phase of aristocracy in the whole world,' yet at the same time he believed that it should be foremost in the democratic ethos. A fault in the few, it became a virtue in the many. 'Every American young man should carry himself,' he inscribes in his notebook, 'with the finished and haughty bearing of the greatest ruler and proprietor. . . . I wish to see American young men, the working men, carry themselves with a high horse.' 'I never yet knew how it felt to think I stood in the presence of my superior. — If the presence of God were made visible immediately before me, I could not abase myself.' 'If I walk with Jah in Heaven and he assume to be intrinsically greater than I it offends me, and I shall certainly withdraw from Heaven.' With Satanic independence and security in his ethereal essence — not with the baseless insolence of caste — Whitman proclaims that he is 'probably larger' than Adam or Eve, the illustrious Greeks, yes, Christ himself, not to mention Columbus and Washington and Fulton, 'because all that they did I feel that I too could do, and more and that multiplied. . . . Not even God is so great to me as Myself is great to me. — Who

melancholy of Rousseau.' (*Uncoll. Poetry and Prose*, i, 121.) In 1851 he objects to Rousseau's disjunction of nature and art, while admiring the man as a 'restless and daring spirit' and 'one of the noblest apostles of democracy.' (*Ibid.*, 243.) Among 'Memoranda from Books and from his own Reflections' (*Prose Works*, vi, 80–81) are a page and a half of biographical fact and comment, in which the *Confessions* is found frivolous, repulsive, and yet fascinating, and the remark is made that 'An American poet may read Rousseau but shall never imitate him.'

Passages merely reminiscent of Rousseau are, of course, innumerable. Professor Holloway quotes, for example, the following comment upon the 'natural man' as Whitman saw him in the Indian Bureau at Washington: 'I should not apply the word savage (at any rate, in the usual sense) as a leading word in the description of those great aboriginal specimens, of whom I certainly saw many of the best. There were moments, as I look'd at them or studied them, when our own exemplification of personality, dignity, heroic presentation anyhow (as in the conventions of society, or even in the accepted poems and plays), seem'd sickly, puny, inferior.'

knows but I too shall in time be a God as pure and prodigious as any of them?' [1] He is hostile not only to 'much-bepraised modesty' but equally to the higher virtue of humility: 'Let fools affect humility in the strength of their conceit: this brain (?) feels and claims the divine life which moves restlessly (?).' All of these quotations are from his early notebooks; but the same ideas, phrased with a strategy less bold, reappear in the writings that he published. Thus, in the Preface of 1855, he declares, 'The soul has that measureless pride which consists in never acknowledging any lessons but its own,' and later, in 'Democratic Vistas,' he pictures a model of personality in which the leading trait is pride:

We descry a well-begotten selfhood — in youth, fresh, ardent, emotional, aspiring, full of adventure; at maturity, brave, perceptive, under control, neither too talkative nor too reticent, neither flippant nor sombre; of the bodily figure, the movements easy, the complexion showing the best blood, somewhat flush'd, breast expanded, an erect attitude, a voice whose sound outvies music, eyes of calm and steady gaze, yet capable also of flashing — and a general presence that holds its own in the company of the highest.

This expansive pride Whitman proceeds to offset with the second elementary principle of the human soul, an expansive sympathy. For he believes that the soul 'has sympathy as measureless as its pride and the one balances the other and neither can stretch too far while it stretches in company with the other.' [2] The meaning of sympathy, in its most inclusive sense, Whitman indicates by describing the poet as the 'complete lover' of the known universe, burning with

---

[1] This would appear to be the *reductio ad absurdum* of Emerson's inadequately guarded doctrines of the Oversoul and of the unity of man. In the phrase 'in time' Whitman joins these doctrines with what he terms the 'evolution-principle.'

[2] It may be remarked that this figure, a kind of elastic tug-of-war, provides for two emotions that actually (to change the figure) tend to oscillate from one extreme to the other. A principle of concentration, or control of emotion, is occasionally assumed in Whitman (as in the passage quoted above), but its nature is never described nor its importance estimated.

desire for contact with 'all perfection and beauty' and joyous in the 'harmony of things with man.' The soul loves the body and all nature. This is his sense in the first Preface; for it was only in later years that he dwelt upon the fraternal relation of human beings to each other. Instead of the 'narrow, constipated, special amativeness' prevalent in the past, Whitman came to feel that he should praise in his poems (specifically in Calamus), and consistently in his prose, the general love of man: 'this never-satisfied appetite for sympathy, and this boundless offering of sympathy — this universal democratic comradeship — this old, eternal, yet ever-new interchange of adhesiveness, so fitly emblematic of America.' Thus, he insists, there is 'not that half only, individualism, which isolates. There is another half, which is adhesiveness or love, that fuses, ties and aggregates, making the races comrades, and fraternizing all.' Perceiving that individualism, as he conceived it, 'would surely destroy itself' unless offset by some strong force, he invoked adhesiveness as the best corrective; but there is no question that in his mind it ever remained second to individualism. He so asserted in the baldest terms; and it is evident even in that curiously subdued picture that he drew, in 'Democratic Vistas,' of a kind of frontier Brook Farm, where each man and woman could bring to fruition his precious idiocrasy:

I can conceive a community, to-day and here, in which, on a sufficient scale, the perfect personalities without noise meet; say in some pleasant Western settlement or town, where a couple of hundred best men and women, of ordinary worldly status, have by luck been drawn together, with nothing extra of genius or wealth, but virtuous, chaste, industrious, cheerful, resolute, friendly and devout. I can conceive such a community organized in running order, powers judiciously delegated — farming, building, trade, courts, mails, schools, elections, all attended to; and then the rest of life, the main thing, freely branching and blossoming in each individual, and bearing golden fruit. I can see there, in every young and old man, after his kind, and in every woman after hers, a true personality, develop'd, exercised proportionately in body, mind, and spirit. . . . Perhaps, unsung, undramatized, unput in essays or biographies — perhaps even some such community already exists, in Ohio, Illinois, Missouri, or somewhere, practically fulfilling itself, and thus outvying, in cheapest vulgar life, all that has been hitherto shown in best ideal pictures.

Such is the goal toward which man has been striving through the ages.

§8

In the foregoing analysis of Whitman's literary theory, I have for the most part refrained, in the interest of clearness, from criticism of its validity. I have sought to bear in mind that Whitman is so provocative of assent or dissent that his expositors are prone either to accept him as an infallible master or to reject him as an impostor. I have sought, above all, to understand what it was that he believed, and to state it, so far as possible in his own words, more clearly than he saw fit to do in his mélanged cogitations. To end with mere exposition, however, would be to rest at the inn instead of pressing on to our destination. In the pilgrimage of the mind, as Whitman himself taught, no man's theory is a sufficient abiding place.

Accordingly, in the following chapter I shall attempt to deal critically with some of the doctrines that Whitman held in common with other theorists of the Romantic Movement, and in the remainder of the present chapter to estimate the prophetic criticism with which Whitman alone persistently concerned himself.

In their attitude toward past, present, and future, critics may be divided into three classes. First are those who look backward, traditional critics, men impressed with the fact that humanity is made up of more dead than living, and with the rights of the dead to a hearing and a suffrage in matters of perennial interest to humanity. Such were Emerson and

Lowell, appraisers of tradition, enemies alike of convention and revolution. A second class contains those who look around, contemporary critics, men consciously or unconsciously impressed with the compelling force of the movement of which they are a part, eagerly responsive to what appears to them most vital in the aspirations of their day or the day just before. Such was Poe, as indifferent to tradition as to convention, content to work out the implications of the movement to which he chanced to belong. The third class is composed of those who look forward, prophetic critics, men dominated with the idea that the future will be different from and better than the present and the past, anxiously looking for signs to assist them in prefiguring the lineaments of the new age. And such was Whitman. The traditional critics attain a certain breadth and centrality, at the risk of prematurely closing their minds; the contemporary critics attain a striking definiteness, at the risk of equally striking narrowness; and the prophetic critics attain freedom from the limitations of past and present fact, at the risk of having their theories belied by the event.

Of sanguine temperament, Whitman set out to be the foremost prophetic critic of his generation. Expressly rejecting the authority of the past and the present, he had small room in his conscious thought for the æsthetic achievement recorded before his own day, though as we have seen he was rather largely acquainted with that achievement. The materials that he deliberately chose to work with were nonliterary: modern science and American democracy. His task was to raise them to a higher plane through a fervid religious spirit, and to translate the result into æsthetic terms. The thing that he prophesied was a democratic-scientific art, religious in spirit, destined to belittle all preceding æsthetic achievement, save possibly his own.

Has the event belied his prophecy? As we approach the last quarter of the century following the Preface of 1855, it is indeed clear that science and democracy have advanced apace, and that literature has reflected their progress; nevertheless, it is equally clear that the exalted expectations that gave such power to Whitman's prophetic criticism seem far less plausible than they were in the romantic epoch before the Civil War. We are not living in a time, and cannot foresee a time, characterized at once by an ardent belief in democracy, a high satisfaction with science, and an all-suffusing religious spirit. Since the late war, disillusionment, skepticism, and cynicism have crowded upon us. Determinism has robbed life of purpose and even of adventure. We are indulging, wearily, the hoary lusts of knowledge, sensation, and power. Romantic enthusiasm, romantic idealism, the romantic sense of 'the dignity of man' have faded away.

> The wealthiest man among us is the best:
> No grandeur now in nature or in book
> Delights us.   Rapine, avarice, expense,
> This is idolatry; and these we adore:
> Plain living and high thinking are no more.

So might a Wordsworth sing if living at this hour. Or so a Whitman:

> O I could sing such grandeurs and glories about you!
> You have not known what you are, you have slumber'd upon yourself
>   all your life,
> Your eyelids have been the same as closed most of the time,
> What you have done returns already in mockeries. . . .

Notwithstanding our advances in candor and hygiene, Whitman would doubtless pronounce the new America as 'morbid' as the old Europe. He would find even our science and our democracy morbid.

The nineteenth-century enthusiasm for science has passed away. It brings no thrill to read to-day, in the lay sermons of Huxley, that 'There is but one kind of knowledge and but one method of acquiring it'; that 'The man of science has learned to believe in justification, not by faith, but by verification'; that 'Natural knowledge, seeking to satisfy natural wants, has found the ideas which can alone still spiritual cravings.' It brings no thrill to read in John Burroughs, at the end of the century, 'Think you the man of science does not also find God? that Huxley and Darwin and Tyndall do not find God?' This sentence is from a pæan for science, 'The Light of Day'; thirteen years later, just before the war, Burroughs wrote an essay, 'In the Noon of Science,' more nearly in our mood. 'I too at times,' he admits, 'feel the weary weight of the material universe as it presses upon us in a hundred ways in our mechanical and scientific age.' 'Our civilization is like an engine running without a headlight.' 'We cannot vault into the saddle of the elemental forces and ride them and escape the danger of being ridden by them.' 'Physical science spoke in Huxley, and doubtless spoke accurately, when he said, "The soul stands related to the body as the bell of a clock to its works, and consciousness answers to the sound the bell gives out when struck." It is not a very comforting or inspiring comparison.' And increasingly, since entering into the noon of science, we have come to feel with Burroughs that science speaks accurately but not comfortingly. In proportion as science has strengthened its control of our minds and lives, we have grown restless and resentful and yet impotent. After more than two centuries devoted largely to placing man in nature, we are ready for an age devoted to getting him out again. Yet we can see no way of releasing man scientifically — the one possible way is impossible. Distrustful of science, we still make it the final court of appeal.

As for democracy, Whitman's other basis for an ideal future, the fact is that our mood is, once more, one of weary acceptance mixed with distrust. Though its claims upon us are less than those of science, we are committed to it for lack of any other promising working plan. Yet we can discern few indications that democracy might show itself a substantial basis for any such grandiose structure as that which Whitman prophesied. To be sure, we have witnessed, and shall doubtless continue to witness, an enormous concern with the average: a larger and larger application of the principle stated in the first of Whitman's extant notebooks, that to be democratic 'is to accept nothing except what is equally free and eligible to any body else.' The result of this equalization, and of the efficient organization taught by science, is a degree of standardization probably unparalleled in history.[1] Everywhere reflective persons fear that the equalitarianism of democracy inevitably tends to depress the superior and raise the inferior — to hold all to the standard of the average, the mediocre. Everywhere the fear is growing that in discarding absolutism we have rid ourselves of the divine right of the sovereign king only to assume the yoke of the divine right of the sovereign people. It is certain, at all events, that while democracy has shown expedition in providing for the average, it has thus far signally failed to attend to the individual — Whitman's main object. The remedy, according to Whitman's mode of thought, lies in a constant elevation of the standard of the average: the potential intelligence and wisdom of the masses will be actualized, in time, by the process of evolution. This, however, we have come to feel is a matter of faith. Our present science lends little support to an inherent 'dignity of man' or to his 'perfectibility.' It is wholly possible that the science of the future will lead us away from democracy toward some form of aristocracy.

The millennial expectations that Whitman built upon science and democracy, we are now well aware, rested upon insecure foundations. But the weakness of his prophecy may be better accounted for otherwise. It is the result of his using, in the main unconsciously, the romantic tradition in which

---

[1] Standardization appears to be most marked in America, especially in the Western States, where but a few decades ago the individualism of the frontier had afforded the amplest room for initiative and diversity. Compare Whitman's ideal community (above, p. 210) with the actual Main Street.

he must historically be placed. Gazing into the future, he saw there the romantic past from which he had averted his eyes. Notwithstanding his profession of modernity, his vision was in essentials that of the eighteenth and early nineteenth centuries, that of the naturistic stream of thought and feeling (with its modifying tributaries) running all the way from Shaftesbury to Emerson. He gives us the deism of Shaftesbury Transcendentalized. The perfection of nature, the natural goodness of man, 'the great pride of man in himself' offset with an emotional humanitarianism — these are the materials of a structure only slightly colored with modernity. His politics, his ethics, his religion belong to the past, even that facile 'religiousness' which he hoped would suffuse and complete the work of science and democracy. Like Rousseau he cried 'Back to nature' and praised at once the ego and the average; and like him he spurned reason and exalted the emotions. Like Walter Scott he was fascinated with the beauty of the feudal order, which he hoped democracy might emulate while developing great personalities. Like Wordsworth he sought communion with his soul in the challenging presence of nature, and sang the glory of the humble and obscure in a language and rhythm intended to correspond with the tenor of their lives. Like Carlyle and Emerson in their most romantic years, he looked to Transcendental ideas for his conception of the soul and the universe. Like Emerson he extolled the virtue of self-reliance, authenticated not only by the romantic tradition but also by the example of the American frontier. In ideal Western personality he saw a kind of homespun equivalent of the old feudal splendor, and in his verse he sought to convey the energy, initiative, freedom, simplicity, and barbaric yawp of the pioneer. He was a European romanticist modified by the American environment. He was the last of the great romanticists and his death in 1892 symbolically coincided with the passing of the frontier.

Consequently, Whitman erred fundamentally when he conceived himself as the first of a new order of bards. He had many great predecessors, but no great successors. We have beheld, to be sure, the miracle of a 'New Poetry' at a time when the muse was supposed to have fled from an ugly materialistic civilization, but it was not a poetry that Whitman could have approved, notwithstanding his influence upon it. The realistic movement that he encouraged was destined, not many years after the last 'Leaves of Grass,' to pervert his doctrine and betray his dearest hopes.

Whitman's relation to the realistic movement is similar to that of Wordsworth, who made his domain the 'real life' of ordinary men and sought to picture 'the infinite variety of natural appearances which had been unnoticed by the poets of any age or country.' Witnessing the activity of the scientific spirit — the presiding spirit of realism in art — Wordsworth held that if the man of science should create any important change in the condition of men or in their habitual impressions, the poet could be counted on to follow in the steps of the man of science — to give life ('flesh and blood') to his discoveries. The poet should effect a 'transfiguration' of the realities supplied by science. For 'Poetry is the breath and finer spirit of all knowledge; it is the impassioned expression which is in the countenance of all Science.' Now, this view of science and poetry, set forth in effete, feudal Europe in 1800, reappears in the ostensibly revolutionary Preface to 'Leaves of Grass' more than a half-century later. 'There shall be love,' writes the American bard, 'between the poet and the man of demonstrable science. In the beauty of poems are the tuft and final applause of science.' Demonstrable science is indeed the 'father' of poetry. A new kind of poetry will naturally result from the activities of the scientific spirit in the nineteenth century. In a later preface Whitman speaks of 'the entire revolution made by science in the poetic method.' In 'A

Backward Glance,' referring to an article on Wordsworth in an English periodical, he asserts that the poet must now emigrate to the larger area opened up by science, and transfigure the newly discovered realities by giving them flesh and blood and breath: 'Whatever may have been the case in years gone by, the true use for the imaginative faculty of modern times is to give ultimate vivification to facts, to science, and to common lives, endowing them with glows and glories and final illustriousness which belong to every real thing.' As the poetry of the past dealt with myths and fictions, the poetry of the New World will deal with 'realities and science'; for he is assured (to return to the first Preface) of 'the superiority of genuineness over all fiction and romance,' of the fact that (to go back even to the early notebooks) 'Man has not art enough to make the truth repulsive — nor of all the beautiful things of the universe is there any more beautiful than truth.' Here Whitman is speaking, surely, with the accent of the latter-day realist, and again when he says, elsewhere, that poetry must give us 'honest shapes,' without distortion or decoration, and that nothing is to be included 'for beauty's sake.'

Discarding thus the unrealities of romance in favor of the realities of science, Whitman joined in the fight which, as W. D. Howells said, 'realism is making to-day against effete romanticism,' and became one of the stalwart champions of a movement which actually Europe, not America, was leading toward triumph — toward a triumph not at all to his liking. His own was a 'mystic realism,' as he styled it, a realism inseparable from the Transcendental tradition. Toward a realism in harmony with science but not in harmony with his religiousness, his attitude was one of uncompromising opposition. 'Fearless of scoffing and of the ostent,' he exclaimed, 'let us take our stand, our ground, and never desert it, to confront the growing excess and arrogance of realism.' Of the type of realism loosely called photographic, he remarked, as Poe had done, that it is useless to try 'to repeat the material creation, by daguerreotyping the exact likeness by mortal mental means.' What he demanded resolutely, on the contrary, was a likeness transfigured by immortal spiritual means.

And yet he confronted the arrogance of realism in vain. It not only held on its way, but drew him with it, absorbed him in its cause. The last of the great Romantics must be conceived also as a precursor of the twentieth-century Realists, who have continued his innovations in diction and verseform, his inclusion of the supposedly commonplace and ugly, his unflinching frankness of statement, and in general that with which these aspects of his art were associated — his scientism. They have neglected, however, his warning against an infidelistic halfway science.[1] They have disregarded the fact that he completed his science with an optimistic emotional religion. At the same time they have neglected his optimistic democratic dogmas. The prevailing mood of realism has come to be pessimistic, so that nothing in Whitman is read to-day with more gusto than those passages in his criticism of modern life in which he reveals reason for pessimism.

These passages recur at intervals in his prose writings all the way from the year 1840 to the close of his career. Meditating at the age of twenty-one his 'wonderful and ponderous book,' he concluded to devote the principal part of the book to condemning the quest of riches and possessions. The evangelical note of this early plan was resumed in the 1855 Preface, permeating the whole of it and especially the passage on worldly and otherworldly prudence, the longest and most coherent paragraph in that preface. In the passage on political liberty there is also a spirited characterization of American politicians, 'swarms of cringers, suckers, doughfaces, lice of politics.' In later years, after more observation,

[1] See above, pp. 204–06.

these politicians proved for him that the elected rulers of democracy are as bad as the rulers of feudal Europe. Democracy, opening up humanity *en masse*, has, alas, brought out the bad along with the good qualities. It appears that 'Man is about the same, in the main, whether with despotism, or whether with freedom.' Indeed, 'There is not a bit of difference,' he exclaims roundly, recalling our shame during the administrations of Fillmore and Buchanan; and he writes an amazing characterization of the representatives of the sovereign people gathered in convention:

The members who composed it were, seven eighths of them, the meanest kind of bawling and blowing office-holders, office-seekers, pimps, malignants, conspirators, murderers, fancy men, custom-house clerks, contractors, kept-editors, spaniels well-train'd to carry and fetch, jobbers, infidels, disunionists, terrorists, mail-riflers, slave-catchers, pushers of slavery, creatures of the President, spies, bribers, compromisers, lobbyers, sponges, ruin'd sports, expell'd gamblers, policy-backers, monte-dealers, duellists, carriers of conceal'd weapons, deaf men, pimpled men, scarr'd inside with vile disease, gaudy outside with gold chains made from the people's money and harlot's money twisted together; crawling, serpentine men, the lousy combings and born freedom-sellers of the earth.

Such are our governors, duly catalogued by an optimist. As for the governed, we may turn to an address made by Whitman before the Brooklyn Art Union in 1851, where, after picturing the Greek ideal of man upon which he says 'imagination loves to dwell,' he presents with indignant satire the American ideal — 'the orthodox specimen of the man of the present time, approved by public opinion and the tailor': tight boot with high heel, trousers big at the ankle, neck swathed in many bands, supporting 'the modern shirt collar, bold as Columbus, stretching off into the unknown distance,' and 'to crown all, the fashionable hat, before which language has nothing to say'; and then, within, 'his utter vacuity of anything more important to him as a man than success in "business" — his religion what is written down in the books, or preached to him as he sits in his rich pew, by one whom he pays a round sum, and thinks it a bargain — his only interest in affairs of state, getting offices or jobs for himself or someone who pays him.' Elsewhere Whitman rejects the conventional standards of morality as 'constipated, narrow, and unphilosophic.' Actual American life he describes as 'canker'd, crude, superstitious, and rotten,' or as 'a sort of dry and flat Sahara.' Our life seems to be, one half of it, a feverish thirst for money; and the other half, a desire for amusement and killing time. No, Whitman is assuredly not blind to 'the highly artificial and materialistic bases of modern civilization, with the corresponding arrangements and methods of living, the force-infusion of intellect alone, the depraving influences of riches just as much as poverty, the absence of all high ideals in character — with the long series of tendencies, shapings, which few are strong enough to resist, and which now seem, with steam-engine speed, to be everywhere turning out the generations of humanity like uniform iron castings.' He concludes that if mechanism is not met with a force-infusion making for spiritualization, then 'our modern civilization, with all its improvements, is in vain, and we are on the road to a destiny, a status, equivalent, in its real world, to that of the fabled damned.'

This sort of criticism begets a lively response in our postwar period, on the part of realistic intellectuals — critics, novelists, playwrights — who have witnessed the further progress of the tendencies and shapings that Whitman had in view. Only, whereas Whitman, in his romantic and pioneer idealism, held to 'essential faith in man, above all his errors and wickedness,' the realists and naturalists of our day find no place for a sovereign soul in a humanity compounded of stupidity and folly and guided only by the fatality of instinct and environment. Inseparably if not happily wedded to science, they cannot follow Whitman in his assurance that truth is that which satisfies the soul; they derive their truth, rather, from economics, biology, and psychology. Their function they conceive to be, not to call forth the slumbering divinity of the average, but to describe with scientific integrity a very undivine average that generally accepts and occasionally revolts from the physical comforts and mechanical amusements provided by applied science.

In the essentials of his prophecy, Whitman, we must conclude, has been falsified by the event. But even if his prophecy had been or should hereafter be justified, it would be of curious interest rather than real importance. The central value of literary criticism is not accurate forecast, but determination of sound principles of writing. It is after all no great matter to predict the special assumptions and partial interests of the next age — the particular form of temporal provincialism that happens to be next in order. The true concern of the critic is not with any type of aberration, but with the enduring values that have been gradually illuminated by the secular aberrations of mankind.

CHAPTER V

THE TWENTIETH CENTURY: CONCLUSION

§1

WALT WHITMAN was the last of the commanding personalities in American criticism of the romantic age. His death coincided not only with the passing of the frontier, but also with the arrival of the Revolt of the Nineties, a movement which, despite its debt to him, inaugurated a realism hostile to the essentials of his creed. Through writers like Hamlin Garland, Stephen Crane, Edwin Arlington Robinson, Frank Norris, and Edith Wharton, all of whom published significant work before the end of the nineties, the realism of the early twentieth century clearly announced itself. In verse this realism received full expression, in the years following 1912, through the 'New Poetry' of Amy Lowell, Robert Frost, Vachel Lindsay, Edgar Lee Masters, Carl Sandburg, and many others; and when this bewildering chorus gradually subsided after 1916, the realistic programme was continued by a large number of prose writers, including Theodore Dreiser, Sherwood Anderson, and Sinclair Lewis. This energetic creative impulse was accompanied by a critical movement antagonistic to the romanticism of the nineteenth century and sympathetic with the aims of realism; criticism more and more became (to use its own big words) impressionistic, expressionistic, sociological, and psychological.

The critical revolt first plainly declared itself in 1913 — the time of the poetic revival — in a book entitled 'The Spirit of American Literature.' The author pronounced America to be not a democracy but 'a vast bourgeoisie'; depreciated its 'household poet' Longfellow as 'third-rate'; exalted Mark Twain and Walt Whitman; found such realists

as Howells and James fine but tame and thin; complained
that American writers as a whole are 'idealistic, sweet, delicate, nicely finished' and 'turn their backs on life, miss its
intensities, its significance'; conceived that 'the whole
country is crying out for those who will record it, satirize it,
chant it'; and joined the American Spirit in calling upon the
Muses for 'twelve novelists, ten poets, and eight dramatists,
to be delivered at the earliest possible moment.' [1] In the
welter of speculation that quickly ensued, the central issue
was the problem of an American culture, a problem that had
been posed in the eighteenth century and discussed with
intermittent vehemence through the nineteenth century.
Whitman, as we have seen, pointed out that America had
achieved political independence in the eighteenth century
and economic independence in the nineteenth, but that her
cultural independence lay in the future. In the half-century
after 'Democratic Vistas' this higher independence appeared
no nearer attainment; indeed, the war with Germany, while
rendering America foremost in the world in respect to political and economic power, only accentuated the impotence of
her culture. It is not surprising that our intellectuals, young
and old, should feel that the immemorial problem of a native
cultural tradition has acquired a certain urgency, and that
they should be making strenuous efforts to solve it.

One cannot but doubt, however, whether the majority of
our critics are likely to fare better than Whitman, inasmuch
as their approach to the problem is essentially his. Like

[1] After John Macy, some of the critics who rose to prominence were Van
Wyck Brooks, Randolph Bourne, H. L. Mencken, Stuart Sherman, Carl Van
Doren, Henry S. Canby, Lewis Mumford, and Harold E. Stearns, certain of
whom performed valuable service through their powers of unhampered observation or refreshing satire. Although some of the foregoing critics differed
widely from one another, a number were sufficiently like-minded to find a place
among the Thirty Americans who in 1922 surveyed *Civilization in the United
States*. In more recent years a host of critics and biographers have sought to
forward, through books and the journals of opinion, the reinterpretation of
American life and letters in terms of modern thought, doubting almost everything except modern thought — in some cases that as well.

Whitman, they are living in the present (that is, the recent past) and looking into a blank future. If few of them will hazard the rôle of the prophetic critic, nearly all are contemporary critics — eager to maintain the open mind, quick to seize upon what seems most attractice and hopeful at the moment. Like Whitman, nearly all of them are in revolt against a past that they do not really know, often do not in the least care to know: their vital memories, for the most past, stop with Whitman himself, behind whom the past is a dim otherness and vast irrelevance. Revolting against romanticism and frontier crudity, they are actually dealing with the problem of an American culture and literature, to a large extent, in the romantic and frontier spirit. They are more interested in the national 'genius' than in the broadly human; they affect self-reliance rather than reliance upon the experience of the past; they are impelled by a mood of adventure more than by a will to reform with the aid of old standards. They keep in the foreground of their minds the desire for national individuality, that desire, typical of the nineteenth century, which everywhere found expression in literature based upon the national experience and in politics based upon the theory of the national state. They still ignore, almost as patently as our post-Revolutionary patriots, the fact that a national culture is a slow growth and cannot be improvised in a century or two. They still ignore the fact that America has never been shut off from the rest of the world, as the old nations substantially were, and that the multiplying mechanisms of communication have rendered solitary development hereafter impossible. They are still unable to realize that the national soul cannot be asserted but must be suffered to assert itself. They are still unable to realize that, while it would be interesting for us to be American, it is far more important for us to be human, and that while we cannot know how to become American, we can know reasonably well how to become human.

Whitman himself, as these contemporary critics fail to remember, more and more came to understand that our proper task is not one of rejection and isolation, but one of acceptance and assimilation. Even in his first Preface he mitigated his burial of the dead past with his declaration that, through evolution, the past lived in the present. By 1881, however, he came to feel that this declaration did not adequately state the bond of past and present, Europe and America. Whether because of deeper insight or, as he suggested, because of the altered vision of old age and invalidism, he was compelled to restate the matter as follows:

Years ago I thought Americans ought to strike out separate, and have expressions of their own in highest literature. I think so still, and more decidedly than ever. But those convictions are now strongly temper'd by some additional points. ... I see that this world of the West [America], as part of all, fuses inseparably with the East [Europe], and with all, as time does — the ever new yet old, old human race — 'the same subject continued,' as the novels of our grandfathers had it for chapter-heads. If we are not to hospitably receive and complete the inaugurations of the old civilizations, and change their small scale to the largest, broadest scale, what on earth are we for?

In a later passage of the same essay, pursuing the idea of hospitable reception, Whitman frankly suggested that perhaps the best thing we can do is 'to saturate ourselves with, and continue to give imitations, yet awhile, of the æsthetic models, supplies, of that past and of those lands we spring from,' not merely England, but in addition 'stately and devout Spain, courteous France, profound Germany, the manly Scandinavian lands, Italy's art race, and always the mystic Orient.' [1] The next year, upon the death of Long-

[1] 'Poetry To-day in America,' *Prose Works*, II, 212, 228. He gave the same advice repeatedly. Holding that we have relied too exclusively upon England, he urged, on one occasion, a reception of Spanish culture ('The Spanish Element in Our Nationality,' II, 116–19) and on two occasions a reception of the culture of 'all former lands' from India and Greece to Italy, France, and Spain. ('British Literature,' II, 274–77; 'Little or Nothing New, After All,' II, 296.)

fellow, Whitman wrote in praise of him as the type of poet — poet of gentle humanity — needed for self-assertive modern America, and endorsed 'what I have heard Longfellow himself say, that were the New World to be worthily original, and announce herself and her own heroes, she must be well saturated with the originality of others, and respectfully consider the heroes that lived before Agamemnon.' If it ever occurred to him to apply this unflinchingly to himself, Whitman may well have questioned whether his own work was, after all, worthily original, whether he had sufficiently saturated himself with the originality of the European writers of the past.[1] The same doubt might well be entertained to-day by not a few of our most prominent creative and critical writers, who have perhaps not even immersed themselves, as Whitman did, in the King James Bible and in Shakspere. They have scant inclination to heed his warning against a smart and superficial modernity, his demand that we use 'hourly' the heritage of the past, and his reminder that 'at present, and doubtless long ahead, a certain humility would well become us.'

Now, this humility is out of the question until we face in all candor the fact that independence of the past is forever delusive. Nothing is more certain than the law of continuity, by virtue of which an age loosely termed revolutionary derives its formative ideas from the age previous. The great revolution at the close of the eighteenth century, for example, manifested in the political realm by the French Revolution

Of these lands we are 'inextricably the heirs.' While there are national differences, the story of mankind, Whitman repeats, is ever 'the same subject continued' — 'the same old humanity — the same old heart and brain.' More and more he looked, in the manner of Matthew Arnold, for correctives to offset national exaggeration and to render possible a more representative humanity.

[1] Possibly this doubt found voice in the following passage in 'A Backward Glance': 'Modern science and democracy seem'd to be throwing out their challenge to poetry to put them in its statements in contradistinction to the songs and myths of the past. As I see it now (perhaps too late), I have unwittingly taken up that challenge and made an attempt at such statements — which I certainly would not assume to do now, knowing more clearly what it means.'

and in the intellectual and artistic realm by the Romantic Movement, not only reacted against certain interests of the eighteenth century, but also cultivated other interests and brought them to fruition. Thus, a poem like 'Tintern Abbey,' while indeed profoundly original, was the result of more than a century of rational sensationalism; and when Emerson in 'Nature' sought to enjoy an original relation with the universe, he actually effected a complex interweaving of Platonism, deism, and German idealism. Whitman's fulfillment of nineteenth-century modes of thought and feeling has been indicated in the preceding chapter. The same continuity might be readily illustrated in any department of human activity in any period of history. And along with continuity we must reckon also with the perennial tendency of thought to return upon itself by reviving ideas and values long neglected. The Renaissance revived elements of ancient humanism, the Romantic Movement revived elements of the Middle Ages and the Renaissance. To recur to the examples above, Wordsworth's verse harks back to Milton and Shakspere and the ballads, Emerson drew heavily upon Plato and the Cambridge Platonists, and Whitman derived hints for his 'free' verse from the rhythmical patterns of the English Bible. Through continuity and revivalism, the past is inescapable.

This is obvious. But the obvious is sometimes curiously ignored, and it is surely one of the more modest functions of criticism to perceive the obvious, and if necessary point it out to creative writers elate in their contemporaneity. Nothing is more necessary to-day, in this age that prides itself upon its superiority to the past even while its faith in progress is faltering, than that we should ask ourselves, in the honest, rational manner that we affect, what past we are actually using, and whether that past contains all that we need.

§2

The past we are actually using, the past that has shaped our current conception of man and the universe, is the age of naturism that stretches from the seventeenth century to the present. On the far side of this age lie the faith of the Reformation, the humanism of the Renaissance, the faith of the Middle Ages, and the humanism of ancient Rome and Greece: more than twenty centuries of experience, containing virtually all the greatest figures in literature. On the near side of the seventeenth century lie the rationalism and skepticism of the epoch before the French Revolution, the aspiring emotionalism of the Romantic Movement, and the rationalism and skepticism of the nineteenth and early twentieth centuries: less than three centuries of experience, expressed in a literature fascinating in its variety but tending to the incomplete and tangential rather than to wholeness and centrality. The present is the issue of this comparatively recent past.

Although, strictly speaking, no movement can well be said to have had a beginning, it may assist our thought if we will follow Huxley in dating our modern time from an inconspicuous event in 1645 — the holding of meetings in London by a few students desirous of 'improving natural knowledge.' For this obscure inception of the Royal Society was the proximate beginning of a movement destined, says Huxley, not only to confer immense practical benefits on men, but also to effect 'a revolution in their conceptions of the universe and of themselves' and to alter profoundly 'their modes of thinking and their views of right and wrong.' [1] Before the

[1] For an admirable characterization of seventeenth-century currents of thought, in relation to literature, see Edwin Greenlaw's lecture on 'The New Science and English Literature in the Seventeenth Century' (*Johns Hopkins Alumni Magazine*, XIII, 1925, pp. 331–59). The dominant tendencies are set forth as: (1) a 'new realism,' or sense of fact, reliance upon observation and experiment, (2) the overthrow of authority in favor of free inquiry, and (3) the growth of faith in progress, impelling men to improve their estate in the mundane world.

close of that century, science had made vast strides, notably
through the genius of Newton, and philosophy had undertaken a fresh start in the rationalism of Descartes, Hobbes,
and Locke, followed early in the next century by the elegant
sentimentalism of Shaftesbury. It became clear to the intellectuals of the eighteenth century that a supernatural
revelation of religious or ethical truth was superfluous, that
the physical universe itself was a perfect revelation of God,
and that man was naturally good and perfectible. Rationalism and sentimentalism, cool analysis and enthusiastic feeling
— these were divergent manifestations of the same tendency,
an extraordinary faith in nature. The way was thus prepared
for the great literary apostle of nature, Rousseau, who employed in her service the weapons of both abstract logic and
a vehement and contagious enthusiasm; and by Rousseau
the way was prepared, throughout Europe, for the Romantic
Movement. Man being naturally good, his instincts right
when unhindered, it was believed that evil must be the result
of social institutions. It is conventions, and not natural
depravity, that render actual life so ugly and unhappy and
untrue, and it is through the assertion of self that man may
win his due happiness and perceive beauty and truth. The
inalienable dignity of man was boldly announced by the
geniuses of the 'Sturm und Drang,' by the Transcendental
philosophy, and by the romantic schools of the several
European countries and of America. In the temporal sphere
sovereignty passed from kings to man, and in the spiritual
sphere from God to man. Perhaps the ultimate romantic
ideal has nowhere been better pictured than in Shelley's
rapturous vision of the day that shall liberate men at last
from 'the pride of kings and priests':

> The loathsome mask has fallen, the man remains
> Sceptreless, free, uncircumscribed, — but man
> Equal, unclassed, tribeless, and nationless,
> Exempt from awe, worship, degree, the king
> Over himself.

Actual life, however, persistently refused to submit to the romantic vision of ideal life, and by obstruction and long postponement it at length broke the facile optimism of the Cause of Man. Probably its main instrument was that very rationalistic spirit which had supplied the doctrines of sentimentalism and romanticism. At first allies, rationalism and sentimentalism had drawn farther and farther apart. Cool analysis of nature was the way of science, enthusiastic feeling for nature the way of romanticism. This disunion proved fatal to the more exalted pretensions of romanticism. The dignity of man, based upon his natural desires, had scarcely been triumphantly proclaimed when it was disproved (so it seemed) by the natural sciences, which proclaimed that not man but nature was sovereign, that, instead of being king over himself and over nature, man was merely one of nature's myriads of subjects. The optimism associated with the emotional justification of the natural man passed into the pessimism associated with the biological justification of the natural man. From Wordsworth the way leads, through Tennyson, to Thomas Hardy. By means of evolutionary science, the actual overcame the ideal, and correspondingly realism and naturalism overcame romanticism.

The fact that realism was a reaction against romanticism must not be permitted, however, to obscure their essential kinship. Both ranged their forces in opposition to the humanistic and religious traditions of the past, and when they also opposed each other were merely engaged in civil warfare. This internal conflict did not and could not result in the complete victory of either side, because at heart the two sides were in agreement. Alike they were animated with the same purpose of placing man in nature, the one praising his dignity in that position, the other revealing his indignity. Their hostility to each other, unlike their hostility to old traditions, had an air of unreality. It is not surprising to find that realism frequently admits romantic elements, and that its progress has been repeatedly interrupted by romantic revivals. Nor is it surprising to find critics to-day, weary of the oppressive rule of realism, calling for more romanticism, since the passage from the one to the other is so easy: they dwell, in discord, under the same roof.

Such is the past that we are using in our present literature. If here in America our conscious memories stop with Whitman, our unconscious memories stop with the foundation of the Royal Society and the philosophy of Shaftesbury. Much of our reading public is still sentimental and romantic in its taste, still willing to assume (at least while a pure, wholesome story is unfolding) that man is naturally good and lovely; and our more characteristic readers are professedly realistic and naturalistic, still willing to assume (at least while a veracious document is progressing) that man is naturally unaccountable and generally ugly. In either case it is assumed that man is an unitary not a dual being, that his 'self' is his supreme concern, and that the creative expression of the self must not be hindered from without by convention nor from within by inhibition. This self, the only good of which we are sure, is characterized by an expansive pride and an expansive sympathy — the two coöperating virtues in the ethics of Rousseau and Whitman. A creed of this kind, said to be authenticated either by the romantic 'heart' or by biological and psychological theory, is conceived as giving full play to the individual and perhaps the needful amount of protection to society.

Now, only the reactionary or fundamentalist mind, zealous in the service of a lost cause, will venture to assert that our modern scheme of man and the universe is totally false. Granting that, like all schemes that have obtained extended credence, it is partly sound and partly unsound, the critical mind in quest of enduring standards will confidently look for the positive contribution of the naturistic movement and endeavor to define that contribution. What has our accumulating naturistic tradition added to the traditions of humanism and religion?

It would be superficial to answer that it has given us an immense amount of natural knowledge, since knowledge has no 'value' in itself, apart from a valuer. We must restate the question, and ask: What has man learned of value to himself? To this we may answer with assurance: he has come to feel and know, as never before, his relation with the physical universe. Judea and Greece, the sources of the older European culture, devoted themselves most effectually to realizing those aspects of man which appear to be independent of nature. It was left for modern Europe, especially since the seventeenth century, to devote itself to realizing those aspects of man which appear to be dependent upon nature. This it has done, especially in romanticism, by frankly recognizing, expressing, and exalting man's natural impulses; and, especially in science and realism, by seeking to understand and faithfully to represent these impulses. To arrive at a realization of man's naturalness, as well as his humanity or divinity, was assuredly of high importance. We must concede that the 'wisdom of the ages' — the old established views of life — rested in part upon ignorance. Our naturistic centuries, in addition to their demolishment of myth and superstition, have done valuable service in acquainting man intimately with the bond that exists between him and external nature. They have thrown a flood of light upon those natural impulses which had been but slightly understood by an old humanism seeking to control them and an old religion ever inclined to extirpate them. We now perceive, as never before, the folly of endeavoring to extirpate these natural impulses and the magnitude of the task of controlling them. We are right in seeking to realize, if not to justify, the ways of nature to man.

It is one thing to question and revise the old established views of life; it is, however, quite another thing to abandon them without stopping to examine their radical credentials. If the old views rested in part upon ignorance of nature, our revolutionary views rest in part upon ignorance of the past. While romanticism has been priding itself upon its universal sympathy and understanding, and scientific realism upon its honest search for truth, both alike have failed to penetrate to the essentials of the old views and to disengage them from the accidents. The modern world has been provincially intent upon its own special achievement and arrogantly indifferent to the achievement of the past. A curious consequence of this fact is a persistent confusion between the values derivable from naturism and the values inherited from humanism and religion. Blindly we ascribe to 'nature and the language of the sense' elements of our experience that are actually the consequence of centuries of human ('unnatural') culture, inherited through books, tradition, institutions, and the like. This was the error of Wordsworth, for example, in 'Tintern Abbey,' though he corrected it in later years, perceiving that even in his Revolutionary ardor the past had been vital in him: 'I . . . carried about me,' he said,

> The experience of past ages, as, through help
> Of books and common life, it makes sure way
> To youthful minds.[1]

Sure way it makes, indeed, not alone to youthful but equally to mature minds, for it enshrines truths that perish never, central truths of life that have no witness in nature but that cannot be explained away by any philosophy of nature. When it becomes possible to define the unacknowledged debt of naturism to the experience of past ages, we shall doubtless be astonished to discover how slight the constructive power of naturism actually is, how small its contribution will be to the synthesis of the future. The need of our time can hardly be a continuance of our uncritical skepticism as to the beliefs of the past, but rather a critical skepticism as to the beliefs of the present.

[1] *The Prelude*, ix, ll. 331–37.

§3

This need is already felt. Some of the most cherished enthusiasms of the naturistic age, such as progress, romanticism, democracy, nationalism, have lost their warmth; the ultimate competence of science is questioned; realistic and naturalistic art appears to have entered upon disintegration and decadence. The great war has brought in its train a mood of disillusionment unfavorable to the reigning ideas of the century that culminated in the war, and a growing sense of the need for both social and intellectual reconstruction. The skepticism formerly applied to the wisdom of the ages is now frequently applied to the wisdom of our own age. Although much of this new skepticism is as puerile and wholesale as the old, more and more of it is drawing to the support of a genuinely critical movement that may be traced back, in this country, to Emerson and Lowell.

Emerson and Lowell, as we have seen, were by no means wholly committed to the modern programme. Their vital memories reached far into the past, Lowell's to Dante and Emerson's to Plato. With an integrity equal to our own, they refused to accept anything on authority and submitted all tradition to free inquiry, seeking to disengage the permanent from the transitory elements in tradition and to reconcile the permanent elements with whatever appeared to be sound in the modern programme. Their task was continued by Charles Eliot Norton, and in the next generation by a number of critics and scholars who have been called 'the new humanists.' [1] 'These all attend to one or another phase of the cleavage between man's way and nature's way — a dualism which, whether it cut between man and external nature, or between the "natural man" and the "spiritual man" within; whether it emphasize the "inner check" in any of its various modes, or, as against the naturalistic "education of the senses," commend to man the study of his own humane tradi-

[1] *Cambridge History of American Literature*, IV, 491.

tion, and summon him to take up the racial torch and hand it on — in any case places man's hope not upon what nature, whether within or without, may do for him, but upon his making himself more completely human.' This is a broad statement of a creed that has in recent years steadily acquired fresh adherents and fresh formulation.[1] The strength of this critical movement may be measured by the vehemence of the attacks upon it by the defenders of the old naturism. They object to the sharp clearness of the humanist creed, yet show their failure to understand it — condemning it, paradoxically, as both classical in its emphasis on form and romantic in its emphasis on imagination, and also as both intellectualistic and moralistic ('puritanical'). If it is indeed all of these, it would seem to be immune from the charge which they press most violently of all: that it is rigid and narrow.

These attacks appeal to prejudices that have been fixed in our minds by naturistic modes of thought. A better way to consider the reconstruction proposed by the new humanism would be to examine its fundamental assumptions.

The first of these assumptions is that assumptions are inevitable, since every conception of life ultimately rests upon them. Absolute skepticism, if there were such a thing, would rest upon the assumption that unlimited doubt is necessary, a position that not even Anatole France was willing to take:

I have feared those two words, full of a formidable sterility, 'I doubt.' So powerful are they that the mouth that has once pronounced them truly is for ever sealed, and can never reopen. If one doubts, one must keep silent; for, whatever one may discourse about, to speak is to affirm. Since I had not the courage for silence

[1] The 'new humanists' named in the *Cambridge History* are Paul Elmer More, Irving Babbitt, John Jay Chapman, and George Edward Woodberry. To these might be added W. C. Brownell, F. J. Mather, Jr., P. H. Frye, William F. Giese, Barry Cerf, Samuel Strauss, Stuart Sherman (especially in his earlier work), Robert Shafer, P. H. Houston, G. R. Elliott, and younger men whose names are less familiar.

and renunciation, I willed to believe and did so. I at least believed in the relativity of things, and the succession of phenomena.[1]

Practically, silence is impossible, absolute skepticism is impossible. Practically, we live by belief, by faith, by that which we provisionally *know*: that which appears to us most nearly to correspond with reality, or rather with experience, or rather still with those portions of experience that we choose to value. Shrinking from the specter of sterility — that everlasting No — we make our affirmations, to-day no less than in the past, identifying our belief with the truth. Of this fact few naturists in our time seem to be aware. For the most part they dogmatically affirm that they can know and explain man and the universe, and patiently proceed to reduce everything in experience to a deterministic monism. In order to attain this conclusion, they assume, first, the final validity of reason, declaring their perfect faith in it, despite the testimony of the history of philosophy that faith in reason may lead to bewilderingly diverse doctrines. They therefore assume, secondly, that the reality to be explored by reason is the succession of phenomena, the realm of physical science; and thirdly, that whatever experience appears to conflict with this reality must be explained — if necessary, explained away — in terms of this natural reality. Such are the assumptions of our current naturistic thought that prides itself upon its avoidance of mere 'faith'; such are the assumptions that underlie the great bulk of our so-called realistic and naturalistic literature, and of the criticism that interprets and encourages this literature. These assumptions we may now compare with the further assumptions of humanism.

Humanism assumes, secondly, that the essential elements of human experience are precisely those which appear to conflict with the reality explored by naturism. It recognizes, indeed, the service of naturism: the service of romanticism in

---

[1] *On Life and Letters*, Third Series, xi. So, too, Plato had taught that a faithful sensationalism must be speechless.

showing the power of the natural man's impulses, the service
of biology in showing the physical union of man with nature,
the service of psychology in showing the instinctive processes
that man shares with other forms of life; for thus has been
demonstrated, if nothing else, the magnitude of the problem
of morality. Yet exactly here, in the realm of the moral or
specifically human, our modern faith is impotent. Nature,
apparently blind and pitiless, indifferent to all that we value
most, affords no light in our search for a *modus vivendi* in a
state of society. In vain do we seek in her for standards of
justice, self-restraint, moderation, gentleness; in vain for a
principle of rational or spiritual guidance adequate for human
life as we know it. The ethical problem cannot be illuminated
by a naturistic philosophy which merely affirms, optimisti-
cally or pessimistically, that man is motivated by natural instinct, or informs us, at best, how his moral habits may be
'explained' by the process of evolution. In the motion
picture of reality that science offers there are no values, but
only quantitative measurements of force, mass, etc. Yet
values are in fact the main concern of man, the perennial object of his ardent striving.[1]

Accordingly, the central assumption of humanism is that
of a dualism of man and nature, as opposed to the monism assumed by naturism. Conceding, with Emerson, the possibility that the contrasting realms of the human and the
natural might be reconciled if we could behold them both *ab
extra* — that in the highest view the ancient maxim 'Know
Thyself' and the modern 'Study Nature' may offer two ap-

[1] Science measures what are significantly called *facts*, i.e., things done,
phenomenal happenings viewed in retrospect. It believes that all the facts can
be found, and that when they have been found, it will also be able to predict
succeeding steps in evolution. These steps could then be measured quantitatively. A few less confident scientists, however, believe that, even if our
knowledge of the past were complete, we could discern nothing in the past that
would enable us to foresee the variations of the future. They thus point to a
differentiating principle of pivotal importance, and confess their inability, as
scientists, to deal with it.

proaches to the same reality — humanism is skeptical of all such speculation based upon the assumption of an underlying unity and is convinced that, practically, the rightful concern of man is his humanity, his world of value and quality that marks him off from a merely quantitative natural order.

In assuming this dualism, humanism appeals to the authority of the actual experience of mankind, past and present. Of the trend of past experience there can be no doubt; both of the old guiding traditions, the Greek and the Christian, however different outwardly, were absolutely at one in their sharp contrast between the human and the natural. Scarcely more doubtful is the trend of present experience; even in an age when the official philosophy is monistic, the working philosophy of the vast majority of mankind is still dualistic. Men are still conscious of an inner conflict, insusceptible of reconciliation, between the expression of natural desire and the will to conform to a standard of values. The failure of naturism to define new values has resulted in the continued application of the essentials of the classical and Christian traditions, even on the part of countless persons who profess the rejection of all tradition. Few indeed are those who are living 'according to nature,' expressing the 'self' (that is, temperament) in disregard of convention without and inhibition within; most men are still living 'according to society,' patterning themselves in harmony with a general code and consequently restraining themselves. It is still the belief of most men (if by no means their invariable practice) that perfection is a worthy end, that it depends upon the control of the natural by the human, and that it necessitates loyalty to standards of truth and justice which cannot be conceived as natural but which are none the less binding. On the one side is the inclination of nature, sufficient for the conduct of the animal creation but insufficient for the conduct of man; on the other side, the authority of conscience (which remains a fact, even when 'accounted for') and the authority of the laws,

written and unwritten, that give direction to the activities of
the conscience. These laws are the product of the convention-
making power that man incessantly exerts, in revolutionary
no less than in stable ages:

> As if his whole vocation
> Were endless imitation.

Of necessity, a natural, spontaneous action is rare, since, even
when only once repeated, it is already in danger of moving
toward a convention or social habit. Unconventionality itself quickly becomes conventional, as one may observe, in
any period, among the young or the old who cultivate eman-
cipation from conventions that do not please them. Thus do
the most natural people bear witness to their humanity.

Finally, humanism assumes the freedom of the will to conform to a standard of values, as opposed to the deterministic
assumption of naturism. While acknowledging that reason
leads readily to a belief in necessity, whether that necessity
be spiritual or mechanical, humanism is unwilling to follow
reason when it proposes a conclusion at variance with the
manifest facts of experience. It is a matter of universal experience that we assume our power to will our next actions;
life appears to be impossible on other terms. Common sense,
as well as intuition, dictates the assumption of choice. This
is the precarious but ineluctible dignity of man, clearly affirmed by Greek humanism and by Christianity, confusedly
promulgated by a romanticism that lost itself in nature, and
still accepted in practice by a scientific age that rejects it in
theory. We may believe, like Browning's Andrea, that we are
in God's hand, or, like the behaviorist, that we are in Nature's
hand, and yet actually we shall proceed to carry out the actions we have determined upon, in the conviction that they
represent our own free choice. While the ultimate criterion
of our actions may be God or Nature, in either case we assume, along with the Victorian Tennyson, that

Our wills are ours, to make them thine,

and long with the mediæval Dante, that

... la sua volontate è nostra pace.

In judging the acts of our fellows in the intercourse of daily life, we assume that they also are free to choose, or, as we prefer to say when their actions affect ourselves, that they are *responsible* for what they do. Our theoretical belief in the sovereignty of Providence or in the fatality of instinct and environment is forgotten in the practical experience of life.

Such have always been the assumptions of humanism. In opposition to the assumptions of naturism — first, that it makes no assumptions, secondly, that reason is the only sure guide, thirdly, that the reality found by reason consists of the phenomenal order, and fourthly, that no specifically human reality exists — humanism to-day, as in the past, assumes, first, that assumptions are unavoidable, secondly, that the essential reality of experience is not natural but ethical, thirdly, that there is a sharp dualism between man and nature, and fourthly, that man's will is free. Reflecting upon life in the light of these premises, humanism arrives at a doctrine and a discipline that may be briefly stated as follows:

1. An adequate human standard calls for *completeness*; it demands the cultivation of every part of human nature, including 'natural' human nature. It suppresses nothing.

2. But it also calls for *proportion*: it demands the harmony of the parts with the whole. Instead of 'accepting life' indiscriminately, it imposes a scale of values.

3. This complete, proportionate standard may be said to consist of the *normally or typically human*. It is concerned with the central and the universal, not the eccentric and the idiosyncratic. It is concerned with a permanently valid ethos, not with any temporary code of conventional society.

4. Although such an ethos has never existed, it has been

approximated in the great ages of *the past*, to which humanism accordingly looks for guidance. It looks chiefly toward Greece, where it still finds its best examples (in sculpture, in Homer and Sophocles, in Plato and Aristotle); also toward Rome (Virgil, Horace), toward the Christian tradition (Jesus, Paul, Augustine, Francis of Assisi), toward the Orient (Buddha, Confucius), toward moderns like Shakspere, Milton, and Goethe. Selecting the 'constants' that appear to be worthy of preservation, humanism seeks to transcend the specialism that limits all ages in the past as well as the present age.

5. Unlike romanticism, which in its quest of a natural ethos repudiated the logical faculty, humanism is always true to its Hellenic origin in its faith in *reason*. It seeks to deal positively with the whole of experience, including those elements of experience that do not fall within the scope of what is termed science.

6. Unlike the conceptions of life that grow out of science, humanism seeks to press beyond reason by the use of *intuition* or *imagination*, following the example of the most poetical of Hellenic philosophers, who resorted again and again to symbol and myth, and the example of the foremost Christian poet when he forsook the guidance of Virgil in favor of that of Beatrice. Humanism holds that, after reason has brought us before the veil that shrouds truth, a power above the reason is needed to cope with what Goethe termed 'the illusion of a higher reality.' This power above the reason is the human or ethical imagination, as distinguished from the natural or pathetic imagination, which is below the reason.[1]

[1] The excellence of Greek art may be said to lie in its success in achieving unified form while suggesting an ethical infinite. The romantic critics employed an insidious flattery when they credited Greek art with executing its humanistic aim 'in the utmost perfection,' in contrast with modern art, which 'can only do justice to its endeavors after what is infinite by approximation.' (A. W. Schlegel, *Dramatic Art and Literature*, Lecture I; cf. Coleridge, *Works*, IV, 29, and Lowell, *Prose Works*, IV, 232–35, *Poetical Works*, IV, 45–46.) This con-

7. The ultimate ethical principle is that of *restraint* or *control*, indicated alike by practical experience and by the light of reason and the ethical imagination. There is a law for man and a law for thing. That which is law in nature becomes anarchy when surrendered to by man — the anarchy of wandering desires and blind impulses, the morbid ebb and flow of unhindered temperament, the restless oscillations of expansive pride and expansive sympathy. This anarchy is the product of romanticism and naturalism in their pure state, that is, when they do not wittingly or unwittingly draw upon the humanistic or religious tradition. As Coleridge perceived,

> The Sensual and the Dark rebel in vain,
> Slaves by their own compulsion!

Freedom and power and happiness cannot be won by those who practice the modern philosophy of what is loosely termed 'self-expression.' They can be won only when the energies of the instinctive self have been harnessed by the ethical self:

> The winged Courser, like a gen'rous Horse,
> Shows most true Mettle when you *check* his Course.

Humanism remembers, to be sure, that the Popean pseudo-classicists as well as the Puritans, instead of checking the steed, generally locked him in the stable, where he might indeed rebel in vain; it remembers always the need of freedom, which it defines as liberation from outer constraints and subjection to inner law. It asserts that this inner law of concentration, when it has eagerly expansive senses and emotional

---

trast between the Greek perfection within fixed limits and the modern imperfection arising from infinite aspiration involves a twofold confusion: first, a confusion of the Christian aspiration toward the Infinite with the romantic yearning for the limitless and indefinite, the one quenching desire and the other exalting it; and secondly, a confusion of the classical aspiration toward an ethical infinite with the romantic yearning for the limitless and indefinite. The scholarship of the nineteenth century has made it clear that the Greeks, even in the 'definite' forms of their sculpture, sought to express, as Professor Gardner says, an 'inexhaustible idealism' — an endless approximation.

energies to command, is the true source of power, of character, of elevation, of happiness.[1]

8. This center to which humanism refers everything, this centripetal energy which counteracts the multifarious centrifugal impulses, this magnetic will which draws the flux of our sensations toward it while itself remaining at rest, is the reality that gives rise to religion. Pure humanism is content to describe it thus in physical terms, as an observed fact of experience; it hesitates to pass beyond its experimental knowledge to the dogmatic affirmations of any of the great religions. It cannot bring itself to accept a formal theology (any

[1] H. S. Canby has well described (*Definitions*, 1922, pp. 165–66) the 'anti-Puritans' of twentieth-century literature who, assuming that all things have been proved false except their desires, make a philosophy of these desires. Their truth they derive from psychoanalysis, which they interpret to be a scientific justification of the frank expression of desires. They are quite unaware, however, that the traditional humanistic and religious values actually hold an important place in the popular books on psychotherapy. Dr. A. F. Riggs, for example, tells us that animals act 'presumably without choice or without reason. On the other hand, the human being presides over the conflict of his own instincts, felt by him as a conflict of emotions. He presides over this conflict with intelligence and with a consciousness of the power and necessity of choice.' 'It is like guiding spirited horses — you guide, they obey, not their own impulse, but your will.' 'It is when intelligence and will are used to realize an ideal through an action which is contrary to instinctive demands, that animal behavior rises to the dignity of human conduct.' (*Just Nerves*, 1922.) In another book Dr. J. A. Jackson and Helen M. Salisbury inform us that 'Character is what we do with our instincts. . . . We may follow our primal desires, we may deny their existence, or we may use them for ends which are in harmony with our lives as we want them to be.' 'What Paul calls the law of his members warring against the law of his mind is simply what we call to-day the instinctive desires coming into conflict with our conscious ideal.' (*Outwitting Our Nerves*, 1922.) In a third book we may read that Jesus, the perfect man, illustrates 'the right expression of power. He exerts it *over* himself, and *on behalf of* others. His self-mastery is complete, so that the claims of body and mind are acceded to or denied at will.' He is contrasted with 'the primitive man, whose instinctive energy pushes forth to destroy rather than to build up.' (G. Coster, *Psychoanalysis for Normal People*, 1926.) All of these books call to us, with the ancient Greek sage, 'Know Thyself,' and exhort us to conversion, which they term sublimation, and to the quest of salvation, which they term mental and physical health (*mens sana in corpore sano*). Their psychology is new, after all, chiefly in showing the power and the subtlety of that instinctive life the control of which renders man human. The humanist may be grateful for this new light on the appetitive principle in the Aristotelian ethics; the religionist, for this new light on the devil.

more than it can accept a romantic idealism) that has been set up in defiance of reason, for it holds that the value of supernatural intuition must be tested by the intellect. Again, it fears the asceticism to which religion tends in consequence of a too harsh dualism of the flesh and the spirit, for, as we have said, humanism calls for completeness, wishing to use and not annihilate dangerous forces. Unlike religion, it assigns an important place to the instruments of both science and art. Nevertheless, it agrees with religion in its perception of the ethical will as a power above the ordinary self, an impersonal reality in which all men may share despite the diversity of personal temperament and toward which their attitude must be one of subjection. This perception, immensely strengthened for us by Christianity, was already present in the humanism of the Greeks, who saw that the unpardonable sin is insolence or presumption, an overweening pride of passion or reason, a failure to be mindful of the Nemesis that lies in wait for disproportionate self-assertion. Humanism, no less than religion, enjoins the virtue of *humility*.

From what has been said, it should be clear that humanism, like Greek philosophy, 'begins with science and not with religion,' and that it is 'a serious endeavor to understand the world and man, having for its chief aim the discovery of the right way of life and the conversion of people to it.' [1]

§4

The working philosophy of humanism includes an æsthetic. Though fundamentally it is the æsthetic of classicism, the modern humanist will so far as possible give it a modern statement.

Beauty may advantageously be considered with reference to quantity and quality, i.e., degree and kind.

1. *Quantity*. The æsthetic of the naturistic age, as the

---

[1] Such is J. Burnet's characterization of the central spirit of Greek philosophy, *The Legacy of Greece*, p. 58.

speculation of Benedetto Croce indicates, has tended to consider beauty only with reference to degree. According to Croce, beauty is merely perfect expression, and expression that falls short of perfection is in so far ugly. This theory is a sophisticated result of the modern rejection of objective imitation in favor of subjective expression; we are no longer to deal with truth of imitation but only with intensity of expression. 'Intensity,' together with its synonym 'vitality,' is now in the forefront of our critical terminology. 'There is a vitality which lies back both of naturalism and of romance,' as a recent American critic has said; and he calls for 'a fourth dimension' that will require criticism to ask of a work of art, not only Is it true? is it good? is it beautiful? but also *Is it alive?* His suggestion is gratuitous: this is the one question that naturism is eager to ask of works of art. Are they alive, vital, intense, like the works of nature; in other words, are they organic and not mechanical? Do they unfold like flowers, at the prompting of an inner urge, and so attain an inevitable form or complete expression? Or has the human agent consciously interposed his own will between Nature and her indirect product, and marred this product?

It must be admitted that the idea of the organic, which even Plato and Aristotle found useful in thinking upon art, has been carried to the point of absurdity by both romanticism and realism. It has virtually destroyed the idea of human purpose or design, which is fundamental in the æsthetic of humanism. It has caused us to suffer the delusion of thinking that selection is not a fact, when it is actually the primary fact in nearly the entire artistic process, from the initial period of preparation to the final period of revision. 'Nearly the entire,' we must say, rather than 'the entire'; for there enters into the work of art, also, an element of the incalculable, something that appears to transcend the normal power of the artist to find what he wants. This something-given, this inspiration, may be conceived as proceeding either from the subconscious activity of nature in us or from the super-conscious activity of a reality congruous with our humanity. It is conceived in the latter manner in the invocations of the classical poets and of the Christian Milton praying for divine assistance; this is the æsthetic aspect of the humility of humanism.

While avoiding the misuse of the biological analogy of the organic, the modern humanist has a sufficient sense of the importance of a vitality that permeates the whole artistic work and assures expression of all the parts that constitute the whole. In addition he has an adequate sense of the need of conscious design and selection, by means of which art, or human form-giving, is differentiated from the turbid flux of nature. He is even more solicitous than the naturist of com-pleteness of expression, of a maximum quantity of beauty, and he believes that it can be attained, not by the identifica-tion of art and nature (the prime æsthetic heresy of modern thought), but by the employment of human powers — clear purpose, hard deliberate effort, and the insight that rewards toil.

2. *Quality.* There are not only degrees but also kinds of beauty. If there were only degrees, we should have to regard all complete, proportionate expressions as equal, regardless of the nature of the expressions; but common sense alone suf-fices to prove that we are inevitably concerned with the na-ture of the things expressed. Common sense tells us that 'The Rape of the Lock' and 'Paradise Lost,' the 'Ode to the West Wind' and 'King Lear,' 'On First Looking into Chap-man's Homer' and the 'Iliad' itself are not equally admira-ble, even though we assume that they are all perfect ex-pressions. The most we can say is that they are perfect ex-pressions in their kind. We know, further, that the question of kind involves those moral and intellectual considerations that Croce seeks to rule out of art. Especially in a represent-ative art like literature, we ask not only, How beautiful is

this poem, this drama? but also, What kind of beauty does it possess? What is the worth of that which it expresses? What is its truth, its goodness? Critical theory has always insisted, down to our naturistic age, upon the need of thus distinguishing between form and content, and if it has often erred by forgetting the intimate relation of the two, it has erred less seriously than our modern theory that identifies them. We cannot rest content with perfection of form; we are bound to consider also what it is that has this perfection and how it compares with other things that likewise have it. The artist selected certain materials for expression; we are to judge his selection no less than his expression.

Now, an artist may select his materials from the several great provinces of experience, namely, the senses, the feelings, the reason, and the ethical will. Since he can hardly hope to explore all of these provinces equally, he will specially interest himself in some of them and relatively neglect others. If he is a romantic, he will emphasize sense impressions and natural feeling and subordinate reason and ethical imagination. If he is a realist, he will emphasize sense observation and reason and subordinate natural feeling and ethical imagination. If he is a classicist, he will emphasize reason and ethical imagination and subordinate the senses and feelings.

This would seem to be equivalent to saying that classicism emphasizes the more important realms of experience and subordinates the less important, and that it therefore offers the finest conception of beauty. We may miss in it the bewildering variety and indeterminateness of romantic emotionalism, together with the exquisite sense perceptions characteristic of both romanticism and realism, but, living in a naturistic age, we are perhaps not in a position plausibly to affirm that authors like Sophocles and Virgil had too little of these. However that may be, the humanist critic, prizing reason and ethical control and insight as the height of human power, must view classical art as the nearest approach to the ideal kind. Exalting what is essential, subordinating what is secondary, it approximates an all-comprehensive, duly proportioned kind of art.

In drawing this conclusion, the modern humanist must deal with the claim that primacy in kind, as well as in degree, belongs to Shakspere. He may seek to show that the enigmatic Shakspere was essentially a humanist, the contemporary, as it has been said, of all those who, avoiding both the natural and the supernatural, dwell upon 'the wide sunlit human level' where 'truth and goodness and beauty remain the same from age to age.' But the annexation of Shakspere to the humanist domain, I think we are bound to feel, is a somewhat high-handed procedure even though partly justified. While he contributed to the humanistic ideal, he did not embody its essentials as Milton did. It is best to face the issue in all candor: to point out that Milton, the greatest English poet since Shakspere, conceded the supremacy of the ancients; that Goethe, the greatest writer since Milton, did the same; that the claim of Shakspere was put forward in a naturistic age, romantic critics urging it with an exaggeration that is now manifest to us; that while Shakspere accords well with Anglo-Saxon and Teutonic predilections, he is comparatively alien to those Latin peoples whose centrality in respect to art it is difficult to deny; that — to go to the heart of the matter — Shakspere was apparently concerned rather with mirroring life than with interpreting it, and therefore tended to submit to actuality rather than to transcend it. If his vision embraced more of life than any other author has contemplated; if he has presented, as Dr. Johnson acknowledged, 'scenes from which a hermit may estimate the transactions of the world, and a confessor predict the progress of the passions,' it is equally true that his works are 'a forest, in which the oaks extend their branches, and pines tower in the air, interspersed sometimes with weeds and brambles, and sometimes giving shelter to myrtles and to roses; filling the eye with awful pomp, and gratifying the mind with endless diversity.' He is like nature — an open secret, vast and varied, confused and enigmatic. If we must refuse to say of Sophocles that 'He saw life steadily and saw it whole,' it is because his tragedies do not include all of life; if we must refuse to say it of Shakspere, it is because, though Argus-eyed, he did not see life steadily enough, did not bring his incomparably abundant materials into that order and harmony of vision that distinguishes art from experience. The image that he offers is partially blurred and elusive; his profoundest commentators, accordingly, are at variance as to his 'meaning,' and his lay readers find little solace in him from the apparent meaninglessness of life itself. Despite the impressive development of his mind and art, Shakspere to the end failed to resolve his inner confusion, which limited the qualitative excellence of his art, or his corresponding outward confusion, which limited the quantitative excellence of his art.[1] For our best examples of sound art, which gives to ample materials firmness of inner meaning and of outward form, in other words fuses quality and quantity of beauty, we must still return to the ancients. Though we have far more knowledge than they had, though existence is to us tremendously more complex, the fact is inescapable that our materials have overwhelmed us, and that in losing control of the essentials of art we have paid an enormous price for the gains we have made in non-essentials.

In thus asserting the primacy of an art that flourished several centuries before Christ, the humanist does not, however, propose a gospel of stagnation. He gives due weight to both continuity and experiment, believes in both tradition and change.

For tradition, rightly understood, implies change; is not

[1] Of this confusion the character of Hamlet is symbolical. More than any other tragic agent in the plays, he is critically aware of the chaos of forces that actuate 'the paragon of animals.'

repetition but development; is a cumulous process in which new elements are constantly assimilated into the old structure or organism. It may be thought of as an evolution, provided that we suffer no deterministic delusions as to progress toward an unknown goal in the future, but keep our eyes steadfastly upon the humane standard envisioned by the labor of the past and inherited by the present only in so far as the present is aware of it. Tradition allows for a principle of variation, as inexplicable and inevitable as in organic science, by virtue of which each age, indeed each artist, possesses a new individuality. It welcomes the registration of this individuality, so long as the superior principle of continuity is not violated by an arrogant and artificial self-exploitation. It believes that an artist who has a valuable 'originality' may safely trust that originality to take care of itself, while he can unite himself with the past in a vital manner only by dint of a humble and ardent discipline.[1] Tradition, it has been well said, 'involves, in the first place, the historical sense, which we may call indispensable to any one who would continue to be a poet beyond his twenty-fifth year; and the historical sense involves a perception, not only of the pastness of the past, but of its presence; the historical sense compels a man to write not merely with his own generation in his bones, but with a feeling that the whole of the literature of Europe from Homer and within it the whole of the literature of his own country has a simultaneous existence and com-

---

[1] 'This is especially true in the arts which we call the fine arts, where technique and tradition are of prime importance; and it would not perhaps be too fantastic to attribute, in part at least, the downfall of painting, architecture, and the handicrafts in the earlier decades of the nineteenth century — perhaps the greatest artistic disaster the world has ever suffered — to this modern enthusiasm for the originality of creative genius, and the desire on the part of every artist and architect and handicraftsman to display as conspicuously as possible his own personality and peculiar gifts. Ever since then the history of art has been the history of conscious and violent revolutions and reactions, instead of that gradual and unconscious modification of an inherited tradition which characterized its development in previous ages.' (Logan Pearsall Smith, *Words and Idioms*, 116–17.)

poses a simultaneous order.'[1] Awareness of this simultaneous order is assuredly far more important, both to the artist and to the critic, than awareness of that merely successive order that Croce proposes, with his law of an historical sequence 'dominating the dance of the intuitions.' Tradition is to be conceived as a living world of achieved art, into which the latest work will be admitted only if it is both new and old, new because of a different angle or personal medium, old because of its memory of time-hallowed truth and beauty. It must give the past the power to speak again, with a new accent. It must prove afresh the immortality of the past, and is likely itself to attain immortality in proportion as it enters into the central current of tradition. If the poet is a man speaking to men, rather than an individual expressing his idiosyncrasy, he cannot hope to address humanity hereafter unless humanity has already addressed him; unless he is aware, as Mr. Eliot says finely, 'not of what is dead, but of what is already living.'

§ 5

The critical method of modern humanism remains to be indicated.

Its first step is historical understanding: it seeks in the beginning to remove whatever historical barrier may exist between us and a work of art. In this object it is in accord with the kind of scholarship that flourishes to-day everywhere, especially in the universities, a scholarship rendered possible by the historic sense that arose in the naturistic movement, which demonstrated the otherness of past ages, the operation of an *Entwickelung* linking the successive ages, and the fact that art is in some sense the product of racial heritage, environment, and the time. Through historical scholarship we are able to work our way back to past ages, to live in them like contemporaries, to read their books as they were origi-

[1] T. S. Eliot, *The Sacred Wood*, 43–44.

nally read in the light of the forms and habits of the particular civilization then existing. Vividly do we see to-day the need of making this return, if our literary criticism is to have a substantial foundation. The great task, however, is to erect a structure upon the foundation, and from this task the humanist will not shrink as the historical critic does:

The historical critic approaches literature as the manifestation of an evolutionary process in which all the phases are of equal value. Essentially, he has no concern with the greater or less literary excellence of the objects whose history he traces — their existence is alone sufficient for him; a bad book is as important as a good one, and much more important than a good one if it exercised, as bad books have a way of doing, a real influence on the course of literature. In practice, it is true, the historical critic generally fails of this ideal of unimpassioned objectivity. He either begins by making judgments of value for himself, or accepts those judgments which have been endorsed by tradition.[1]

When true to his calling, the historical critic is not concerned with what is best irrespective of time but merely with what is fittest at the moment. He asserts that we must have complete knowledge before we can have judgment of values, thus postponing judgment to a future that can never arrive. He forgets, perhaps, that he would have no calling if humanity did not insist that literature is of value. Humanism is here, as always, with humanity; it believes that literature exists because it has value, and it seeks to determine wherein that value resides.

Before judgment of value is possible, however, the critic must take a second preparatory step: he must supplement the understanding born of knowledge with the understanding born of sympathy. Holding his standards of judgment in abeyance, he must endeavor to read the book not only as if he were a contemporary of the author but as if he were the author himself. Through a more cultivated æsthetic sensibility and a fuller willingness to submit himself to the author's

[1] J. Middleton Murry, *Aspects of Literature*, 3.

spirit than the erudite historian is likely to possess,[1] he will seek to reproduce in himself the author's vision, to re-create the æsthetic experience of which the book is the external expression, to revive in its totality the intention of which it is the issue. Biographical knowledge will help him, here, far less than a sympathetic release of his faculties in response to the book. He will be well aware of the fact that sympathy, like knowledge, is never complete, and that his judgments will therefore contain, like the truths of science, an element of uncertainty; but he will refuse to take refuge from uncertainty in an impressionistic self-exploitation. Having come to understand the book as fully as possible, he will proceed to the specific task of criticism: judgment of the book's value.

First, its value, its beauty, considered quantitatively. He will ask, In what *degree* has the artist succeeded in carrying out his æsthetic intention? This he can answer by comparing the book, or physical work of art, with the artist's intention as revealed to him by knowledge and sympathy. If book and intention coincide, the book is entirely beautiful. If the book falls in some measure short of the æsthetic experience it was intended to represent, its beauty is to that extent imperfect. Perhaps nearly all books are in some measure imperfect, since authors, like other human beings, mar their achievement through such weaknesses as haste and laziness, halting their efforts before they have fully carried out their intention. The ugly consequences are obscurity, diffuseness, misplaced emphasis, inconsistency, cacophony, and the like. The criterion of quantitative beauty, it will be observed, is supplied not by the critic but by the artist himself, or, to be more exact, by the artist's intention.

Secondly, the critic will judge of beauty qualitatively, asking What *kind* of beauty does the book have? In answering this question, he can no longer accept without question

---

[1] See the passage on erudition and critical elasticity in Arnold's *On Translating Homer*, Eversley edition, 245–46.

the artist's intention, as if one intention were as good as another. While artists are prone to resent the questioning of their intentions, presupposing that these intentions are admirable and that only their success in carrying them out is open to debate, they rarely hesitate to question the intentions of other artists. Sincerity of intention and efficiency of execution do not constitute a sufficient test of excellence in the æsthetic any more than in the moral realm. The critic must test also the object itself. Is it sound or false, and if sound, how does it compare with other sound objects?

The criterion in this case is not the artist or the critic but truth or nature — the nature of things, things as they really are. This has been the aim of all the great movements in the history of art; they have all been professedly realistic. In its general intention, what we term realism to-day differs not at all from past art; its intention is philosophical, it differs only in the philosophy that it uses. That philosophy, as we have seen, finds its master truth in the phenomenal order described by the natural sciences, and is radically in agreement with the romantic philosophy that delighted in singing epithalamia in celebration of the emotional union of man and nature. Wordsworth, like the modern realist, asserted that the object of poetry is truth, and his truth was certainly closer to the truth of the realist than to that of Aristotle, whom he cites in the same passage as having said that 'Poetry is the most philosophical of all writing.' The philosophy of classicism (not the pseudo-classicism that perverted the ancient doctrines and provoked the romantic revolt), while it superficially agreed with romanticism in holding that the real is the ideal, fundamentally disagreed in holding that the ideal is ethical and therefore irreconcilable with nature. The philosophy of humanism finds its master truth, not in men as they are (realism) or in men as worse than they are (naturalism) or in men as they 'wish' to be (romanticism), but in men as they 'ought' to be — 'ought,' of course, not in the usual restrictedly moral sense, but with reference to the perfection of the human type. Hence, in the words of a contemporary critic at home in both the ancient and the modern world, a critic deserving of quotation at length:

The true literary critic must have a humanistic philosophy. His inquiries must be modulated, subject to an intimate, organic governance, by an ideal of the good life. He is not the mere investigator of facts; existence is never for him synonymous with value, and it is of the utmost importance that he should never be deluded into believing that it is. He will not accept from Hegel the thesis that all the events of human history, all man's spiritual activities, are equally authentic manifestations of Spirit; he will not even recognize the existence of Spirit. He may accept from Croce the thesis that art is the expression of intuitions, but he will not be extravagantly grateful, because his duty as a critic is to distinguish between intuitions and to decide that one is more significant than another. A philosophy of art that lends him no aid in this and affords no indication why the expression of one intuition should be preferred to the expression of another is of little value to him. He will incline to say that Hegel and Croce are the scientists of art rather than its philosophers.

Here, then, is the opposition: between the philosophy that borrows its values from science and the philosophy which shares its values with art. We may put it with more cogency and truth: the opposition lies between a philosophy without values and a philosophy based upon them. For values are human, anthropocentric. . . .

An ideal of the good life, if it is to have the internal coherence and the organic force of a true ideal, *must inevitably be æsthetic.* There is no other power than our æsthetic intuition by which we can imagine or conceive it; we can express it only in æsthetic terms. We say, for instance, the good life is that in which man has achieved a harmony of the diverse elements in his soul. . . . Plato's philosophy is æsthetic through and through, and because it is æsthetic it is the most human, the most permanently pregnant of all philosophies. Much labor has been spent on the examination of the identity which Plato established between the good and the beautiful. It is labor lost, for that identity is axiomatic, absolute, irreducible. The Greeks knew by instinct that it is so, and in their common speech the word for a gentleman was the καλὸς κἀγαθός, the beautiful-good. . . .

It only remained for Aristotle to discern the nature of the relation between artistic 'imitation' and the ideal for the Platonic system to be complete and four-square, a perpetual inspiration and an everlasting foundation for art and the criticism of art.[1]

§6

Having sketched the æsthetic theory and the critical procedure of the new humanism, we may return, finally, to its practical relation with the problem of an American literature and culture. Humanism maintains that it is idle to aspire to an Americanism based upon hostility toward and ignorance of the past; that if we are ever to be worthily American we must first be worthily human; that the attainment of humanity is a task calling less for construction than for reconstruction; that the old established views of life must be revived and corrected by those who will take pains to examine the radical credentials of those views. Although such a reorientation should be sought simultaneously in all the higher departments of human activity — in philosophy, in religion, in art — it may be sought with the largest prospect of success in art, specially the art of letters. Chaotic though our literature is to-day, it is nevertheless more vital than either our 'scientific' philosophy or our sentimental and materialistic religion. It has ample energies that might be controlled and shaped for use, instead of being diffused and lost, as at present, in tangential experiment. Unlike technical philosophy and formal religion, it already possesses an enormous, eager audience, thanks partly to the mechanical inventions of the naturistic age. A cause as well as a result, our literature is not only expressing but determining the thoughts and feelings of millions of readers.

Before a new order of creative literature can arrive, however, the way must be prepared by criticism. The modern

[1] Murry, *op. cit.*, 7–10.

poet or novelist who flatters himself that he is creating something new will generally be found to be following, toward the dim inane, one of the old paths marked out by his naturistic predecessors. Vaunting himself upon his individualism, his independence of all tradition and authority, he is none the less incapable of eluding the past, and a narrowly limited past at that. How, save through criticism, can he become aware of a larger, richer, deeper beauty, how else come to see the need of drawing back toward the center of life and art, how else perceive that in his quest for novelty he must carry with him the permanent and the universal and thus reconcile change with tradition? How, save through criticism, can he be provided with an audience who will understand his efforts to do something better than move toward the limbo of the eccentric, the *cul de sac* of the falsely original, and who, understanding him, will give him support and encouragement to continue more earnestly than before? Even genius of the first order doubtless needs a sensible amount of preparation, a state of the public mind that it can express and intensify; and a lesser artist is wholly dependent upon it. If such an artist to-day were to attempt a restoration of the pivotal values of art, he would presumably be damned with silence, or with the remark that he did not 'belong' to our enlightened modern world, or with meaningless cries of 'Victorian! Puritan!' He could not even count upon the support of the educators of youth, the scholars in the colleges, to whom the past is matter for historical record rather than a school of judgment. It is a deplorable fact that the young literary aspirant, whether he graduates from practical journalism or from the noisy haven of 'college activities,' is aware of only two possibilities of success in his art: he may be a vital realist or he may be a sophisticated romantic — in either case a little more eccentric than his predecessors.

In a recent anthology,[1] the editor points out that already

[1] *American Criticism, 1926*, the first of a series to be published annually.

'our critical spirit is prodigiously fecund.' It is strenuously trying, he says, quoting Matthew Arnold, 'to make an intellectual situation of which the creative power can profitably avail itself'; and this it is 'actually accomplishing,' he declares on his own account, not through its 'actual performances or apparent direction,' but simply through its 'native vigor.' To write thus, however, is to subscribe to the current confusion of quantity with quality. We do not need more, but better criticism, if we are to have better readers and better writers. It is difficult to see how a mere continuance and multiplication of our usual types of criticism could ever rouse from sleep this 'noble and puissant nation' of ours, destined, according to the anthologist, to fulfill Milton's prophetic vision. Certainly our 'apparent direction' is not toward the kind of nobility that Milton had in view, nor toward the kind of intellectual situation that Arnold desired: for we are alien from the essential doctrine and discipline that guided both the Puritan humanist and the Victorian humanist. We are naturists, and our criticism is historical, psychological, expressionistic, impressionistic.

Adopting the spirit and method of science, our historical and psychological critics concern themselves with description and explanation, with fact instead of value, with cause instead of result. One of our 'sociological' critics, for example, is satisfied when he has shown in a study of Sherwood Anderson 'how impossible it would have been for him to have written another tragedy like "Othello," another novel like "Persuasion"'; and one of our 'psychoanalytical' critics restricts his function to tracing 'Poe's art to an abnormal condition of the nerves and his critical ideas to a rationalized defence of the limitations of his own taste.' These are ambitious tasks, they are even interesting tasks; but they do not in the least forward the central aim of criticism, which is the determination and the application of standards of value. 'Othello' and 'Persuasion,' the works of Poe and of Sherwood

Anderson, these remain what they were: unvalued expressions. Our impressionistic critics, the followers of Anatole France, are even less helpful, dealing as they do with themselves rather than with works of art. Obedient to the romantic cult of uniqueness and to the skeptical spirit encouraged by science, they throw over the task of evaluation and with admirable candor tell us that they are interested only in self-expression, that is, in new creation rather than in criticism of what has already been created. They tell us that truth is 'the adoration of second-rate men,' and that they wish to be first-rate men like Carlyle and Macaulay, poor judges but great artists — 'They could make the thing charming, and that is always a million times more important than making it true.' These impressionists we should give leave to be as charming as they can, but for criticism we must turn elsewhere. If we turn to the expressionists, the followers of Croce, we shall find a theory useful so far as it goes. In the spirit of romanticism, they regard each work of art as a unique expression, and in the spirit of science, they measure its beauty quantitatively. In doing so, however, they endeavor, unlike the impressionists, to escape from themselves into the work of art and to judge it as the artist himself might have judged it, asking: To what extent does it express the intuition that gave it birth? This is a very sensible and pertinent question, properly the first question we must ask of a work of art. But it is not the only question. We must make bold to ask also, Is it true? Is it good? What kind of truth does it offer, and what is its ethical quality? These are the last questions that humanity has traditionally asked of works of art, and we must ask them to-day if we are to prepare an intellectual situation of which the creative power can profitably avail itself.

'We stand to-day' (to quote our anthologist once more) 'in the center of a vast disintegration. In America the situation is complicated by the peculiar problems of our own culture.

Our forces and problems must be organized before the artist can do his work. Perhaps the reason why the creative spirit has never (in literature) experienced a full flowering in America, and is at present enervated in Europe, is that the artist exhausts his creative energy in a squandrous [sic] and unavailing struggle before this synthesis can be reached.' No longer is the situation in America really 'peculiar.' No longer is America the only great frontier nation, no longer is it solitary in that provincialism that Poe and Emerson and Whitman deplored, no longer is it alone in its severance from the vital traditions of the past; Europe likewise has lost her moorings and is drifting without apparent direction, although her unconscious tradition, her profound under-current, is far stronger than ours. Everywhere, the need of the age is integration, the establishment of a significant relation between the present and the past. We are sufficiently aware of the arbitrary elements in the integrations of the past; it is time for us to become aware of the arbitrary elements in our present thought that are delaying the integration of the future.

THE END

INDEX